Visual "Literacy"

Visual "Literacy"

Image, Mind, and Reality

Paul Messaris

Westview Press
Boulder • San Francisco • Oxford

Portions of this work have appeared as "Visual 'Literacy': A Theoretical Synthesis," *Communication Theory* 3, no. 4 (1993), and "Does TV Belong in the Classroom? Cognitive Consequences of Visual 'Literacy,'" in *Communication Yearbook,* ed. Stanley Deetz (Newbury Park, Calif.: Sage Publications, 1994) and are reprinted by permission.

Published in 1994 in the United States of America by Westview Press, Inc., 5500 Central Avenue, Boulder, Colorado 80301-2877, and in the United Kingdom by Westview Press, 36 Lonsdale Road, Summertown, Oxford OX2 7EW

Library of Congress Cataloging-in-Publication Data
Messaris, Paul.
  Visual "literacy" : image, mind, and reality / Paul Messaris.
    p.   cm.
  Includes bibliographical references and index.
  ISBN 0-8133-1667-7. — ISBN 0-8133-1937-4 (pbk.)
    1. Visual literacy—United States—Psychological aspects.
2. Visual communication—United States—Psychological aspects.
I. Title.
LB1068.M47   1994
370.15'23—dc20   93-26069
                                                                                    CIP

Printed and bound in the United States of America

The paper used in this publication meets the requirements of the American National Standard for Permanence of Paper for Printed Library Materials Z39.48-1984.

10   9   8   7   6   5   4   3   2   1

For Carla

Contents

5 Awareness of Artistry and Manipulation   135

The Detection of Artifice, 138
Unconcealed Artifice, 147
Visual Manipulation, 154

6 Conclusion: Other Questions, Other "Literacies"   165

Images and the Appearance of Reality, 166
Images and Cultures, 168
Familiarity with Visual Subject Matter, 176
"Production Literacy," 180

Figures

Acknowledgments

For more than two decades, The Annenberg School for Communication has been an extraordinarily supportive environment for scholarship in visual communication. It is a pleasure to express my gratitude to the two faculty members who designed the school's program in visual communication and who were my own mentors in this area, Larry Gross and the late Sol Worth. I am also thankful to the two deans, George Gerbner and Kathleen Hall Jamieson, whose commitment to visual scholarship at Annenberg has kept the program strong through the years.

There are several colleagues, both current and former, whom I would like to thank for their support during the planning and writing of this book. At Annenberg, Ray Birdwhistell and Charles Wright gave me encouragement when I needed it most, and Oscar Gandy, Bob Hornik, Klaus Krippendorff, and Amos Vogel provided valuable comments and advice. Elsewhere, Gretchen Barbatsis, John Bell, Derek Bousé, Georgette Comuntzis-Page, Renée Hobbs, Stuart Kaplan, Phil Kipper, Stuart Liebman, Steve Prince, Brian Stonehill, Nia Sukanto, Harold Switzgable, Sari Thomas, Mike Willmorth, and Cindy Zuckerman all gave me the benefit of their experience and interest in the issues I have tried to deal with here. I have also drawn continued inspiration from the many colleagues and friends who participate in the annual Visual Communication Conference, founded by Bob Tiemens and Herb Zettl.

Like most people who teach in areas in which they also do research, I have found that the classroom is often the most productive forum for the development of new ideas, and I would like to thank the many students, both undergraduate and graduate, who have taken my courses in visual communication and responded with intelligence to what I had to say. I am particularly indebted to the former research assistants who helped me at various stages of the development of this book: Christine Santini, Bipasha Shom, Seema Shrikhande, Jisuk Woo, Jim Woods, and Barbie Zelizer.

The book's cover art was made available through the kindness of Toby Haggerty and Mario Van Peebles as well as the generosity of Kathleen Hall

Jamieson. Grateful thanks to all three. Finally, many thanks to David Graper, Andrea MacDonald, John Massi, Deb Porter, Ellen Reynolds, and Donna Schadt for providing technical support at Annenberg; to Jim Davison of the Republican National Committee, Anne Gaines of E. C. Publications, and Jon Knowles of the Planned Parenthood Federation of America for their generous assistance in the process of securing illustrations; to Cindy Hirschfeld and Meredith Sund of Westview Press for their efficient handling of the book's preparation and production; and to Gordon Massman, senior editor at Westview Press, who has made my dealings with the press a uniformly pleasant experience.

Paul Messaris

1

Four Aspects of Visual Literacy

A colleague of mine who teaches film history once described the following incident. He had shown his class the famous surrealist film, *Un Chien Andalou,* made in 1928 by Luis Buñuel and Salvador Dali. In this film's hard-to-forget opening scene, a woman, shown in medium close-up, looks out at the viewer. Behind her stands a man, whose hands reach around the woman's body. One hand holds open her left eye. The other hand holds an old-style straight razor. There is a shot of the night sky, with a long, narrow cloud bisecting the disc of the full moon; then the razor slices into the eye, and a viscous blob of liquid oozes out. Some time after the day of this film's screening, one of the students in my colleague's class came to see him in his office. She asked him a variety of questions about other aspects of the course, and then, somewhat hesitantly, she brought up *Un Chien Andalou.* In class, the opening scene had been discussed in terms of its not-very-subtle symbolism and in connection with the variety of ways in which male filmmakers have fantasized about violating women's bodies. But this young woman's question dealt with the film on a different level: "How," she wanted to know, "did they get that woman in the film to let them cut into her eye?"

Although my colleague remembers distinctly that this was the phrasing of his student's question, it turned out that what she was interested in was the technical means through which this sequence had been produced. She knew, of course, that there had been some "special effect," but she couldn't figure out what it was, and she seemed quite surprised when my colleague pointed out to her that the effect was nothing more than a simple matter of editing: The cutting of the eye occurs in a separate shot, and this shot is an extremely tight close-up, making possible the substitution of a dead animal's eye for the eye of the woman. It is the simplest of movie tricks; and yet, in the eyes of this viewer, it created such a powerful impression of a seamless reality as to leave her with the conviction that she had seen the "real" woman's eye being sliced. (Perhaps I should add, for those who haven't seen this film, that it is in black-and-white and is typically projected either with no sound at all or with a jaunty tango on the soundtrack.)

We can probably take it for granted, of course, that in this specific case obliviousness to the editing and to the camera's framing of the scene was heightened by the hair-raising subject matter. But lack of awareness of artifice—and of editing in particular—is hardly unique to this one instance. Since the earliest days of analytical thinking about movies, writers (many of them filmmakers themselves) have noted the compelling illusion of a whole reality that can be summoned up by some forms of editing and framing, and they have speculated about the reasons for and sources of this kind of effect. Is it a response that viewers have learned, through cumulative exposure to the conventions of the medium, or are its roots in some way more "primal"? Would someone who had never seen a movie before succumb to this illusion or not? Why? This is one of the sets of questions I will try to answer in this book by discussing editing as well as some of the other elements that go into the creation of a convincing visual representation of "reality." At the heart of this discussion is the following concern: How is it that pictures, both moving and still, can conjure up a world of almost palpable objects and events despite the many differences between the appearance of the real world and the appearance of any kind of picture, no matter how realistic?

These questions intrigue me, as they have intrigued so many others, for their own sake—but also because of their broader implications. My colleague who told me the story about *Un Chien Andalou* was not simply reflecting on the fascinating properties of pictorial perception. To him, the main point of the story was that it illustrated the need for visual education. Much of his teaching had been dedicated to the elucidation of principles by which the visual media may be used to misinform, distort, and manipulate, and he was somewhat disconcerted to find that a highly intelligent, well-educated student in one of his own courses was evidently capable of succumbing to the most elementary forms of visual deception. As someone with personal memories of Nazi propaganda, he pointed out that some of the fabrications in newsreels of that period were no more complicated in their technique.

The educational goal that my colleague was advocating (greater experience in the workings of visual media coupled with a heightened *conscious awareness* of those workings) is often referred to as visual "literacy." Strictly speaking, of course, the term "literacy" should be applied only to reading and writing. But it would probably be too pedantic and, in any case, it would surely be futile to resist the increasingly common tendency to apply this term to other kinds of communication skills (mathematical "literacy," computer "literacy") as well as to the substantive knowledge that communication rests on (historical, geographic, cultural "literacy"). So, somewhat reluctantly, I am going to use the term "visual literacy" in this book. More specifically, I intend to examine four relatively distinct aspects of this general topic.

1. *Visual literacy as a prerequisite for the comprehension of visual media.* The images in visual media (single pictures as well as movies and television) often differ considerably from the appearance of the real world. Because of these differences (e.g., the lack of color in outline drawings or the sudden shifts in point of view caused by movie editing), some writers have argued that the ability to interpret visual media requires prior experience. In this kind of argument, the term "visual literacy" would refer to the familiarity with visual conventions that a person acquires through cumulative exposure to visual media.

2. *General cognitive consequences of visual literacy.* Proponents of visual education often argue that experience with visual media is not just a route to better visual comprehension but also may lead to a general enhancement of cognitive abilities. To put it differently, the cognitive skills that are brought into play in the interpretation of television and other visual media may be applicable to other intellectual tasks as well. For example, it has been proposed, as we shall see later, that experience with film and television may improve children's understanding of spatial relationships in the real world.

3. *Awareness of visual manipulation.* Regardless of the validity of the possibilities outlined above, visual education might make a viewer more resistant to the manipulations attempted by TV commercials, magazine advertising, political campaigns, and so on. In other words, even if learning about the visual devices used in picture-based media does not have any effect on a viewer's comprehension of pictures or on one's other cognitive abilities, it might still make the viewer more *aware* of how meaning is created visually—and therefore less likely to be taken in by abuses of this process. (This is the form of visual literacy envisioned by the colleague who told me the story about *Un Chien Andalou.*)

4. *Aesthetic appreciation.* Finally, awareness of the ways in which visual media give rise to meaning and elicit viewers' responses can also be seen as providing a basis for informed aesthetic appreciation. Knowing how visual effects are achieved may lessen the vicarious thrills we might otherwise derive from visual media, but such knowledge is self-evidently a prerequisite for the evaluation of artistic skill.

The four propositions outlined above give a reasonably comprehensive account, I think, of the range of positive consequences most commonly imputed to the enhancement of visual literacy. The order in which I have listed them is not accidental; it corresponds to my own assessment of each proposition's degree of validity, ranging from "very low" for the first to "very high" for the fourth. This ranking reflects what I consider to be an essential point about the nature of picture-based media as means of communication: Unlike the conventions of written language or, for that matter, speech, pictorial conventions for the representation of objects and events are based on information-processing skills that a viewer can be assumed to possess even in the absence of any previous experience with pictures.

From this characteristic—which, in my view, is peculiar to pictures and distinguishes them sharply from other modes of communication—it follows almost tautologically that the first of the four propositions listed above is not very likely to be correct. It also follows that the indirect consequences of visual literacy for other areas of cognitive functioning must at best be limited to the reinforcement of preexisting skills rather than the creation of new ones. However, precisely because visual literacy comes more naturally than skill in reading or in understanding speech, conscious awareness of the process of interpretation and response may be more fugitive in the case of pictures than it is with language or with other modes of communication. On this assumption, the argument that explicit education about visual media can make a viewer more resistant to visual manipulation and more aware of artistic merit seems to me particularly compelling.

The idea that attention to visual literacy can enhance aesthetic sensitivity and immunity to manipulation is anything but controversial (e.g., see Brown, 1991; Davies, 1991; Foss and Kanengieter, 1991; Lloyd-Kolkin and Turner, 1989; Metallinos, 1992). I suspect, however, that many readers with a scholarly interest in these matters would disagree with my contention that the skills of pictorial interpretation are derivatives of cognitive skills that may be assumed to preexist independently of a viewer's experience with pictorial media. In the academic literature on this subject, the idea that visual understanding requires visual literacy is often taken for granted.

This idea can be traced through a number of converging strands in writings on art, photography, movies, and other kinds of images. An early inspiration for this idea was an essay written in the 1920s by the distinguished art historian Erwin Panofsky. Titled "Perspective as Symbolic Form," this essay attempted to demonstrate that the Renaissance system of linear perspective, which was commonly thought of as having succeeded in capturing visual truth on canvas, is actually an arbitrary representational style (a "symbolic form") containing significant departures from how things look in real life. Among the departures mentioned by Panofsky was the fact that Renaissance perspective cannot reproduce some of the real-world cues by which we judge distance (a topic to which we will return later in this chapter). But what seems to have mattered most to him was the discrepancy between the flat surface of the picture, with its rectangular perspective grid, and the curved surface of the retina, on which no line is straight (Panofsky, 1991, pp. 28–31).

The logic behind Panofsky's last point was not particularly sound: Why *should* the picture plane, which is meant to represent the world *outside* the eye, bear any kind of isomorphic relationship to the surface of our retinas? Nevertheless, his essay had an enduring influence in the thinking of art historians, and it set the stage for arguments about visual literacy as a precondition of pictorial interpretation. The single most influential source of such arguments has undoubtedly been the work of E. H. Gombrich, especially his 1960 book *Art and Illusion*. Starting from a premise similar to Panofsky's—i.e., the many discrepancies between the appearance of pictures and the appearance of the real world—Gombrich went on to examine the historical and cultural variability in the conventions of pictorial representation, from which he drew the conclusion that different visual cultures may have quite different standards as to what constitutes a realistic rendition of the world in an image. Gombrich also explicitly assumed that someone who had never before encountered a particular pictorial style—e.g., black-and-white photographs or outline drawings—might initially not be able to make sense of it.

This aspect of Gombrich's argument resonated with a number of nineteenth- and early twentieth-century stories by missionaries, anthropologists, and other world travelers to the effect that people in societies without photographs had occasionally expressed puzzlement on first encountering such pictures. (See Deregowski, 1980, for a good review and discussion of such accounts.) This informal evidence and the line of reasoning developed by Gombrich (not only in *Art and Illusion* but also in such later works as *The Image and the Eye* [1982]) have become the basis of a widely held belief in the arbitrariness of images (i.e., the idea that their resemblance to reality is largely—or even entirely—a matter of cultural convention) coupled with a corresponding view of the essential role of visual literacy in understanding them (e.g., see Elgin, 1984, pp. 914–921; Korac, 1988; Morgan and Welton, 1992; Wartofsky, 1979, 1984).

Among the various writers who have contributed to the evolution of such views, perhaps the most extreme has been philosopher Nelson Goodman. He argued that because it is impossible—in philosophical terms, at least—to specify any necessary and sufficient rules of correspondence between pictures and their referents, it follows that pictures are just as arbitrary in their connection to what they represent as language is—and that, in consequence, almost anything can serve as a picture of almost anything else if a culture so wills it (Goodman, 1976). An implication of this position is that the apparent realism of some kinds of pictures is due to the viewer's cultural conditioning rather than to the pictures' relationship to the appearance of reality. For example, Galassi (1981) has argued that the reason early photography struck viewers as being so true-to-life was that the new medium copied certain compositional conventions of earlier handmade pictures that people had come to accept as "natural."

Although still pictures have been the primary focus of formal scholarship along these lines, similar views have also taken hold, usually on a more informal level, among students of movies and television. As in the case of still pictures, arguments about the need for "film literacy" or "TV literacy" are routinely supported by anecdotes about first-time viewers of these media who reportedly had trouble following the events depicted in them. For example, film theorist Béla Balázs describes the case of an early twentieth-century English colonial administrator who lived for many years in parts of the world where movies had not yet penetrated. However, he had read about the nascent medium in newspapers and magazines, and when he finally returned home he eagerly went to the movies for the first time. Although some children sitting near him clearly had no trouble following the picture, he himself reportedly found it utterly impossible to understand (Balázs, 1952, p. 34).

As we shall see presently, evidence of incomprehension of movies or TV by inexperienced viewers has also emerged from research with children, although issues of general cognitive development complicate the applicability of this research to the basic question of prior media exposure. Whether on the basis of such evidence, then, or on the basis of theoretical argument, writers following Balázs have taken the position that a viewer needs to go through a period of visual adaptation before being able to understand the image in a movie or TV program (e.g., see Carey, 1982; Cohen, 1987; Frith and Robson, 1975; Gumpert and Cathcart, 1985; Wilson, 1983). For example, such writers assume that in order to be able to interpret the image on the screen adequately, a viewer must have learned, through sufficient previous exposure, the conventional uses and meanings of such things as close-ups, subjective camera, flashbacks, and so forth.

As one critic of this literature has noted, among many scholars these notions may be said to have attained the status of "contemporary received wisdom" (Carroll, 1988, p. 141). Nevertheless, there has also been a notable contrary tradition, particularly among writers with a background or interest in the psychology of perception (e.g., see Cassidy and Knowlton, 1983; Gibson, 1982, pp. 225–293; Hochberg, 1983, 1984; Kennedy, 1984; Kipper, 1990). Indeed, it is a fact worth pondering that E. H. Gombrich himself—who to this day is routinely cited as supplier of the proof in arguments about the supposed arbitrariness of pictorial representation—explicitly rejected this notion in the very book in which he is supposed to have proven it (Gombrich, 1960). Instead, Gombrich assumed that even when pictures do differ significantly from the appearance of unmediated reality, it is conceivable that they may not require any *new, picture-specific* cognitive skills for their interpretation. From this assumption it would follow, too, that a first-time viewer might be able to adjust to such pictorial styles "with surprising speed" (Gombrich, 1960, p. 53).

Since Gombrich made this assumption, it has been supported by a continually growing body of systematic research. Partly because of this research, but also for theoretical reasons, I do not share the view of visual literacy held by such writers as Nelson Goodman. Although I do think it is true that viewers get better at the interpretation of visual media as they acquire more experience with them, I also think that to a substantial degree the formal conventions typically encountered in still or motion pictures should make a good deal of sense even to a first-time viewer. A concrete example will serve to illustrate this point.

One of the most durable and widely used visual conventions, encountered frequently in film and television but also in photographs and other kinds of still images, is the use of angle of view as a means of making someone look powerful or powerless (Zettl, 1990, pp. 216–219). In film and television, this convention entails the well-known principle of using a low camera angle (shooting from below) to make the person(s) in the shot appear more powerful, menacing, threatening, and so on, depending on the exact context; and, conversely, using a high camera angle (shooting from above) to make the person(s) in the shot appear weaker, and so on. For example, the anti-abortion demonstrator in a Planned Parenthood ad (Figure 1.1) appears more overbearing because we see him from below. High and low angles used in this way are perhaps most likely to be encountered in action/adventure movies or TV programs, but the low-angle technique is also quite popular with producers of political advertising and propaganda, the classic example of the latter being the portrayal of Hitler in Leni Riefenstahl's *Triumph of the Will* (1934).

There is a considerable amount of careful scholarly research on high and low angles (see reviews by Kepplinger, 1991, and Messaris, 1992), and although there is some question as to how this device works in different contexts (e.g., see Bordwell and Thompson, 1986, p. 171), the conclusion that emerges is that the device is indeed effective. But why does it work? Why do viewers respond to this use of camera angle in the manner called for by the convention? What previous knowledge or experience must viewers have in order to make an appropriate response?

If the assumption that pictorial interpretation requires a prior visual literacy were generally true, the answer to these questions would be that viewers would have to have had a number of previous encounters with this use of camera angle, in the course of which they would eventually have acquired a sense of its meaning. As one writer puts it, "We derive meanings from kinds of shots and other filmic techniques because we have learned the codes and conventions of television and film practice. We unconsciously compare high-angle with low-angle shots and know how to distinguish between the two and what they both indicate" (Dyer, 1989, p. 131).

Thus, we could imagine a child gradually coming to associate low angles with shots of superheroes in moments of triumph and thereafter responding to the angle in and of itself in the appropriate way. We could also imagine a parent or other older viewer helping the child develop an understanding of

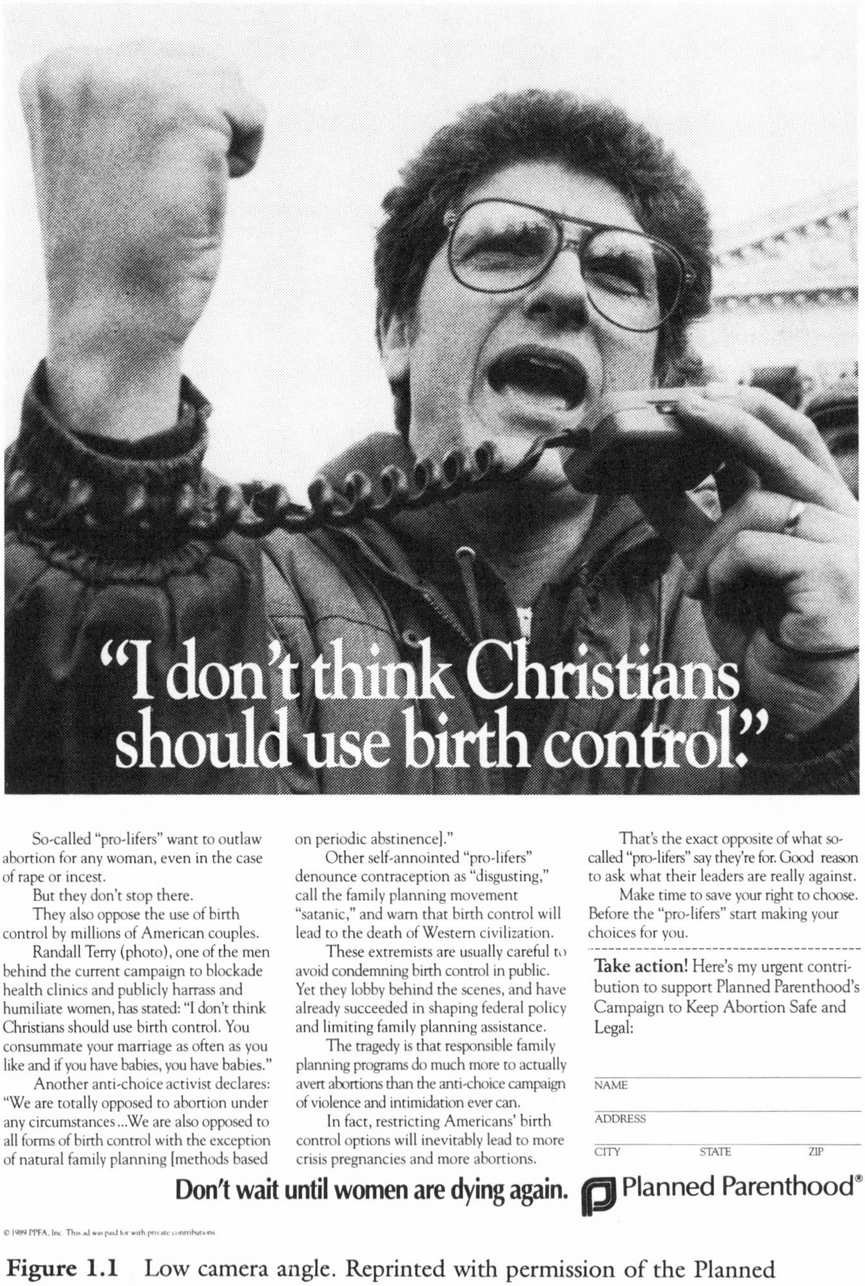
"I don't think Christians should use birth control."
So-called "pro-lifers" want to outlaw abortion for any woman, even in the case of rape or incest.
But they don't stop there.
They also oppose the use of birth control by millions of American couples.
Randall Terry (photo), one of the men behind the current campaign to blockade health clinics and publicly harrass and humiliate women, has stated: "I don't think Christians should use birth control. You consummate your marriage as often as you like and if you have babies, you have babies."
Another anti-choice activist declares: "We are totally opposed to abortion under any circumstances...We are also opposed to all forms of birth control with the exception of natural family planning [methods based on periodic abstinence]."
Other self-annointed "pro-lifers" denounce contraception as "disgusting," call the family planning movement "satanic," and warn that birth control will lead to the death of Western civilization.
These extremists are usually careful to avoid condemning birth control in public. Yet they lobby behind the scenes, and have already succeeded in shaping federal policy and limiting family planning assistance.
The tragedy is that responsible family planning programs do much more to actually avert abortions than the anti-choice campaign of violence and intimidation ever can.
In fact, restricting Americans' birth control options will inevitably lead to more crisis pregnancies and more abortions.
That's the exact opposite of what so-called "pro-lifers" say they're for. Good reason to ask what their leaders are really against.
Make time to save your right to choose. Before the "pro-lifers" start making your choices for you.
Take action! Here's my urgent contribution to support Planned Parenthood's Campaign to Keep Abortion Safe and Legal:
NAME
ADDRESS
CITY
STATE
ZIP
Don't wait until women are dying again.
Planned Parenthood®
© 1989 PPFA, Inc. This ad was paid for with private contributions.

Figure 1.1 Low camera angle. Reprinted with permission of the Planned Parenthood® Federation of America, Inc. Copyright © Al Tielemans.

this device by enabling the child to check her or his interpretation against an adult yardstick (see Messaris, 1983). Both of these ways of learning the meaning of a communicational convention (contextual cueing and adult tuition) also occur in language, and in this respect the acquisition of competence in visual interpretation may be similar to the learning of a language. However, there is something else about the camera-angle example that distinguishes it sharply from the conventions of language.

I assume that I am saying the obvious when I point out that the use of camera angle to emphasize power or weakness is not an *arbitrary* convention (in other words, it is not like the *words* "powerful" or "weak," whose forms are unrelated to the concepts they denote). Rather, this visual convention reproduces the structural features of real-life situations: looking up at powerful people and looking down at weak people (cf. Schwartz, 1981), a realm of experience that is likely to be particularly relevant during the formative years of childhood. In other words, this visual device is based on perceptual habits a viewer can be expected to have developed in everyday, real-world experience, even without any previous exposure to visual media.

It follows, therefore, that first-time or inexperienced viewers should be able to make sense of the low-angle device (when it appears in the appropriate context) much more readily than they could comprehend a linguistic convention. It also follows that the need for visual-literacy training as an aid to comprehension of this device should be correspondingly low. Conversely, explicit training may be even more necessary for building awareness of intentionality and artifice in the case of the camera-angle convention than in the case of language. For example, in a political ad, the verbal statement that a candidate is a "strong leader" may proclaim its intentions more obtrusively than does a shot of the candidate on a podium, seen from below.

Of course, camera angle is only a single example of visual "language." In order to establish the more general point that pictorial conventions as a whole are based on preexisting mental processes for the interpretation of nonpictorial experience, we must examine these conventions systematically. Such an examination, together with an overview of available empirical evidence, is the subject of the next two chapters. However, the reader who is more interested in the practical consequences of visual literacy (discussed in Chapters 4 and 5) may find it useful to have, at this point, a brief synopsis of the nature of pictorial conventions and their relationship to nonpictorial interpretational skills. This discussion will be followed by an overview of the rest of the book's argument.

Still Images

We will begin by examining still images (drawings, paintings, photographs), then proceed to a discussion of film and television. A convenient way to frame this examination of still images is to ask the following question: Assuming we could find someone who had never seen pictures before (just as Balázs's colonial administrator had never seen movies), is there any a priori reason that the person should not be able to interpret a picture? In other words, what obstacles to interpretation might we *expect* pictures to pose to a person with little or no previous pictorial experience? Obviously, one possible obstacle is lack of familiarity with the cultural content of the pictures— i.e., with the objects or events or situations depicted in them—but that type of barrier is not peculiar to pictures as such; it would apply equally to other media, as well as to direct, unmediated encounters. The more essential barriers, as far as pictorial communication is concerned, are those having to do with representational conventions peculiar to this medium.

The considerable previous literature on this issue (e.g., Gombrich, 1960; Snyder, 1980; Wartofsky, 1984) has pointed to three broad categories of pictorial conventions that we might expect, a priori, to pose interpretational obstacles to a first-time or inexperienced viewer: (1) many types of pictures (e.g., unshaded outline drawings, black-and-white photographs) fail to reproduce the range of colors and degrees of illumination of the real world; (2) any picture that attempts to represent the third dimension must do so on a flat, two-dimensional surface; and (3) certain pictorial styles (e.g., sketches, stick figures) omit many details of the shapes of persons and other objects. All three of these categories denote significant discrepancies between the appearance of pictures and the appearance of reality, and, in the absence of any further information, we might want to conclude that a first-time viewer would probably not be able to make much sense of pictures containing these conventions before having gained some experience with them.

As it happens, however, this conclusion would be premature. There is, as I have indicated, a growing body of systematic research on the interpretational abilities of pictorially inexperienced viewers, and the findings converge on the following points: Of the three categories of conventions listed above, only one—the rendition of three dimensions by two-dimensional means—has been found to cause any appreciable degree of trouble to inexperienced viewers. Neither of the other two categories of conventions presents a significant obstacle. In other words, previous experience is not a prerequisite for the interpretation of outline drawings, black-and-white photographs, sketches, or stick figures—to name only four kinds of pictures.

What could account for these findings? What is it that allows inexperienced viewers to circumvent the barriers posed by such "obviously" unrealistic conventions as lack of color, lack of shading, and incomplete form? Conversely, what is it about the collapsing of three dimensions into two that makes comprehension so much more difficult? As Hagen (1980) pointed out in an earlier review of this literature, the investigators who have produced these findings have not typically tried to give an encompassing and coherent answer to these questions. A major reason for this gap in the literature is the fact that, until fairly recently, scientific knowledge on the topic of visual perception *in general* (as opposed to the more specific problem of pictorial perception) did not point to any clear solution of these difficulties. Since the early 1980s, however, major advances in the theory of vision, most notably by the late David Marr of MIT (see Marr, 1982), have resulted in reconceptualizations of this topic that have crucial implications for our understanding of what goes into the interpretation of a picture. I will argue here that current conceptualizations of the general visual process would predict precisely those patterns of pictorial interpretation by inexperienced viewers that were outlined above.

The specific aspect of vision theory from which this connection emerges has to do with the brain's "translation" of the retinal image into a mental representation of identifiable objects in three-dimensional space. In Marr's account—or, rather, in the simplified, nontechnical version with which I am going to work here—this process involves three successive steps. In the first step, visual information is transmitted from the retina to the brain. Essentially a two-dimensional array of light and color values, this information is processed by the brain to detect the outlines of objects and the edges of surfaces. The end result is a mental representation that can be thought of as corresponding to an outline drawing of the scene the eyes are looking at. On the basis of this outline representation, the brain proceeds to figure out the scene's three-dimensional properties and to identify the various objects in it.

The crucial point, as far as the perception of pictures is concerned, is that "inattention" to details of shading and color is part of every human being's standard mental apparatus for inferring three-dimensionality and object identity in a visual scene. Therefore, we should not be surprised to find that lack of shading and color in the specific case of pictures does not pose significant interpretational obstacles to uninitiated viewers. As has already been noted, this finding is precisely what researchers on pictorial perception have come to, not only in studies of adult viewers living in environments with limited exposure to pictorial media (e.g., Cook, 1981; Kennedy and Ross, 1975) but also in ingenious experiments with animals (e.g., Zimmerman and Hochberg, 1970) and in a classic case of a child raised in New York City with no exposure to pictures (Hochberg and Brooks, 1962).

Once the brain has extracted an outline representation from the retinal image, a second step in the interpretational process assigns depth to the various parts of the outline—i.e., calculates distances between the viewer and each part of the scene. This extraction of the third dimension from the two-dimensional outline representation is a complicated process involving several different kinds of information. The most crucial of these for present purposes are the following four:

1. Binocular disparity—i.e., the difference between the image formed in the left eye and the image formed in the right eye. According to the well-known principle of stereoscopic vision, this difference can give the viewer a powerful sense of depth, especially when the eyes are focused on close objects.
2. Motion parallax—i.e., the amount of change brought about in the retinal image by a change in the relative position of the viewer vis-à-vis the object or scene being viewed. The standard example of how motion parallax works is what happens when we look out of the window of a moving train: Objects close to us move across our visual field more rapidly than do distant objects.
3. Texture gradients—i.e., apparent changes within our retinal image of the density of a regular pattern or texture in the scene we are looking at. The clearest example of this phenomenon is the case of linear perspective: When we look at a pattern of straight, parallel lines stretching away from us, the visual image we receive is one of increasing density as distance increases until all the lines appear to converge in a single "vanishing point." The same general principle is also in evidence, although perhaps less obviously, when we look at any surface bearing a regular pattern: tiles, pebbles, grass, and so on.
4. Occlusion—i.e., the blockage of the view of part of one object by another object. This is a trivially obvious but nonetheless compelling clue as to which of two objects is closer to us. Note, however, that the depth information yielded by this clue is strictly relative. It informs us that one object is closer than another but can give us no sense of *how much* closer.

What do these facts about depth perception in real-world vision tell us about the more specific question that concerns us here—viz., inexperienced viewers' ability to infer depth in pictures? As should be readily apparent, two of the four components of real-life depth perception described above, binocular disparity and motion parallax, cannot possibly be present in pictures (ordinary, nonholographic still pictures). That absence in itself might be expected to cause some trouble to a viewer not accustomed to making judgments of depth without these two crucial aids. But the problem is not simply one of having fewer depth cues to work with. It is also the case that the remaining two types of information, texture gradients and occlusion, are of limited utility as cues to the general three-dimensional properties of a visual space. The problem with occlusion has already been noted. As for texture gradients, although one can readily think of situations in which they might give a perfectly adequate sense of the spatial characteristics of a scene (e.g., a picture of a room interior with uniformly tiled floor and walls), one can just as easily imagine scenes with no patterned surfaces whatsoever (e.g., many nature scenes).

Because of these limitations, we would expect inexperienced viewers to have trouble seeing depth in pictures; we would also expect to find that the creators of images have developed alternative means of conveying depth information. The latter issue will be examined in detail in Chapter 2. As for the former, there is indeed research to indicate that depth perception may be a problem for inexperienced viewers. The best-known instance occurred in a series of studies by Hudson and others, in which pictorially inexperienced viewers (mostly from isolated rural areas) tended to interpret a picture of a hunting scene as being relatively flat (i.e., containing all its objects in a single plane), whereas viewers who had greater pictorial experience were much more likely to see the picture as a representation of three-dimensional space (e.g., Hudson, 1967).

The final stage of visual perception to be considered here, step three in the overall process we have been discussing, is object identification. In this last step, the outlines of objects, whose distance from each other and from the viewer has been determined in step two, are now used to infer the objects' identities. Although this process is not yet understood as well as the ones we have examined thus far, it seems fairly certain that the process entails a "reduction" of objects' outlines into a more elementary representational form, in which only the basic underlying structure is retained and many incidental details are discarded. These more basic structural representations are then matched against a "dictionary" of object structures in the brain's memory. It follows that two different outlines will be labeled as the same object as long as the underlying structures yielded by the outlines are the same. In real-life visual perception, an obvious example would be our ability to identify a person under varying conditions of illumination—bright, with many details visible, or dark, with many details missing.

These principles suggest that our ability to interpret such incomplete images as sketches and stick figures may be an extension of an everyday, real-life perceptual skill rather than something we have to learn with specific reference to pictorial conventions. We might also expect, therefore, that sketches and other incomplete images should not greatly curtail the ability of inexperienced viewers to identify objects in pictures. As has been noted, the available research corroborates this expectation, even in the case of highly attenuated pictorial representations (e.g., Cook, 1981).

In general, then, both the previous research and the theoretical argument developed here converge on the notion that there is considerable continuity between picture perception and everyday, real-life vision. Although the lack of two important depth cues and the limited usefulness of the other two may make pictorial depth perception difficult for inexperienced viewers, the recognition of objects in pictures seems unproblematic under a broad range of circumstances. Furthermore, many pictorial conventions that might at first blush seem quite "unrealistic" appear in fact to be interpretable on the basis of any viewer's real-world visual skills.

Even in the case of depth perception, as we shall see in Chapter 2, it would be hard to argue that the informational cues typically used by more experienced viewers constitute an arbitrary, exclusively pictorial set of conventions. Finally, it should be added that much of what has been said above also applies to an important aspect of the interpretation of film and television—namely, the viewer's recognition of the objects in a single image. It should be evident as well that because film and television, unlike still pictures, are capable of incorporating the major depth cue of motion parallax, depth perception in these media should be less problematic for the inexperienced viewer than it is in the case of still pictures.

Film and Television

Film and television are complex modes of communication involving the interplay of pictures, speech, and music, as well as other kinds of visual and aural elements (e.g., written titles or sound effects). Our focus here will be primarily on the relationships among the images, although we will occasionally examine sound, too. In discussing how the succession of images is used to create meaning in film and television, it is useful to make a distinction between two kinds of situations—on the one hand, editing or other kinds of transitions within a single location and time frame (e.g., successive views of different characters in a scene from a fiction film, various features of a landscape in a nature documentary, or a sequence of moves on the playing field in a sports broadcast); and, on the other hand, transitions across time, place, or both (e.g., scene changes in a fiction film or transitions from newsroom to on-site coverage in news broadcasts). Each of these two general situations involves its own distinctive set of conventions for making the events on the screen intelligible to the spectator.

Among the array of devices employed by films and TV programs for same-place/same-time transitions, three general categories will be discussed here. Collectively, these three categories give a fair representation, I think, of how meaning is created in this kind of transition. The three categories of convention are: (1) creation of an image of a coherent object, action, or space through the successive presentation of partial views; (2) rendition of characters' unverbalized thoughts and feelings through the juxtaposition of facial close-ups and appropriate contextual cues; and (3) modulation of emphasis and emotional tone in a scene through variation in camera positioning vis-à-vis the scene's action.

The first of these categories encompasses a variety of devices intended to help the viewer piece together a coherent sense of the world in front of the camera from the partial views presented on the screen. There is evidence that early filmmakers were somewhat hesitant about departing from the all-encompassing, single-viewpoint image characteristic of the first movies (Jesionowski, 1987; Musser, 1991). There was apparently some fear that breaking up the action through editing (e.g., cutting back and forth between two characters in conversation) might confuse the viewer. Perhaps as a consequence of this apprehension, when this kind of editing took hold in Hollywood cinema, it was accompanied by several well-known rules intended to help viewers maintain their orientation. These rules include the use of an encompassing "establishing shot" at some early point in the action; confining successive points of view to one side of the action (the "180-degree-line" rule); and keying shot transitions to characters' off-screen glances (so that a shot following an off-screen glance represents what the character is looking at).

The extent to which these aids to comprehension are in fact necessary is not clear. What does seem to be true, however, is that within the framework they create, the mental activity of synthesizing a sequence of partial views into a coherent whole is not problematic even for inexperienced viewers of film and television—contrary to the assumptions of early filmmakers. Compelling evidence on this point comes from ongoing research by Renée Hobbs and her colleagues on first-time viewers of video narratives in an isolated village in Kenya. The first phase of this research examined the villagers' interpretations of two versions of a videotaped story, one unedited, the other incorporating the kind of editing we are concerned with here. Comprehension of both versions was high, and no significant loss of comprehension was caused by the editing (Hobbs et al., 1988).

Evidently, then, a movie viewer's ability to make sense of this general visual convention must rest on a preexisting, real-world cognitive skill—namely, the process through which all human beings beyond infancy construct a coherent sense of their immediate environment by making successive glances in various directions (see Hochberg and Brooks, 1978, pp. 281–288). This process, which will be discussed in more detail in Chapter 3, is rarely replicated exactly in movies, but the empirical evidence allows us to say, at least, that when such things as the 180-degree-line rule are observed, the analogy is close enough for practical purposes.

The second category of conventions of same-place/same-time editing (or, more generally, image juxtaposition) to be considered here has to do with the visual rendition of characters' unspoken thoughts or feelings. When a character's subjective experience is itself visual, as in dreams, memories, or hallucinations, it can be shown directly on the screen through such devices as the flashback. Because these devices often involve a transition in time or place, however, they will be discussed later, together with other forms of space/time transition. When subjective experience is not primarily visual (e.g., when it involves love, hate, and various other emotions), film and television are relatively deficient compared to verbal narratives in representing the inner life of people. This deficiency is undoubtedly one reason for the nonvisual convention of subjective voice-over narration in fiction films and TV programs.

The most straightforward visual device for the representation of nonvisual subjective reality is probably facial expression. In fact, it has been argued that the importance of facial expression in movies has made audiences more sensitive to this aspect of communication, even in their everyday lives, than they would otherwise be (Balázs, 1952, pp. 39–45). However, as research on real-life facial expression has indicated, the face by itself is typically an incomplete informational cue (Birdwhistell, 1970). To make sense of facial expression, we need to combine its "message" with the information provided by the rest of the body (gesture and posture) as well as the broader context in which the expression occurs. This interplay of context and facial expression was studied extensively by one of the earliest film theorists, Lev Kuleshov, who also reportedly performed several experiments demonstrating what may be called the "Kuleshov effect": When a close-up of a person's face is juxtaposed with shots of various emotional situations (a corpse in a coffin, a prisoner being let out of jail, etc.), viewers interpret the same facial expression differently depending on the shot it is juxtaposed with.

Kuleshov's theorizing and experiments, performed in the Soviet Union in the 1920s, were based on an already established convention of Hollywood cinema—the juxtaposition of a face and a significant object or situation—which has remained a central device for the portrayal of fictional characters' emotional responses. More recently, this device has also come to be used in nonfiction film, television interview programs, and political advertising, sometimes in morally questionable ways (e.g., potential distortion of an interview subject's true position). These issues will be discussed in more detail in Chapter 5. For the moment, the essential point about this convention is that it is based on an interpretational skill—viz., combining the evidence of face and context—that all adequately socialized people develop in their real social environments, regardless of the presence or absence of visual media.

The third type of convention we are going to look at here also appears to be based on principles of real-life social perception, although here the relationship is not always so direct. In our earlier discussion of camera angle, it was argued that the standard use of camera angle to emphasize power or weakness is derived from the analogous real-life experience of looking up at bigger, more powerful people and looking down at smaller, weaker ones. A similar argument can be extended to a broader range of visual conventions having to do with the placement and orientation of the camera vis-à-vis what is being filmed or videotaped. More precisely, it is the relative placement or transitions in placement that provide the cues.

This variable is the director's principal tool for controlling the nature of the viewer's involvement with the events on the screen. For example, at the climax of a scene, the camera may move closer; relatively tighter close-ups may also be used to emphasize the protagonist and encourage the audience's identification with that character. For the same reason, the protagonist may be framed more directly; at the conclusion of a film, as the tension is released, the camera may pull away from the action. What all these very frequently encountered practices have in common is that they appear to derive their meaning from the way in which intimacy and involvement are related to distance and orientation in real life. For this reason, Meyrowitz (1986) has suggested the label "paraproxemics" for this cluster of conventions, a term derived by extension from "proxemics," the area of communication research dealing with the social meaning of interpersonal distance and orientation. Meyrowitz's label is a formal expression of the notion that here, too, film and TV conventions appear to be constructed on the basis of pre-existing cognitive principles for the perception of our physical and social environment.

Up to this point, then, we have seen that some of the most fundamental devices through which meaning is created in still and motion pictures derive their meaning from analogous real-life perceptual habits rather than from purely arbitrary conventions. In the case, however, of the other major category of film and television devices to be discussed here—viz., transitions in which location and/or time frame change—there can be no analogy to real-life perception, because place and time are always continuous in reality. (Of course, movielike discontinuities can occur in dreams, and the idea that there is a kinship between movies and dreams is among the oldest notions in film theory. But relatively few filmmakers have ever tried to pursue this analogy systematically, and the actual logic of most time and space transitions in mainstream movies is actually quite different from the principles described by systematic investigators of the visual component of dreams, e.g., Freud, 1952, pp. 60–72; see Tomlinson, 1991.)

In seeking the basis of intelligibility of space/time transitions in film and television, a useful starting point is the distinction between fictional material (most feature films, TV sitcoms, soap operas) and nonfiction (news broadcasts, sports, game shows). The significant point about this distinction is that when there is a change in location, time frame, or both in a nonfictional context, it is typically "explained" in words. For example, the anchor of a news program will orally introduce location footage or an on-site reporter; a sports announcer will say "Let's get another angle on that" or "Let's take another look at that" to set up an instant replay; the voice-over in a nature documentary will announce the changes of location and season or new phases in the life-cycle of an animal; and so forth. In general, then, it seems that the sequencing of images in nonfictional space/time transitions typically conforms to the logic of verbal narration. Of course, some juxtapositions of images might make sense to viewers even without the accompanying words, but it seems doubtful that the conventions entailed in these transitions constitute a *new* language as opposed to an extension of the principles of verbal narration.

Similar doubts can be raised about space/time transitions in fiction films and TV programs. In the century that has elapsed since the birth of cinema, the conventions associated with transitions of this sort have gone through a number of different evolutionary phases (I will discuss some of this history in more detail in Chapter 3). The driving force behind the evolution of these conventions has been a consistent, seemingly inexorable tendency to rid the transitions of any explanatory devices. This tendency has been documented by systematic research (Carey, 1982), but even the most casual viewer of old movies can hardly be unaware of the contrast between the instantaneous scene changes of today's films or TV programs and the intertitles, trains and boats, calendars and clocks, or other transitional devices of the past.

How can we account for the fact that viewers are able to make sense of "unexplained" transitions? Should this ability be seen as a form of visual literacy? When D. W. Griffith and other early filmmakers first began to experiment with the removal of intertitles and other transitional devices, they sometimes assumed that viewers would have been conditioned to understand instantaneous transitions because of the presence of such transitions in the novels of Charles Dickens and other literary narratives (see Williams, 1980, p. 35; also Eisenstein, 1944, pp. 213–216). Whatever validity this assumption may have had at the time, in today's world the idea that a filmmaker could presume upon the audience's familiarity with literary conventions seems rather quaint. However, the assumption that space/time transitions in visual narratives might be based on the same principles of intelligibility as certain literary prototypes leads to a productive broadening of the focus of our topic.

In all modes of communication, not just in film or television, it is possible to make a distinction between two complementary sources of meaning: the code and the context. Codes are rules of correspondence between form and meaning. In the case of language, for example, our knowledge of the code is what allows us to infer tense from the form of a verb, to recognize the predicate from its structural position in a sentence, and to attach meanings to the groupings of sound which constitute each individual word. In the case of images, some examples of codes already described in this chapter are the rule of occlusion for inferring depth; the principle by which camera angle is related to a sense of power and weakness; and, in the present context, the image of a calendar shedding its pages as an indicator of the passage of time. Although it may sometimes appear that interpreting communication is simply a matter of applying the appropriate codes, the fact, of course, is that human communication always entails an interaction between code and context. This interaction makes it possible for intended meanings to be inferred despite ambiguities in the code, misuses of the code, or external sources of "noise." This interaction, or, more precisely, the fact that interpretation can be based on context is, as I see it, the reason that both verbal and visual narratives have been able to dispense with explicit explanatory devices for certain kinds of transitions.

The atrophying of codes is hardly confined to the sorts of devices with which we are directly concerned here. For example, the English language has been able to drop rules for indicating distinctions of gender (the masculine and feminine forms of the word "cousin" in the original French) and number (the singular and plural forms of "you" in Middle English) because aspects of context, such as the listener's knowledge about the speaker's family or the number of listeners present, can usually be counted on to compensate for the loss of code (see Baugh and Cable, 1978, pp. 242–243; Williams, 1975, pp. 244–249). It seems to me that a similar process has been at work in the area of cinematic space/time transitions. The tendency to eliminate explicit explanatory devices amounts to a progressive shifting of the burden of explanation away from the transition itself and onto the context.

Given these considerations, the notion that viewers' ability to make sense of space/time transitions in contemporary films and TV programs requires prior familiarity with a visual language or grammar—i.e., with a set of medium-specific codes—seems self-evidently untenable. The principal consequence of the historical trend described above is that there are hardly any transitional codes left for viewers to be familiar with. To the extent that interpretation of these transitions depends on familiarity with principles of narrative progression, we might want to speak of a "narrative literacy" (see Meadowcroft and Reeves, 1989). However, it is unclear how *visual* such a skill would be, because: (1) there may be no sharp distinction between the kinds of space/time shifts one finds in visual narratives and those that occur in everyday verbal storytelling; and (2) even in visual narratives, narrative progression is often a matter of dialogue.

At the same time, however, mere familiarity with the real-life equivalent of the events portrayed in a fiction film or TV program is often a sufficient basis for a contextual interpretation of space/time changes. For example, at the conclusion of Stanley Kubrick's *The Shining* (1980), there is a scene in which the injured protagonist is stumbling through deep snow, late at night. Exhausted, he slumps to the ground. Then suddenly it is day and he is dead. This leap forward in time, which is here accomplished through a straight cut, is representative of a type of transition that older films would probably have handled through a dissolve (giving a clearer separation of the two time frames) or through such devices as an insert shot of the sun rising (i.e., an explicit indicator of the passage of time). But even in the absence of any devices of this sort, any viewer should be able to grasp the meaning of the sequence from *The Shining* on the basis of two universally available items of contextual knowledge: (1) night is followed by day; (2) prolonged exposure to severe cold can lead to death (especially if someone is already injured).

The possibility that this kind of contextual knowledge—i.e., knowledge that is not dependent on previous exposure to film or television—can serve as an adequate basis for inexperienced viewers' interpretations of space/time transitions has been tested by Hobbs and her colleagues in a follow-up study to their earlier investigation of point-of-view changes in editing. As with the original study, the follow-up was done in Kenya among first- and second-time viewers of video. The study was based on a short film produced locally by the researchers that depicted events and circumstances with which all the viewers were thoroughly familiar. Although the film contained a number of space/time transitions, including a flashback, these viewers' comprehension of the narrative was virtually flawless (Hobbs and Frost, 1989).

As in the case of same-place/same-time changes, then, there are both theoretical and empirical grounds for believing that space/time transitions in film and television do not confront first-time viewers with the kinds of interpretational obstacles whose existence is sometimes taken for granted by scholars who write about these matters. It is true that there is some anecdotal evidence (such as Balázs's story about the confused colonial administrator) that points to an opposite conclusion, and I would not want to dismiss such anecdotes as exaggerations or fabrications. However, I would argue that it is highly unlikely that the miscomprehensions reported in these anecdotes were caused by *visual* obstacles as opposed, for example, to lack of familiarity with the circumstances depicted in a particular movie. (Recall that Balázs's colonial administrator had been absent from his homeland for many years.) It is also worth emphasizing that the two studies by Hobbs and her colleagues constitute the only systematic body of research to date on inexperienced *adult* viewers' interpretations of cinematic conventions.

More generally, then, there are good reasons for being very skeptical of the hypothesis that a specifically visual literacy is a prerequisite for understanding the kinds of visual conventions used in most mass-mediated movies or TV programs. Rather, as I will argue in more detail in Chapter 3, the intelligibility of these conventions appears to be largely a matter of analogy to real-life perceptual cues (in the case of same-place/same-time editing), verbal explanation (nonfictional space/time transitions), or contextual information (fictional space/time transitions). Furthermore, as Chapter 2 will demonstrate in more detail, reproduction of real-life perceptual cues (with the notable exception of depth information) also seems to account for the intelligibility of a wide range of still-image conventions. In the remainder of this chapter, I want to give a brief outline of what I see as the implications of these arguments in two major areas: first, the broader cognitive consequences of visual literacy; second, the relationship between visual literacy and awareness of visual artistry and manipulation. As I have done thus far in this introductory chapter, I will be summarizing arguments presented in more detail later in this book (Chapters 4 and 5, respectively).

Cognitive Consequences of Visual Literacy

That visual literacy has been unjustly neglected by our educational institutions is an idea one encounters frequently, not only among educators and communication scholars but also outside the academic world (e.g., see Pittman, 1990). This idea often takes the more specific form of a comparison between language and images. Our educational system is too concerned with words, this argument goes, and considerations of balance require that we pay more attention to other modes of communication. Because images have become so ubiquitous as a result of the various technologies of the mass media, surely visual literacy in particular should be a major focus of any attempt to achieve this kind of balance.

If the consequences envisioned by holders of this view are primarily artistic—i.e., enhancement of aesthetic awareness—or critical—enhancement of awareness of the workings of commercials, political ads, and other forms of overt or covert persuasion—then I agree completely that the present state of education in visual literacy is generally inadequate. However, advocates of visual-literacy education often argue that a more visually oriented educational system would also lead to broader cognitive benefits, providing students a new set of mental tools with which to understand the physical and social environment (e.g., see Chideya, 1991; Greenfield, 1984). Put another way, what this argument assumes is that images, like language, are a distinct means of making sense of reality and that visual education will give students an alternative, but equally valuable, form of access to knowledge and understanding. As my students sometimes ask: "Why can't term papers and theses be done visually instead of verbally, especially in courses in visual communication?"

Here, it seems to me, the equation between images and language has been taken too literally. To argue that there should be more of a balance between linguistic and pictorial education doesn't mean such a balance would enable us to do with images all the kinds of things we now do with words. Furthermore, as the line of reasoning I have been trying to develop up to this point implies, even if images do have a potential role to play as cognitive tools, it does not necessarily follow that this function is dependent on prior visual education.

A useful way to begin an examination of these issues is to make a distinction between two rather different functions or aspects of communication, which I will label, very simply, analysis and description. Description entails an account of a particular series of events or of the features of a particular object or situation. Analysis differs from description in two major ways that concern us here: First, it often deals with generalities, classes of objects, situations, or events rather than individual cases; second, and more important, rather than simply reporting events or the characteristics of objects or situations, it is concerned with establishing the conditions under which these events or characteristics can be expected to occur. Description and analysis are routine and sometimes overlapping features of our use of language. For example, in a single stretch of conversation we might describe the harrowing circumstances of a family member's recent hospitalization and then go on to discuss the probable causes of the ailment, the effectiveness of various known cures, the likelihood that new cures will be found, and so on. But how compatible are these two functions of communication with the characteristics of images?

As far as what I am calling description is concerned, I don't think there could be much argument about its compatibility. Conveying information about the features of particular objects or the details of particular events is so central a part of what we do with images that even raising the question in this connection may seem peculiar. However, when it comes to analysis, we face a very different situation. Analysis, in the sense in which I am using the term here, often deals with general categories rather than individual items, and it is characterized by a focus on causality, contingent relationships, hypotheticals, estimates of likelihood, and so forth. For all these aspects of meaning, verbal language contains conventions (individual terms or syntactic devices) that indicate explicitly what kind of statement is being made. In the case of images, however, such conventions are almost totally lacking.

I say "almost" because images do seem to have a limited capacity for making certain kinds of explicit generalizations. For example, the generic images of men and women on bathroom doors, or the generic cigarette in "no-smoking" signs, are explicit symbols for classes of objects rather than for any individual man, woman, or cigarette. But the range of generic images is limited to the world of concrete objects or events (e.g., we can show an individual cause of illness—say, a picture of someone smoking—but there can be no generic image illustrating the abstract term "cause"), and within that world it is further limited to classes of *similar* objects or events (i.e., we can have a generic "person" and a generic "cigarette" but not a generic "object"). In the absence of explicit means of conveying generalizations, the creators of images will sometimes use such devices as a sequence of individual cases, on the basis of which the viewer herself or himself is supposed to infer the implied generalization. To take an example from the world of advertising (in which analytical statements are hardly a primary concern, of course), a much-discussed campaign for AT&T featured an ad in which several individual people were shown communicating with their loved ones over the telephone, the implied message being that AT&T brings "people," in general, together (see Arlen, 1980, for a detailed discussion of this ad campaign).

Similar devices are routinely used as substitutes for types of meanings that images cannot express explicitly. For example, a recent TV ad consists of a number of vignettes in which husbands or wives who are initially reluctant to return their spouses' early-morning affections become extremely responsive after using Scope mouthwash. This "before-after" contrast as a symbol of causal transformation has become highly conventionalized in visual advertising, and it might seem to be an adequate visual equivalent of a feature of analytical language. However, the equivalence is at best very weak. For one thing, there is evidence that the kind of visual device we are considering here—i.e., a juxtaposition of images from which the viewer is supposed to infer a causal claim or other type of analytical statement—can be problematic even for experienced viewers (people who watch TV regularly) unless it is accompanied by narration or a caption that makes the point verbally (see Messaris and Nielsen, 1989).

A more significant reason these devices are poor substitutes for genuine analytical discourse—and the reason my examples had to be drawn from the "quasi-analytical" area of advertising—is that the real world is rarely as uniform or as predictable as the world of advertising. The type of device used in the AT&T and Scope ads—a series of vignettes in which the product brings about a desirable outcome—may be an adequate tool of analytical communication when all events in a certain category are similar or when a certain cause always has the same effect. But the moment we go beyond such a simple state of affairs, we run into trouble. For example, how would we use this type of device to convey the following, fairly routine analytical statement: "This product is not always effective, but it is more effective than its competitors"? Would we start with a series of nine effective before-after sequences, add one ineffective one, and then contrast this series with another batch of before-after sequences for each of the competitors? I think this example has already brought us well into the realm of absurdity, even though we have barely begun to penetrate the extraordinary range of complexity that analytical language is capable of.

The first time I discussed these issues in one of my classes, a student asked me, "But what about a filmmaker like Eisenstein? Don't his films do what you say visuals can't do?" Since then I have come to realize that one of the most effective ways of illustrating these points is in fact to refer to the scenes in which Sergei Eisenstein attempted to "editorialize" (e.g., the heavy-handed sequence from *October* (1928) in which objects of worship from around the world are strung together, one after another, to make the point that all religions, "high" or "low," arise from the same primitive impulses). As Prince (1990) has pointed out, the editing techniques Eisenstein and other early filmmakers developed in sequences such as this are essentially the same as those used in the kinds of TV advertising discussed above—and the present-day ads seem more sophisticated in this respect. In view of the dazzling visual inventiveness of the more purely narrative portions of Eisenstein's films, the relative crudeness of his "editorializing" suggests that it is indeed the nature of the medium—specifically, its lack of explicit indicators of causality, contingency, and the like—that makes it unsuitable as a vehicle of analytical communication. With respect to the topic of visual literacy, then, I repeat that, whatever other benefits students might receive from a more visually oriented educational system, a new analytical "language" is not likely to be one of them. It follows, therefore, that the more appropriate place to look for cognitive consequences of visual literacy is in the descriptive function of communication, an area in which images are very much at home.

In discussing the cognitive implications of the descriptive symbol systems of images, it may be useful to begin with one more comparison between images and language. As a system of symbols for representing the objects and events of the world around us, language is sometimes seen as conferring upon its users a "worldview," a distinctive slant or perspective on those objects and events. The reasoning behind this assumption about language is based on the fact that the connection between words and the things they stand for is arbitrary, in the sense that there is no resemblance between the symbol and its referent. In the absence of such a resemblance, linguistic communication depends on the establishment of a relatively fixed set of categories and labels for the phenomena to which such communication will make reference. What this amounts to is the imposition on reality of a set of distinctions and categories, and because any two languages may differ with regard to the distinctions they make, their users' views of reality could conceivably be shaped accordingly.

Perhaps the best-documented example of this kind of difference between languages is the fact that the number of basic color terms in some languages is much smaller than that which a speaker of English takes for granted (e.g., there are languages with only two color terms, black and white). Equally clear instances of divergent linguistic classification systems can be found in various languages' terminologies for shape and size, animals and plants, and space and time. It is sometimes assumed that, in and of themselves, these differences prove that language shapes worldview, and more than one prominent anthropologist has used language as the basis for descriptions of such things as the "primitive mind" or the "Oriental view of reality." However, there have also been several attempts to test the consequences of terminological differences empirically, beginning with such studies as Carroll and Casagrande (1958) and including more recent work by researchers such as Kay and Kempton (1984). This research suggests that, although the idea that language differences lead to radically different conceptions of reality may be a romantic exaggeration, a smaller-scale "fine-tuning" of people's sensitivities to shape, color, and so on does seem to occur. As we shall see in Chapter 4, there is evidence that cross-cultural differences in systems of linguistic representation of reality reflect the different requirements of various cultures' physical and social environments. In this sense, then, a language's representational system can be seen as a means of adapting a child's developing cognitive/perceptual framework to the task of life in a particular cultural milieu.

Keeping in mind this background material about language, we can now go on to look at images. The idea that the representational conventions of a culture's images might shape the worldview of the members of that culture (more precisely, of the children growing up in that culture) may seem, on the face of it, an obvious proposition. In this obviousness, however, there is also the danger of tautology—i.e., of seeing the images themselves as evidence of the worldview. I have insisted on the importance of outlining the equivalent notions in the case of language because it seems to me that these can serve as our guide regarding the kinds of criteria we should apply in our examination of images. As I hope my discussion of language made clear, the notion that a representational system might shape its users' world-view is contingent on the presence, within that system, of a particular way of "carving up" an area of reality (e.g., a particular way of dividing up the color spectrum, a particular way of classifying shapes). Applying this criterion to images, we would be led to look for instances in which a certain representational style made a consistent set of distinctions within the flux of experience.

Examples of this kind of thing are not hard to find. As far as color is concerned, there are numerous instances of pictorial style in which the spectrum is consistently reduced to a palette of no more than three or four encompassing terms (e.g., archaic Greek vase painting, seventeenth-century Japanese prints, Native American art of the Pacific Northwest). A more complicated and more interesting example is described in a very influential cross-cultural study of art styles by John L. Fischer (1961). In a comparison between relatively egalitarian and relatively hierarchical societies, Fischer found that the art of the former was characterized by the repetition of similar design elements (people, animals, or abstract figures), whereas the art of the latter was characterized by the presence of a variety of different elements.

The obvious hypothesis that emerges from this finding is that these art styles might have served to "bias" social perspectives in the direction of lesser or greater awareness of interpersonal differences, respectively.

Cases such as the one described by Fischer are certainly most intriguing, and because the concept of worldview is often associated with social perception rather than with physical perception, this seems to be a particularly apt illustration of the process whose existence we are considering. However, I think we have to be very cautious in generalizing from such an example. Although at least some pictorial styles evidently do meet the criterion of distinctly partitioning reality, our discussion of language points to two further considerations that may be appreciably more problematic. First of all, it should be recalled that in the case of language the presence of a fixed categorization scheme is an unavoidable necessity arising from the arbitrary nature of linguistic signification. But images, as I have labored to show, are substantially analogic representations of the things they stand for, and this distinction has a very crucial implication. It means that, in principle, images are capable of representing the entire range of variation in a realm of experience and need not collapse this range into a more limited number of categories. Thus, although certain visual styles may exercise consistent limitations in their color palettes or in the range of variation of pictured objects' shapes, no visual style *has* to exercise such limitations in any particular area of representation. In an age dominated by photographic technology, lack of such limitations is probably the rule rather than the exception.

In other words, I am suggesting that a child growing up with the mass-mediated visuals of today's world is not being exposed to the kind of consistent partitioning of visual experience from which a "biasing" of vision might be expected to arise. Let me be the first to acknowledge, however, that this argument applies only to the *representational conventions* of images—in other words, that aspect of images for which linguistic analogies are usually thought most appropriate. If, however, we were to examine the *narrative content* of visual media, I have little doubt that we would encounter any number of category schemes with a potential for structuring audiences' worldviews—most notably, perhaps, the typical action drama's assignment of most of humanity to the category of non-hero.

A second reason for skepticism regarding the potential effects of images on viewers' perceptual frameworks stems from another important difference between images and language. Language is a mode of communication that all fully socialized people participate in routinely and actively, as both producers and receivers of messages. But in most societies—and certainly in all modern industrialized societies—the routine production of images is the province of a relatively small number of individuals and organizations. The bulk of the population is confined most of the time to the role of receiver. In the case of language, therefore, the categories of the representational system have a force and an obligatory character that as far as most people are concerned is missing from images. In other words, if internalization of the categories of a representational system is contingent on active use of those categories, the kind of shaping of cognitive/perceptual frameworks that appears to be attributable to language may be considerably less likely to occur in the case of images.

With respect to visual literacy, then, the view of images as a form of language is probably not very useful in thinking about the benefits of a visual education. Making students more aware of the representational conventions of images is not likely to give them access to an analytical apparatus they would otherwise have lacked, and it does not seem very likely to lead to the kind of adaptive restructuring of cognitive/perceptual frameworks that appears to occur in the case of "real" language. Nor is such visual training likely to make much difference in students' ability to extract descriptive information from images, because the representational conventions of images, unlike those of language, are typically based on informational cues that people learn to deal with in their everyday encounters with their real visual environments. If linguistic analogy is not the way to go in searching for possible cognitive consequences of visual education, is there another avenue of exploring these issues that might be more productive?

What may seem to be the obvious answer to this question is suggested by the work of Howard Gardner and others on the nature of human intelligence. Gardner (1983) has argued very eloquently that intelligence should be thought of not as a single phenomenon but rather as comprising a number of distinct types of mental ability, such as linguistic intelligence, mathematical intelligence, musical intelligence, and so forth (see also Gross, 1973b). In Gardner's theory, these various forms of intelligence are typically associated with distinct symbol systems, but the match is not always precise. In particular, although there is no specifically pictorial intelligence in Gardner's system, there is a more encompassing category, which he calls "spatial intelligence." At the heart of spatial intelligence is the ability to envision mentally the relationships among objects or parts of objects in three-dimensional space (e.g., what a particular structure might look like from various angles of view, how well one shape might mesh with or fit into another, etc.). It should be clear that this form of intelligence plays a role not only in art (painting, sculpture, dance) but also in geometrical thinking, in the design and construction of any solid object (furniture, buildings, machinery), and in much of our everyday interaction with the physical environment. Because vision is so important to these skills and because spatial intelligence contributes to picture-making ability, might spatial intelligence be an area of cognitive functioning enhanced by experience with images?

Our earlier discussion of how viewers make sense of still images and movies suggests at least two clear ways in which such a relationship between pictorial experience and spatial intelligence could be assumed to come about. As we have already seen, still images are not capable of reproducing the full range of depth cues that people use in real life. In Chapter 2 I will argue that as one consequence of this inadequacy, experienced viewers of images may become more sensitive to the remaining depth cues and may also learn to exploit certain types of information that do not ordinarily operate as real-world depth cues but that can serve as bases for inferences about depth in certain situations. If this argument is valid, it opens up the possibility that pictorial experience might also lead to a sharpening of viewers' abilities to judge depth in the real world. To the extent that enhanced depth perception can affect the more global category of spatial intelligence, we have one potential route connecting pictorial experience with more general cognitive skills.

A second way in which such a connection might conceivably come about emerges by implication from the earlier discussion about the interpretation of point-of-view changes in movies. If I am right that our ability to make sense of this aspect of editing is an extension, with some "stretching," of an everyday perceptual activity—deriving a coherent sense of space from successive partial views—then this "stretching" may have real-world consequences in terms of the viewer's general spatial intelligence.

Both of these possibilities may seem quite reasonable. However, as with the other cognitive-effects assumptions we have looked at, there is reason here for considerable skepticism. The problem in this case has to do with the exclusively visual character of pictorial experience. There is considerable evidence from research in developmental psychology that the development of spatial skills requires a combination of visual and physical experience—i.e., actually manipulating an object, walking through a certain space, and so on (Gregory, 1990). Still images and movies are obviously incapable of providing concomitant physical involvement of this sort. Consequently, no matter how logical a connection we can draw between various skills of pictorial interpretation on the one hand and spatial intelligence on the other, it may simply be the case that no transfer of skills is possible from the former area to the latter.

Fortunately, this is one aspect of our more general cognitive-effects topic on which there is some directly relevant research. For example, in a study concerned specifically with the lack of a physical component in the TV-viewing experience, Wachtel (1984) looked at the historical trends in Swiss children's scores on a spatial-intelligence test during the period of the introduction of television to Switzerland. Not only was there no increase in these scores, but there was actually a downward trend, which Wachtel interprets as possible evidence that television may have made children less active in the exploration of their environments. Of course, there are other possible interpretations of such findings, and there are also other, more elaborate studies of these issues, which we will examine in due course in Chapter 4. For the moment, however, it must be repeated that both theory and research leave us in considerable doubt concerning the likelihood that real-world spatial intelligence is affected by experience with images.

Awareness of Artistry and Visual Manipulation

Having spent several pages expressing skepticism about a potential consequence of visual literacy in which many proponents of visual education believe quite strongly, I want to conclude this introductory chapter by making it clear once again that there are other possible consequences in which I myself am a strong believer. As I have already suggested, the consequences I have in mind here are enhanced aesthetic awareness and enhanced awareness of the visual devices used for persuasive and other manipulative purposes. These matters are discussed in detail in Chapter 5; all I am going to do here is give a brief outline of some major points in order to illustrate the kind of approach I intend to use.

The issue of aesthetics, in particular, requires very little introduction because the general argument is very straightforward. My major assumption is that the perception of skill in the visual arts, or in any other medium, provides a type of vicarious satisfaction that is central to the aesthetic experience. Because the perception of skill clearly depends on an awareness of the conventions that the artist is following or breaking, enhanced awareness of conventions—which, as I see it, would be the basic aim of a visual-literacy curriculum—can be expected to enhance aesthetic appreciation. To bring this point down to the level of concrete instances, I will use as examples a pair of scenes from relatively recent films illustrating two opposite situations: on the one hand, violation of a convention that is normally never violated; and, on the other hand, resurrection of a convention that hardly anyone follows any more.

The first example is from Fred Schepisi's film *Iceman* (1984). This film begins with an arctic expedition's discovery of the frozen, perfectly preserved body of a stone-age hunter (played by John Lone). This protohuman is brought back to life, and he escapes from the people who have been supervising him and finds himself in a large underground laboratory, through whose labyrinthine corridors he charges wildly in search of a way out into the open air. Throughout this lengthy sequence, the director uses a visual device I don't think I have ever encountered in another movie. The camera begins by showing the hunter as he runs down a corridor and peers into a room. Then there is a quick pan away from him, and suddenly we are in a subjective shot, seeing what he is seeing as if through his own eyes: the various objects in the corridor rushing toward us, or the inside of the room coming into view. The camera appears to continue in the subjective mode for a while, but then, as we go around a corner or look about inside a room, we find ourselves facing the hunter once again. The important point about all of this is that it is done in one continuous shot, with no editing: The camera goes from an objective point of view (of the hunter) to a subjective view (of what he sees) and back to an objective point of view within the span of a single, unedited shot.

The effect of this device, as my description suggests, is extremely disorienting. One moment we think we are seeing what the hunter is seeing, and the very next he himself appears in the frame. This sequence gives us a sense of what it would be like to have a sudden encounter with ourselves, coming around a corner or walking into a room. Because disorientation is exactly what the character in this scene is supposed to be feeling (in fact, he is twice shown recoiling in utter bewilderment from his reflection in a mirror), this is an excellent example of a device that manages to generate in the audience the same emotions that a character on the screen is experiencing. But what exactly is it that causes viewers to interpret this device in the manner I have described—i.e., as an "impossible" sequence of views?

I have occasionally shown this sequence in an introductory communications course, and my experience has been that students who have not dealt with such matters before find it very difficult to give an answer to this question. In fact, however, the answer is quite simple. What the director has done is to take a firmly established editing convention—a convention so rigidly adhered to that one might justifiably consider it inviolable—and violate it. The convention is that transitions from objective to subjective views are separated by a cut. Any viewer who has grown up with movies and television will have encountered numerous instances of this convention and will undoubtedly have come to take it for granted. However, as the case of my students suggests, familiarity does not necessarily lead to conscious awareness of the rule, even when one sees that rule being broken. This is an example, therefore, of an area where explicit instruction in visual literacy can clearly make a difference. A viewer who has only tacit familiarity with this rule will certainly be able to evaluate the laboratory sequence in terms of how exciting it is, how poignant, and so on. But for the viewer whose knowledge of the rule is conscious and explicit, evaluation of this scene acquires an added dimension. Such a viewer is also able to make an informed judgment about the *means* the director used to make the scene exciting and poignant.

I don't mean to imply, of course, that visual education will lead to enhanced aesthetic sensibility only if viewers are previously completely unaware of the conventions they have been exposed to. Even in cases in which the original form of a convention is fairly obtrusive and has entered a viewer's awareness, there may be a gap between that awareness and the ability to detect variations on the convention. This situation is illustrated in our second example, which has to do with the conventions used in flashbacks, hallucinations, and certain other kinds of narrative transitions.

During much of the history of Hollywood cinema, it was a common practice to introduce flashbacks with the familiar device of a blurring or warping of the image, presumably intended as a visual analogue of the mental disorientation an emotionally charged return into the past may bring about. A similar device was also commonly used for other kinds of transitions out of the stream of ongoing reality, such as hallucinations and dreams. However, it goes without saying that this device is now obsolete, and it seems inconceivable that any filmmaker would employ it today without appearing either hopelessly archaic or deliberately campy. In fact, in one of my classes a perfectly serious blurred-image flashback from a film of the early 1960s, John Ford's *The Man Who Shot Liberty Valance*, was greeted with a wave of merriment.

The loss of this convention has probably not had much effect on the intelligibility of these transitions; it appears that viewers are quite able to figure out the nature of the transition on the basis of the narrative context. However, as far as expressive function is concerned, it can be argued that the obsolescence of the blurred-image convention amounts to a real loss, because it deprives directors of a ready-made means of expressing something that images cannot always convey very successfully—namely, the inner emotions of the character who is experiencing the transition. An interesting solution to the dilemma implicit in these circumstances—the difficulty of choosing between a blatant, old-fashioned expression of subjective experience and no expression at all—occurs in a scene from Paul Verhoeven's *The Fourth Man,* made in 1983.

In this scene, the film's protagonist (played by Jeroen Krabbe) is taking a train ride, in the course of which he experiences either a hallucination or a supernatural vision, depending on how one interprets the overall structure of the film. The way this transition is introduced is very much in line with the traditional conventions for going into flashbacks, hallucinations, and the like: There is a triggering event (the protagonist sees something), the camera moves in for a tight shot of the protagonist's face, and, as the transition begins, pulses of light and darkness move across the screen. However, whereas in a typical film of the 1940s or 1950s (and in *Liberty Valance*) this warping of the image would have been handled as an optical "effect" produced by a lens attachment, here it is the result (ostensibly, at least) of something that happens in the action itself: The train goes over a bridge, and the bridge's girders cast a fluctuating pattern of light and shadow into the protagonist's compartment and across his face. So the director has managed to retain the old convention and use it to create a very effective sense of disorientation, at the same time making the warping of the image appear to be a "natural" outcome of the events on the screen rather than a regression to the "artificial" optical effects of yore. I should add that the same students who laughed at the flashback from *Liberty Valance* expressed nothing but admiration for this scene.

As it happens, however, when these students were asked to describe their evaluations of this scene explicitly, most did so in terms of the scene's suspenseful tone rather than its formal structure, and no one mentioned the specific device of the warped screen. These students were all undergraduates in their second week of a general introductory course on communications. When I showed the same scene to my graduate students in visual communication, in contrast, the relationship to the traditional blurred-image convention was brought up almost immediately. Here, then, is a case in which explicit awareness of the more obtrusive, traditional form of a convention was evidently not sufficient to lead to a concomitant awareness of the conventional basis of a less-obtrusive variant. Because ability to modify and extend received conventions plays such a central role in criteria of artistic evaluation, it seems to me that this example goes to the core of what the aesthetic aspect of visual literacy is all about.

From another perspective, both this example and the previous one point to another major reason why an educator might be interested in visual literacy. Judging from the responses of my students, I can say that both of these scenes are capable of eliciting considerable emotional involvement and strong reactions. Yet the means through which they do so are evidently outside of the awareness of most viewers. This combination of a strong reaction and an obscure agent is, of course, part of the basic "contract" between the audience and producers of escapist entertainment. But even when the audience is a willing participant in visual manipulation, the potential consequences are not always benign. Accordingly, it seems to me that one of the major contributions a discussion of visual literacy can make is to develop a systematic account of techniques of visual manipulation and to explore audiences' reactions to and awareness of these techniques. I have attempted such an account in Chapter 5 (see also Messaris, 1990, 1992). Here I will give a brief overview of three broad categories of formal devices commonly used by producers and directors to manipulate the viewer's response: (1) camerawork based on the paraproxemic principle; (2) the creation of false continuity in editing; and (3) associational juxtaposition in composition or editing.

1. *The paraproxemic principle.* As I indicated earlier, I am borrowing the term "paraproxemics" from Meyrowitz (1986), who used it to describe camerawork that derives its effectiveness from an analogy to the real-world domain of spatial communication or "proxemics." For example, it is commonly assumed that because of the real-world association between physical closeness and psychological intimacy, the audience's sense of intimacy with

an on-screen character may be enhanced if that character gets more close-ups than the others.

An interesting extension of this principle involves the use of subjective camera, i.e., showing the action in a movie or TV program through the eyes of one of the characters in the story (see Branigan, 1985). Because it literally gives the spectator that character's point of view, this device is typically used to encourage empathy and identification. For example, the subjective point of view in the "Twilight Zone" ad (Figure 1.2) gives us a sense of what it would be like to see that kind of face when *we* look into the mirror. Subjective point of view is also commonly found in TV commercials, where it can serve to put the viewer in the shoes of a character receiving advice from an expert or other knowledgeable person. As we shall see in Chapter 5, the effectiveness of this technique has been tested by Galan (1986), who found that commercials employing subjective camera were more persuasive than their "objective" counterparts. Furthermore, Galan also found that the viewers of these commercials did not seem to be aware of the visual variable that she was manipulating.

This latter aspect of Galan's findings suggests that subjective camera—and, perhaps, the more general principle of "paraproxemics"—may be one area of visual manipulation in which there is room for enhancing the level of visual literacy of the general audience. If awareness of these devices also leads to a more critical attitude, we may assume that one benefit of literacy in this area would be a greater immunity to such ploys in advertisements. However, the implications of an awareness of paraproxemics are likely to be most crucial not in advertising but in certain fiction films and TV programs.

Take the case of ABC's "The Final Days," a dramatization of Richard Nixon's last days in office (originally broadcast on October 29, 1989). Perhaps the most affecting section of this docudrama was the final scene, in which the newly resigned president and his wife are escorted by their successors, the Fords, to the helicopter that will take them away from the White House. The ceremonial walk to the helicopter is drawn out considerably on screen, and it is presented through a combination of objective shots of the participants and subjective shots—presumably through the eyes of Richard Nixon himself—of the helicopter looming up ahead of them. They reach the helicopter, they get on board, and then, for the first time in the program, the point of view switches to Mrs. Nixon. We get a close shot of her face, holding back emotion, after which we see, through her eyes, the scene's final shot: her husband, viewed from behind, standing in the door of the helicopter, giving his famous victory salute to the people assembled outside. It is perfectly understandable why the director of this scene should have chosen to present it in this visual style—i.e., in such a way as to encourage the audience to identify with the Nixons. At the same time, however,

34

Figure 1.2 Subjective point of view in a print ad.

to the extent that such identification may also have encouraged viewers to adopt Richard Nixon's point of view on the reasons for his departure from office—i.e., the idea that Congress and the press were to blame—the director's visual choices in this instance cannot be seen as *simply* a matter of style.

On a very different political or ideological level, issues of paraproxemics have also been raised with regard to the way movies present relationships between male and female characters. As several scholars in the area of film studies and related disciplines have pointed out (see Prince, 1988, for a review), camera positioning, including subjective camera style, has been routinely associated in Hollywood cinema with a predominantly male point of view and the objectification of females. The camera typically "allies" itself with the male protagonist, presenting his female counterpart from his perspective. A grotesque extreme of this visual style occurs in slasher movies, in which we, the viewers, are repeatedly invited to witness the spectacle of a cringing female victim through the eyes of the male aggressor. It is this kind of application of paraproxemics that we might expect a visually literate viewer to be led to resist most strongly.

2. *False continuity.* The principle of "false continuity" is one of the fundamental premises of the illusionistic power of film and television. It is the basic principle behind most narrative editing: Two shots joined together in the context of a broader narrative are "read" by the viewer as being part of a coherent stream of space, time, and action, even if the shots were in fact taken at widely separate times and places or if the actions within them were completely unrelated in reality. This principle is equally a part of fictional and nonfictional narratives, but it is the nonfictional case in particular that raises questions of visual manipulation and the need for critical viewing.

A relatively benign instance of this possibility has been reported in several studies dealing with the use of "reaction shots" (i.e., shots of the opponent inserted into the stream of a candidate's remarks) in televised presidential debates (e.g., Messaris, Eckman, and Gumpert, 1979; Morello, 1988a, 1988b; see also Tiemens et al., 1985). Close examination of these shots often finds little evidence that the candidate shown in the reaction shot was actually responding in any obvious way to his opponent's remarks. Yet there is some indication that, even in the absence of obvious behavioral responses by the candidates, the editing structure in and of itself may enhance the sense of clash between them, in viewers' eyes. For example, it appears that one of the three 1976 debates, in which the director used twice as many reaction shots as in the other two, was perceived as more confrontational by viewers, even though a shot-by-shot analysis did not reveal any evidence of more intense confrontation between the candidates in this particular debate. What could have happened here, then, is that viewers were led by the editing to see a connection between two events, the behavior of the speaker and of his opponent, that may not have existed in reality.

In its clearest form, the principle of false continuity may be observed in operation in those situations in which shots of nonfictional events are assembled after the fact for inclusion in a documentary, newscast, or interview program. The classic example of the kind of misrepresentation such a situation can lead to is illustrated very nicely in a scene from the film *Broadcast News* (1987, directed by James L. Brooks) in which an unscrupulous TV newsman enhances the impact of a rape-victim interview through the insertion of a reaction shot of his own teary-eyed face taped after the actual interview was over. Such after-the-fact taping of the interviewer's reactions and questions is, of course, standard practice in TV news, but similar problems can obviously arise whenever purportedly real images are rearranged in some way.

Judging from my own experience, visual manipulation of this sort is very hard to detect on first viewing. The tendency to succumb to the illusion of false continuity appears to be very strong, and, as in the case of paraproxemics, it seems to me that one reason for this effectiveness may be that the devices in question are anchored in the principles of human perception and are not simply arbitrary conventions. In fact, the tendency to see separate images as a continuous event may even operate in cases in which we know that the images have been put together to make a certain editorial point. This possibility was exploited in a humorous way in a parody music video in which repeated images of George Bush saying "Read my lips" are suddenly followed by a shot of him grinning broadly. Less humorously, a political ad put together by Richard Nixon's team in the 1968 presidential campaign showed his opponent, Hubert Humphrey, smiling, juxtaposed with images of destruction in Vietnam and rioting in the United States (see Jamieson, 1984, p. 245). In cases such as these, concealment of editing is clearly not an issue, but the viewer's tendency to see continuity in the images may still support the rhetorical point.

3. *Associational juxtaposition.* This principle is the basis of one of the most common techniques of print advertising, involving the juxtaposition of an image of the product with an image of a person, object, or situation toward which the intended audience can be assumed to have positive feelings. For example, a roadside billboard I used to walk past on my way home from work once displayed the following image: in the background, a young woman and a young man eyeing each other seductively; in the foreground, a can of a popular brand of malt liquor; and, across the bottom of the picture, the words "It works every time."

The specific intent of this juxtaposition is too blatant to require explication. In more general terms, we can say that what this kind of visual device aims for is to transfer the viewer's (presumably positive) response from the background image to the image of the product. The goal of the ad is to create an association in the viewer's mind between the product and the image it is paired with (see Craig, 1992, pp. 166–170), hence the term "associational juxtaposition." Aside from being used in magazines, billboards, and posters, associational juxtaposition is also popular in the area of political advertising—e.g., in the oft-used image of a candidate standing in front of the flag (see Ebong, 1989). It was employed more inventively in George Bush's 1992 campaign video, "The Presidency," in which Mr. Bush's image was interwoven with images of some of the most admired former presidents—whose own images, in turn, were juxtaposed with flags, the White House, the Statue of Liberty, and so on (see Figures 1.3 and 1.4).

Does associational juxtaposition work? We can take it for granted, I think, that its continued use in advertising must be supported by a substantial body of proprietary research. But there is also some published research with a bearing on this question. As Stout (1984) has pointed out, the theoretical model on which associational juxtaposition in advertising is typically based is that of Pavlovian conditioning, according to which repeated exposure to a pair of stimuli, one positively valued (the unconditioned stimulus), the other neutral (the conditioned stimulus), eventually leads to a conditioned (i.e., artificially induced) positive response toward the initially neutral stimulus. There is considerable evidence that this kind of manipulation of response can be effective for both human and animal subjects. Within this body of evidence, there is also some research that specifically supports the notion that Pavlovian conditioning can work with pictorial stimuli (most notably, perhaps, a pair of studies in which subjects were turned into boot fetishists through repeated exposure to sexual images paired with pictures of boots; see Rachman, 1966; Rachman and Hodgson, 1968).

In an informal attempt to gauge the extent to which viewers are aware of the uses of associational juxtaposition in magazine advertising, I have tested some of my students' ability to identify the types of products that are likely to be associated with certain highly conventional forms of advertising imagery. The procedure I used was to show the students a set of advertising images with product labels and all other copy removed and to ask for an estimate of what was most likely to have been advertised in each case. For example, one of these images was a view of a mountain in the Rockies, with a lake in the foreground and a forest in the middle distance but no people, roads, buildings, or other evidence of humanity anywhere in sight.

In earlier research, I had found that, when this kind of scene—a pristine, "empty" landscape, usually in the mountains—appears in a general-circulation magazine, it is very frequently associated with cigarette advertising. It is in fact one of the more common categories of associational imagery in U.S. magazines, rivaling even such encompassing themes as wealth or sex (Messaris, 1989). Nevertheless, despite the ubiquity of this kind of imagery and the obviousness of the strategy behind it, only about a third of my students were able to connect the mountain scene to cigarettes. (Most thought that it

Figures 1.3 and 1.4 Associational juxtaposition. *Source:* "The Presidency," a video shown at the 1992 Republican National Convention. Reprinted with permission of the Republican National Committee.

was a travel or resort ad, although the most common conventions in that area are actually quite different from this one.) Of course, this is a relatively conservative test of awareness of visual manipulation; a viewer might readily recognize associational juxtaposition when confronted with it directly and yet retain no subsequent memory of the specific strategy used. I mention this "finding," therefore, only to suggest, once again, that the "obviousness" of a particular strategy of visual manipulation may not always translate into viewer awareness.

* * *

In general, research on viewers' awareness of visual conventions and manipulation is still something of a rarity in academic scholarship, despite the fact that visual literacy has become an area of considerable concern. A similar scarcity of systematic empirical evidence is characteristic of most of the other topics that I will be discussing in this book, with one notable exception— namely, the issue of inexperienced viewers' interpretations of still images. Although I certainly believe in the value of testing speculation against data, I have not hesitated to deal with issues on which the only data available to me were my own chance impressions and unsystematic observations. The principal aim of this book is not so much to review what others have said or found as it is to develop a theoretical perspective, one that goes against certain widely held views on the nature of visual communication.

A paradigmatic statement of these views is contained in an article by Murray Krieger (1984) on the work of E. H. Gombrich, whose book *Art and Illusion* is frequently—and, according to Gombrich himself (1984), wrongly—cited as having demonstrated conclusively the arbitrariness of pictorial conventions. Krieger refers to the "antique distinction in aesthetics between natural and conventional signs, that is, between signs which look like their referents and signs related to their referents only by convention: in short, between pictures and words" (p. 184). He goes on to argue that Gombrich's work has led us to see that "all representation—even that apparently depending on its resemblance to external reality"—should be "viewed as responding to the perceptual and cultural norms brought to it—in short, . . . as conventional signs" (pp. 184–185). He concludes: "All signs must be read, not—as with the natural-conventional sign distinction—some signs seen and some read" (p. 185).

As far as our understanding of the nature of visual communication is concerned, this conflation of language and images seems to me to be the exact opposite of what a productive approach should look like. As I see it, what makes images unique as a mode of communication is precisely the fact that they are *not* merely another form of arbitrary signification. Learning to

understand images does not require the lengthy period of initiation characteristic of language learning, and permeability of cultural boundaries is
much greater for images than it is for language. Krieger is right, of course, in
questioning the "antique" notion that pictures simply "look like their referents." But that is exactly what makes the problem of pictorial representation
such an intriguing puzzle. Pictures can make sense to inexperienced viewers
despite all the many manifest discrepancies between image and reality (lack of
color, lack of "realistic" shape, or whatever). To conclude from these discrepancies that images are simply another arbitrary language is to bypass the
problem, not to solve it. In addition, such a conclusion goes against
the research evidence, which, in the case of still images, is considerable. As
Gombrich himself has noted in a response to Krieger's article, the kind of
position Krieger exemplifies is typically unconcerned with or ignorant of the
relevant empirical research (Gombrich, 1984, p. 197).

My aim in this book, then, will be to try to explain just how it is that we
are able to see "reality" in images despite their frequent lack of any compelling resemblance to the appearance of the real world. As this overview has
indicated, I believe that the distinctive feature of pictorial signification is that
it is built on our everyday, real-world skills of physical and social perception.
This property makes images a unique mode of communication, clearly distinct from language and the various other modes. From this property, too,
distinct implications can be drawn regarding the impact of visual literacy on
our cognitive abilities, aesthetic sensibilities, and responses to manipulative
uses of media. These consequences differ from those of literacy proper, just
as the mental processes invoked by these two modes are different. In short, I
am arguing for an approach that casts off the burden of unproductive analogies and sees images for what they are: sources of aesthetic delight, instru-
ments of potential manipulation, conveyors of *some* kinds of information—
but not a language.

2

The Interpretation
of Still Images

What does a viewer need to know in order to be able to interpret a picture? The answer to this question depends on the kind of interpretation one is concerned with. Two important aspects of interpretation—namely, aesthetic appreciation and the detection of manipulative intent—will be examined in Chapter 5. In the present chapter, my primary focus is on the viewer's ability to recognize the objects, events, and situations depicted in images. Consequently, I shall be dealing almost exclusively with representational pictures. However, I want to begin with a brief look at nonrepresentational visuals—more precisely, pictures with no external, real-world referent.

The first thing to be said about them is that pure examples of pictures of this kind are quite difficult or even, it may be argued, impossible to come by. It is true that the history of "high art" in the twentieth century has been characterized by a cumulative attempt to rid pictures of external referents. But it is questionable whether such an attempt can ever be entirely successful—whether anything meaningful would remain if all real-world associations were removed from the stock of interpretational conventions on which both artist and audience must rely. It is not just that the shapes and colors of even the most resolutely nonrepresentational picture are likely to evoke, however vestigially, the shapes and colors of the real world. Even if this were not so, it seems inevitable that many of the broader categories in terms of which pictorial structure is typically interpreted—e.g., balance, symmetry, complexity, dynamism—are inextricably rooted in our interactions with the world of real, nonpictorial objects and events (see Arnheim, 1988; Bang, 1991; Saint-Martin, 1990). Nevertheless, let us assume, if only temporarily and for the sake of argument, that one could indeed rid a picture of all nonpictorial referents. What would the interpretation of such a picture involve, and what knowledge would it require?

If the establishment of an external referent is removed as a goal of pictorial interpretation, what remains as the principal focus of the interpretational process is the development of a sense of the picture's internal structure. To a greater or lesser extent, depending on the degree of originality of the picture's creator and of the interpreting viewer, the conditions for understanding this structure may be defined by the picture itself. At the same time, however, because meaningful perception cannot occur in the absence of relevant precedents, the perception of the picture's structure will also necessarily entail comparisons with the structures of other pictures. Assuming that such a thing as a nonrepresentational picture does exist, then, we have one example of a situation in which interpretation is bound to require previous experience with pictures.

But this kind of interpretational process is obviously not confined to our (possibly hypothetical) example of a picture without any external referent. On the contrary, it is likely to be a part of our encounter with any kind of picture, regardless of what else that encounter may involve. Although we may look at a picture because we're interested in a product it is advertising, or because we want to follow the adventures of our favorite cartoon character, or because it reminds us of our trip abroad, we're also likely to have some awareness of the picture's design and composition, how well the colors go together, and whether the illustrator or cartoonist or photographer did a better or worse job than other people working in the same genre. Indeed, it should be evident that similar interpretational processes are likely to be involved in viewers' responses to visual displays of all kinds—including such things as rugs, wallpaper, and architectural facades—rather than just to pictorial displays. (Not that this distinction is always clear, of course.) More generally, then, it can be argued that the interpretation of nonrepresentational pictures exemplifies in pure form an aspect of interpretation that all kinds of visual displays are likely to elicit in some measure. It should be evident that this aspect of interpretation coincides with the conception of aesthetic appreciation put forth in Chapter 1. Further discussion of these issues will therefore be postponed until Chapter 5.

Abstract Representation

As I have already suggested in my brief remarks about the possibility of removing all external referents from a picture, visual displays can be considered representational not just by virtue of whatever concrete things they may portray (people, places, and so on) but also by virtue of their evocation of such abstract properties of real-world visual experience as balance and symmetry. The distinction I am proposing here between "concrete" and "abstract" representation is fraught with complications, but it is a useful distinction to try to make because it leads to some revealing considerations about the way we make sense of pictures. A convenient illustration of this distinction is provided by Rudolf Arnheim in a discussion of the visualization of concepts.

Arnheim described a class exercise in which students were required to draw pictures representing, among other things, a good marriage and a bad marriage. One student drew two circular figures, the first one consisting of smoothly curving lines, the second of spikes. Another student drew a pair of interlocking yin-yang figures, on the one hand, and on the other a pair of figures separated by some distance (Arnheim, 1969, pp. 120–129). The characteristic feature of these drawings is that they represent their subject, the contrast between good and bad marriage, purely in terms of its abstract qualities. They do not use the alternative, concrete procedure of juxtaposing scenes from good and bad marriages (a couple smiling at each other versus a squabbling couple, a couple embracing versus a couple avoiding each other).

Even from my verbal descriptions, it is probably clear which of the drawings made by Arnheim's students were meant to represent a good marriage and which portrayed a bad marriage. The question is: What accounts for one's ability to make sense of these pictures and of such pictures in general? The ability to deal with abstract concepts in visual form is a skill that is consciously cultivated today by artists, critics, and informed viewers, and it seems a safe assumption that, as a result of this cultivation, such people are better at this skill than the average woman or man in the street. However, this pictorial skill is not without parallels in real-world vision, the most obvious evidence being our ability to describe and respond to unfamiliar objects or events in general terms (e.g., complexity of form, rhythm of movement) even if we can't say exactly what they are. To what extent any such real-world skills of visual interpretation are transferable to the interpretation of the kind of pictures we are discussing here is an open question. One crucial difference between the two realms is that the pictures are already abstract, whereas in real-world vision abstraction is a mental response to a concrete visual stimulus (i.e., one replete with information). However, there is some intriguing research suggesting that this difference may not be as consequential as it initially appears.

The research in question began with a study by Fischer (1961) on the relationship between artistic style and the character of society. Fischer assumed that the structural tendencies apparent in a society's visual artworks would mirror, metaphorically, the social-structural principles prevailing in that society. For example, equality in a society's social relationships should be reflected by symmetrical compositions in a society's art; the presence of rigid distinctions among members of a society should be reflected in its art by distinct boundaries around the compositional elements. These assumptions were tested on a sample of some thirty preindustrial societies, all of them relatively small and homogeneous; the results were uniformly positive.

Assuming that Fischer's results were in fact due to the reasons he hypothesized rather than some other cause, they give us reason to believe that processes of abstract representation (and, presumably, interpretation) are not necessarily dependent on previous pictorial tradition. The societies Fischer studied (e.g., Ashanti, Bali, Navajo) did not share a common pictorial culture, so the observed similarities among them in their use of visual abstractions (such as symmetry or enclosure) must mean that the ability to use these abstractions ultimately derives from real-world visual processes rather than from specifically pictorial precedent. (I am assuming that invariant features of the physical environment in which all human beings live result in substantial cross-cultural similarity in human vision, although of course some degree of cultural variation is known to exist [Segall, 1979], an issue discussed in the concluding chapter of this book.)

Fischer's findings have been supported by a number of other researchers working with societies and types of art not included in his original sample (e.g., the designs on ancient Greek pots [Dressler and Robbins, 1975]; hooked rugs from Newfoundland [Pocius, 1979]). Furthermore, the general conclusion drawn here from Fischer's research—namely, that the metaphorical use of such abstract visual design features as symmetry and enclosure may be based on real-world visual processes—is implicitly assumed by certain art-historical theories. These theories have argued that similar social circumstances (e.g., an orientation toward change) find expression in similar features of artistic style (e.g., the use of diagonals, thought of as indicative of motion) among societies with no common artistic heritage. (See Hatcher, 1988, for an overview of this kind of theory.) Here, however, the evidence tends to be much more vulnerable to problems of selective sampling and unreliable interpretation.

As this brief discussion of the research of Fischer and others may already have suggested, what I am calling the abstract representation of reality does not occur only in abstract pictures such as those described in the example from Arnheim. Rather, it can be an aspect of the meaning of a picture that also has a concrete subject. Symmetry, for example, obviously can be present in pictures with concrete figurative content as well as in nonfigurative designs. Fischer argued that his theory should hold regardless of what kind of overt content there might be in a picture, and the various studies cited in connection with his work have dealt with both kinds of pictures, the purely abstract and those that combine abstract and concrete representation. It should be evident, moreover, that such combinations need not be simply additive. It is true that one can analyze the abstract meaning of a picture's style without regard for any concrete figurative elements the picture may contain, but in this society, at least, the more typical expectation is that the abstract and the concrete will work together. The style, one is told, should match the substance.

A good example of how such matching is supposed to occur is provided by the later works of Georges Seurat. Surely one of the most scientifically inclined painters in the Western tradition, Seurat had worked out a detailed scheme for matching the compositional structure, the light values, and the colors of a picture to the mood of its subject (Homer, 1964, pp. 180–234; see also Lee, 1990). A sad mood, for instance, was to be represented by lines drooping or sloping downward, by a predominance of dark areas on the canvas, and by "cool" colors (i.e., colors towards the blue/violet end of the spectrum).

These principles, especially as they relate to the picture's linear design, are particularly apparent in Seurat's *Le Chahut* (1889–1890), a picture of high-kicking dancers, and *Le Cirque* (1890–1891), in which an acrobat is shown balancing with one leg on the back of a galloping horse. The buoyant mood in both pictures is expressed not only through subject matter but also through bright, warm colors and through upward-tilting lines in people's eyebrows, eyes, and mouths, in arms and legs, and in details of dress and architecture. (See Homer, 1964, pp. 220–234, for an analysis of these two paintings.) The logic behind these principles is no doubt readily apparent, but it is important for our purposes to emphasize that, for Seurat, it was not artistic precedent but real-world associations (the effects of gravity on the human body, the way facial features change as emotion changes) that justified these principles.

Similar principles of abstract representation may also be at work in another large category of visual displays—namely, graphs, bar charts, and so on. As with the pictures from Arnheim discussed above, these graphic displays may be seen as involving two kinds of information: an abstract visual representation (which, in this case, is always concerned with one kind of subject: quantitative relationship) and contextual markers (in the form of words, numbers, conventions of usage) specifying the particular issue to which the abstract visuals should be applied (e.g., a company's sales volume, a patient's temperature, the relative merits of different brands of painkiller). As with Arnheim's abstract visuals, it seems possible that, in this case, too, our ability to make sense of the shapes in the chart or graph may draw upon our real-world experience with juxtapositions of large and small objects, rising and falling surfaces, and the like. As before, this is not to say that specific experience with such visual displays does not facilitate interpretation or improve one's ability to deal with the more complex forms such displays may take. However, I am arguing that in all these cases of abstraction, even when the visual material is as difficult, relatively speaking, as a graph or a chart, a specifically pictorial "literacy" may be less of a prerequisite for interpretation than is usually assumed.

Concrete Representation

Whether it is true or not that real-world visual processes may be applicable to the abstract aspect of pictures, common sense would seem to suggest that, when it comes to the interpretation of a picture's concrete content, no special interpretational skills should be required beyond those required by reality itself. The basis of this common-sense assumption, of course, is the idea that pictures with concrete content look like whatever it is they represent. As it happens, however, this common-sense assumption has been attacked frequently and vigorously by writers interested in these questions. These critics have pointed out that there are many kinds of pictures that really don't look very much like the things they represent—and many aspects of visual reality that *no* picture, however realistic the intent behind it, can copy. On the basis of such observations, it is typically concluded that real-world visual skills are inadequate, even irrelevant, for the task of picture perception.

This latter point of view seems to be quite common among people with a scholarly interest in these subjects, so I have organized this section as a response to it. I shall begin by giving a list of ways in which pictures do not or cannot reproduce real visual experience. Then I shall examine the extent to which these discrepancies between pictures and reality pose an obstacle to the use of real-world perceptual habits in picture perception. The discussion will also serve as an opportunity for a brief review of the nature of pictorial conventions and their variation across time and culture.

To begin with, then, here is a list of major discrepancies between concrete-representational images and the appearance of the things they represent:

1. Pictures cannot reproduce the full range of brightness levels to which the eye is exposed in the real world.
2. Pictures cannot reproduce the full range of colors to which the eye is exposed in the real world.
3. Many pictures (e.g., outline drawings) do not contain information about changes in brightness on the surfaces of objects.
4. Many pictures (e.g., black-and-white photographs) do not contain information about the color of objects.
5. Ordinary still pictures (i.e., not 3-D pictures or holograms) cannot reproduce the stereoscopic effect (and attendant depth information) one gets when one looks at the real world with two eyes.
6. Ordinary still pictures (i.e., not movies or holograms) cannot reproduce the effect of motion parallax (and attendant depth information) one gets when one looks at the real world from shifting points of view.

7. Many pictures (e.g., Persian miniatures) do not reproduce the real-world diminution of an object's apparent size with increasing distance from the spectator.
8. Many pictures (e.g., ancient Egyptian paintings) do not adhere to the real-world constraint that things can only be viewed from a single point of view at any one point in time.
9. Many pictures (e.g., political cartoons) contain major distortions of the features of their subjects.
10. Many pictures (e.g., stick-figures) entail major omissions of the features of their subjects.

The items in this list will be discussed under three headings: "light and color" (items 1–4); "depth" (items 5–7); and "object recognition" (items 8–10).

Light and Color

A real-world scene (e.g., an outdoor view containing sun and shade) can present the eye with a considerable range of degrees of brightness. Neither paintings nor photographs are capable of exactly reproducing this aspect of reality. The pigments they use are typically limited to a considerably narrower range of brightness levels. What kind of obstacle does this limitation pose to pictorial interpretation? To what extent does it make interpretation contingent on the learning of picture-specific conventions?

These problems have been addressed by E. H. Gombrich (1960, pp. 33–62), at the very beginning of *Art and Illusion,* his pioneering analysis of conventions of pictorial representation. Gombrich points out that in real-world vision, the abruptness of change in brightness levels and the relative amount of contrast matter more to the viewer than the absolute amount of contrast. Therefore, even if the brightest spot in a picture is much darker than the corresponding spot in reality would have been, a convincing sense of brightness can be conveyed to the viewer by delineating that spot sharply and giving it a background with low internal contrast against which it can stand out. A viewer who had never seen a picture before might require some adjustment to this unfamiliar reduction in the range of brightness, but the adjustment should be rapid and unproblematic, because the interpretational task posed by the picture calls for mental skills which the viewer has already developed in interactions with the real visual surround.

With regard to this aspect of pictures, then, Gombrich's analysis can be seen as an argument against the notion of visual literacy, if the term is taken to imply the existence of a picture-specific set of interpretational skills that viewers have to learn through extensive experience with pictures. It should be noted, however, that Gombrich's emphasis in this discussion is equally on the problems confronting the *creators* of pictures, from whose perspective the satisfactory translation of light and shadow into pigment has entailed the long-term, continuing evolution of representational conventions. To the viewer, these conventions may be transparent, but to the picture makers involved at each stage of the way they were the result of a hard-won struggle to discover what would work (or, more accurately, what would work better than what had gone before). For example, it was not until quite late in the Renaissance that artists were able to produce satisfactory night scenes (e.g., Titian's *Martyrdom of Saint Lawrence*, painted in the 1540s).

Because brightness is a component of our experience of color, light and color often constitute a single issue as far as the representational task of the painter is concerned. As implied above, problems having to do with the naturalistic representation of these elements seem typically to have been addressed relatively late in those pictorial traditions that have been concerned with them. For example, the rendition of atmospheric effects in landscape painting seems not to have occupied Roman painters before the first century B.C., more than three centuries after their predecessors in the Greco-Roman tradition had solved the problem of representing a human figure in a natural pose from a single point of view (Picard, 1968; Ramage and Ramage, 1991; Leach, 1988). The makers of Japanese woodblock prints, who readily adopted Western linear perspective in certain types of pictures by the middle of the eighteenth century, were generally resistant to the use of Western shading until a hundred years later (Fagioli and Materassi, 1985; Sullivan, 1989). In the Western tradition itself, it was not until the late nineteenth century and the work of Seurat and his followers that the rendition of atmospheric light and color was placed on a basis as systematic as that which spatial representation had achieved in the early 1400s (see Weale, 1982, pp. 150–153).

There are several possible reasons for this phenomenon. Lack of suitable technical means may be one of them—the dramatic late fifteenth-century developments in northern Italian techniques for representing light and color, for example, seem to have been contingent on the introduction of oil-based paint from northern Europe. Another factor retarding the development of naturalistic approaches to light and color may have been a recurring clash between representational and decorative tendencies in these pictorial traditions (see Dunning, 1991, pp. 16–19, for a good discussion of this distinction.) Thus, there is evidence that the introduction of naturalistic shading into ancient Greek painting was retarded by artists who were concerned with preserving the pure colors and elegant outlines of earlier styles of representation (Bruno, 1977). In Persian miniatures, in which the decorative aspect of color and design is very strong, sources of light were depicted in pure gold against uniform backgrounds (i.e., with no indication of the effect of light on the surround), even though skillful modulation of colors was demonstrated in other features of pictures (Welch, 1972). Somewhat ironically, the movement away from naturalism in late nineteenth-century European painting was motivated in part by admiration for the flat, unmodulated colors of Japanese prints from the days before Western influence finally resulted in large-scale Japanese adoption of shading (Berger, 1992; Ives, 1974). But aside from all of these possibilities, there may be another reason for those cases in which naturalistic impulses gave priority to the rendition of form and space over light and color—namely, that in real-world vision itself, many details of lighting and color are irrelevant to what Aristotle called the main task of vision: figuring out *what* is out there and *where* it is. A brief review of recent theory concerning real-life visual perception will make this point clear.

In recent years, researchers have made major advances toward a satisfactory conceptualization of the process of vision. A major impetus for these advances has been a theoretical framework summarized in an extremely influential posthumous book by David Marr (1982). Marr's theory is concerned with the transformations visual information undergoes as it is processed by the brain. For our purposes, his account can be described (with considerable simplification) as involving three major phases, the second and third of which will be described in later sections of this chapter. In the first phase, which concerns us here, the input consists of the light and color information recorded by the retina (the light-sensitive grid of nerve endings at the rear of the eye, where light is focused by the eye's lens). Because the retina contains no means for recording the distance from which a particular light ray originated, the information it makes available to the brain can be thought of as a two-dimensional array of light and color values. The brain's task is to derive from this two-dimensional array a sense of identifiable solid objects in specific locations relative to the viewer.

According to Marr, the first phase in this process is concerned with changes in intensity within the two-dimensional array of light. These changes can be caused by three major variables in the scene at which one is looking: (1) discontinuities in the intensity of light striking different parts of the scene (e.g., the bright and dark parts of a landscape resulting from scattered clouds); (2) differences in the brightness of the visible surfaces of objects (e.g., stripes on a tie or on a zebra); and (3) discontinuities in the geometry of visible surfaces. This third variable is crucial to the brain's ability to construct a sense of a three-dimensional world from the flat array of light recorded on the retina.

What this third variable provides is an indication of where the edges of objects are and where objects and surfaces undergo major changes in shape. For example, if the viewer is looking at an object such as a table or chair standing in front of a wall, major changes in the light-intensity of the image will correspond to the object's silhouette (assuming there is some difference between the object and the wall in terms of level of illumination and/or surface reflectance). According to Marr, then, the first phase in the construction of a three-dimensional percept consists in a transformation of the information provided by the retina into a series of outlines corresponding to the various discontinuities discussed above. Marr labels the result of this process the "primal sketch." As this label indicates, the information contained in it may be thought of as roughly similar to the information in an outline drawing.

It should be evident from this brief summation that, in order to use the primal sketch as a basis for inferences about the boundaries and shapes of objects and surfaces, the brain must be able to discriminate among the three sources of variation in light intensity listed above. One of Marr's major achievements was the satisfactory description of a plausible mental mechanism for this process. However, for present purposes, his crucial point is that the subsequent derivation of a three-dimensional percept from the information contained in the primal sketch's outlines is largely independent of the information provided by the first two of these three sources of variation.

To put it differently, the processes involved in constructing a three-dimensional percept operate primarily on one part of the initially available visual information—viz., on those changes in light intensity corresponding to changes in the geometry of the perceived scene. Processing of light and color changes associated with the nature of light falling on the scene or with the coloration of objects and surfaces occurs independently of the derivation of the third dimension. This important principle, which Marr refers to as "modularity," is central to his theory and will be referred to again below.

This conception of visual perception has several implications for our understanding of the perception of pictures. To begin with, it is in accord with the observation that naturalism in the pictorial rendition of form and space is frequently unrelated to naturalism in the rendition of light and color. More specifically, now, this conception leads to the hypothesis that the *absence* of naturalistic light and color from a picture need not prevent the application of real-world interpretational processes to that picture. As long as the picture provides the viewer with satisfactory information about the geometry of the depicted scene, the real-world interpretational processes that handle such information can be brought into play.

What exactly constitutes satisfactory information will be discussed in further detail below. What we can say at this point, however, is that, if the argument made here is correct, then there is no reason to believe that absence of naturalistic light or color, in and of themselves, should prevent a pictorially inexperienced viewer from being able to understand the content of a picture. The notion that black-and-white photographs, monochrome watercolors, outline drawings, and so on, require special interpretational skills because of their lack of naturalistic color and/or shading is not supported by the work on vision cited above.

Depth

We now turn to the second of the three headings under which I have proposed to conduct this discussion of the relationship between concrete-representational images and the appearance of the real world. The term depth is used here to refer to the distance between a viewer's eyes and any point in the visual field. Because the retina does not record depth, much research on real-world visual perception has been concerned with figuring out how depth is inferred by the brain. Similarly, because ordinary pictures are flat, considerable artistic energy has gone into devising satisfactory cues for conveying a sense of depth. The obvious question, for our purposes, is how closely the depth cues employed in pictures match the depth cues used by viewers in reality.

Theories about real-world vision are still quite tentative with respect to the exact details of most of the processes used by the brain to infer depth (Bruce and Green, 1990; Wade and Swanston, 1991). However, a more general understanding of these processes has existed for some time now, and it is possible to construct a list of major depth cues with some confidence. We have already examined the basic components of such a list in Chapter 1. Here I will add some further details.

1. *Binocular disparity.* Ordinarily, people look at the real world through two eyes, and because the two eyes have slightly different points of view, the images formed on their retinas will differ. This difference, commonly referred to as binocular disparity, can serve as a depth cue: In general, the greater the difference, the smaller the depth. A precise description of how this process ("stereopsis" or "stereoscopic vision") works has been given by Marr and Poggio (described in Marr, 1982, pp. 111–159).

2. *Motion parallax.* Ordinary real-world vision involves continuous changes in the position of the viewer's eyes relative to the visual surround. These changes result in corresponding displacements of the retinal image ("motion parallax"), which can be used as depth cues: Roughly speaking, displacement is inversely related to depth, although the details are much more complicated (see Johansson, 1982; Prazdny, 1980).

3. *Occlusion.* If our view of a certain object is partly obstructed by another object, we can infer that the obstructing object is nearer to us than the one whose view is being obstructed. However, this depth cue (occlusion) is limited: It can inform us that one object is farther away than another, but not *how much* farther (either in absolute or in relative terms).

4. *Texture gradients.* If a surface has a uniform texture (e.g., a regular pattern of floor tiles, a brick wall with evenly-spaced bricks, a lawn with a uniform grass cover), the more distant parts of that surface will form denser retinal images than the closer parts. Furthermore, the retinal image of the

texture will change in predictable ways when there is a change in the viewer's orientation towards the surface. J. J. Gibson and his followers have assumed that these texture gradients in the retinal image are used by the brain to infer depth and orientation (Gibson, 1986). However, the degree to which this is true is unclear, and, in any case, the applicability of this depth cue is obviously limited to those cases in which a scene contains one or more uniformly textured surfaces.

5. *Contours*. As noted in our discussion of light and color, the first step in the brain's extraction of depth information from the retinal image consists of the derivation of outlines of objects and surface discontinuities. According to Marr, it is these outlines (their changes over time, their interruption by other outlines, and so on) that serve as the basis for the operation of most of the depth cues; and one of Marr's and his colleagues' major contributions to vision theory has been the exploration of ways in which the actual shape of an outline might itself provide information about depth. Of particular relevance is Marr's description of a process by which the three-dimensional properties of certain solid objects can be inferred from their contours (Marr, 1982, pp. 218–225). Marr's specification of what kinds of objects this process can be applied to is very precise but too technical for this discussion. For our purposes, the important point is that human and animal forms meet the criteria. In other words, if Marr is correct, outlines or contours in themselves should allow the brain to see humans and animals as three-dimensional objects.

6. *Shading*. As a surface's orientation relative to a light source changes, the apparent brightness of the surface changes too. It seems likely that such changes can serve as depth cues, although probably weak ones. In any case, the inferential processes that might be involved are understood only imperfectly.

Turning to pictures, now, it should immediately be obvious that the first two depth cues listed above, binocular disparity and motion parallax, cannot be incorporated in ordinary, flat, still pictures. Does this mean that pictures cannot possibly be interpreted through the use of real-world inferential processes? If real-world vision required all the depth cues to be present together, the answer to this question would be yes, and the case in favor of a specifically pictorial literacy in this area would be clear. However, at this point the principle of modularity, mentioned above, becomes especially relevant. As Marr (1982, p. 102) has shown, there is good reason to believe that the processes described above occur independently of one another, so that depth can be inferred from any one of them (if its criteria of applicability are met) regardless of whether the others are operating. Consequently, those depth cues that *can* be incorporated into pictures can function for the viewer as they would in reality, even though binocular disparity and motion parallax will always and necessarily be absent. (See Kubovy, 1986, for a very thorough discussion of these issues with reference to Renaissance perspective.) The next thing we must ask, then, is what role the remaining depth cues actually play in various pictorial traditions.

Of the depth cues listed above, the one that is perhaps most widely encountered, in pictures from a broad range of cultures and historical periods, is that of outline or contour as a cue to the three-dimensional properties of representations of humans or animals. According to Marr, the inference of depth precedes identification. In other words, this depth cue allows the brain to see solid objects *before* their identity (as a man or woman, as a particular person, as a type of animal) has been established. As we shall see below, identification of an object is based on this three-dimensional percept rather than on the object's outline, because outlines change with every change in point of view, whereas the three-dimensional properties are always the same. Whenever pictures represent humans, animals, and certain other forms through outlines, the real-world strategies of depth perception can be brought into play for those parts of the picture in which these forms occur. What about the other parts?

Pictorial cultures differ widely in the extent and nature of their concern for them. In some pictorial styles, there is no apparent concern with representing a three-dimensional space enclosing the figures in a picture, even though the figures themselves may be rendered with considerable naturalistic detail. For example, in petroglyphs found in the Kalahari Desert in southern Africa, highly naturalistic representations of animals occur in isolation, without any background. Furthermore, there are many types of pictures in which an enveloping space is present only in the sense that the spatial relationship among figures is indicated. Both in ancient Egypt and in ancient Greece, the typical depth cue used in such cases was occlusion, and, given the limited spatial concerns of such pictures, the presence of occlusion should be enough to permit real-world processes of three-dimensional vision to operate. However, when we come to pictorial traditions having more encompassing spatial concerns embracing the representation of landscapes, cityscapes, and architectural interiors, with or without people in them, the situation becomes considerably more complicated.

A standard reference point for the analysis of this aspect of spatial representation is the representational system typically referred to as "Renaissance perspective." (Despite the name, the system was formulated as early as the second century A.D. by the Alexandrian geographer Ptolemy [see Edgerton, 1976, p. 93ff] and was certainly in use, albeit atheoretically, even earlier in Rome [Richter, 1970, pp. 52–53; see also White, 1987, pp. 260–261].) The principles of this system are also in effect in most kinds of photographs. Pictures conforming to this system typically contain several types of depth cues, not all of which are *required* by the basic principles of the system. If human or animal figures are present in a picture, their outlines will constitute depth cues, as indicated above. If the picture is a painting or a photo-graph, as opposed to a line drawing, shading is also likely to provide some information about the three-dimensional properties of various surfaces (faces, for example). Typically, however, these are not the principal depth cues that come to mind in connection with the Renaissance mode of picto-rial representation. Rather, the depth cues typically thought to be character-istic of this representational mode are the following two:

Linear perspective. Lines that in real life would be parallel to each other and receding away from the spectator are represented on the picture plane as converging to one or more "vanishing points." Because the relationship be-tween depth and degree of convergence is regular, this cue is thought of as providing a precise sense of space.

Relative size. In pictures conforming to Renaissance principles, there is an inverse relationship between depth and the size in which objects are por-trayed. The notion here is that, if the viewer of the picture is familiar with the real sizes of pictured objects, the sizes in which they are portrayed in the picture can serve as a precise source of information about the relative depth of each.

Readers familiar with these issues will already have noticed that neither of these presumed depth cues appears as such in the list of real-world depth cues given above. Does this mean that we are now dealing with specifically pictorial depth cues—and, therefore, with evidence of a pictorial literacy re-quired for the interpretation of these kinds of pictures? In answering this question, one should begin by noting that both of these Renaissance depth cues are in accord with the visual information that the equivalent real-world situations (receding parallel lines; objects at different distances from the spectator) make available to the eye. Why, then, have they not been listed as real-world depth cues in the first place?

In the case of linear perspective, we need to make a distinction between two different situations: on the one hand, linear perspective involving *sev-eral* evenly spaced lines (e.g., a Venetian blind viewed at an angle); on the other hand, a single pair of converging lines (e.g., the two sides of a road receding into the distance). It should be apparent that the former instance is simply a special case of the kind of visual pattern to which the texture-gradient depth cue would apply (see Marr, 1982, p. 235). Therefore, there is no need to list it separately. However, when it comes to the latter kind of visual configuration, there is some doubt about whether it does indeed function as a real-world depth cue—i.e., whether two converging lines en-countered in our real environment make much of a contribution to the brain's computation of how far away things are from us. Consequently, if we had evidence that the *pictorial* use of this latter form of linear perspective is an effective depth cue for experienced viewers, we might want to take that evidence as pointing to one component of a picture-specific literacy. This possibility will be addressed shortly.

The second supposed depth cue that concerns us here, relative size, is a result of the same overall representational principle that gives rise to texture gradients and linear perspective. However, in terms of the mental computation that would have to be involved if it were indeed to be used as a depth cue, it differs from these cues considerably. In order for relative size to operate as a depth cue, the viewer must already have identified the objects whose sizes are being compared, whereas the texture-gradient depth cue and, indeed, all the other depth cues, are thought to operate before object identification has occurred. This is an important point, and it corresponds to a major theoretical leap in the work of Marr and his colleagues. They have shown that the construction of a three-dimensional percept is probably accomplished largely on the basis of the primal sketch's outlines (i.e., before the brain knows what the outlines represent) and that object identification is actually predicated on the existence of a three-dimensional percept. Assuming that this theory is correct, we have to conclude that relative size is unlikely to be a real-world depth cue in the normal sense, because depth perception occurs before object identity (and the meaning of relative size) has been established (cf. Hochberg, 1984, p. 850).

This conclusion goes against commonly held belief. As it happens, though, it is supported by a well-known piece of empirical evidence. In Adelbert Ames's famous demonstration involving a distorted room built so as to give the eye misleading linear-perspective information, people at different distances from a spectator are seen as varying in *size,* not distance; if relative size were operating as a depth cue, the appropriate adjustment would have been made. The relative-size cue has also been tested by itself, without the confounding linear perspective, but even here the evidence for its use was minimal: Viewers who were given a monocular image of two people at different distances against a plain background saw a considerable difference in size but very little difference in distance (Gregory, 1970, pp. 28–29). Here is a case, then, of a presumed depth cue that in fact is unlikely to play a major role in real-world vision. If it could be shown, therefore, that relative size does function as an effective depth cue for viewers of pictures, it would constitute a second example of a picture-specific convention.

A third potential depth cue that may be specific to pictures is best discussed by turning to another pictorial tradition: Persian miniatures. Although these eventually came under the influence of Europe and adopted the Western conventions discussed above, traditionally they were made according to a strikingly different set of principles, both with regard to the representation of receding parallel lines and with regard to the relationship between object size and depth. In traditional Persian miniatures, neither of these features serves as a depth cue: Receding parallel lines are *shown* as parallel, and objects are drawn to the same scale, regardless of their position in the space represented by the picture. What serves as a depth cue instead, in addition to occlusion, is height on the picture plane: The more distant an object is supposed to be, the higher up it is painted in the picture.

It should be evident that this convention has a basis in real life: If a person is standing on a level surface, objects resting on that surface will occupy higher positions in the visual field the farther away they are. Again, however, it is not clear how large a role this potential depth cue plays in real-world vision. (What *is* clear is that, if the single variable of height in the visual field were an automatic depth cue, it would often lead to erroneous computations of depth.) In pictures, however, the use of this depth cue is common. Aside from Persian miniatures, in which it is found in its pure form (i.e., as the only source of information about the *amount* of distance between objects), it also occurs in some styles of Chinese and Japanese pictures, and it is a principal component of several Western representational systems. Once again, then, if it can be shown that the ability to use this depth cue successfully depends upon familiarity with these pictorial traditions, this depth cue can be considered a legitimate example of a picture-specific interpretational convention. Research with a bearing on this question, as well as on related possibilities discussed above, will be examined presently.

Object Recognition

The process of object recognition (i.e., how we know *what* it is we're looking at, as opposed to how far away it is or what its shape is) is our final topic in this discussion of relationships between concrete-representational images and the appearances of the things they represent. This process is understood much less clearly than either depth perception or the perception of light and color. Existing theories tend to be either clearly unsatisfactory or too sketchy to take us very far. A major exception is the work of Marr and Nishihara on the use of information contained in an object's outline for the derivation of a three-dimensional representation of that object and a sense of the object's identity (see Marr, 1982, pp. 295–328, for a relatively nontechnical account). A premise of this theory is that it is extremely unlikely that the brain could recognize objects by matching their perceived outlines against a "catalogue" of possible outlines stored in memory. The reason behind this premise should be easy to grasp. Any one object (or type of object) can be viewed from an infinite number of different directions, and each direction would correspond to a different perceived outline; therefore, our brain would have to store an infinite number of outlines in memory if all possibilities were to be available for matching. However, because the object itself, as a three-dimensional entity, remains the same regardless of where we view it from, if matching could be done on the basis of a three-dimensional representation then only a single prototype would be required to be stored in memory.

The problem then becomes one of deriving a three-dimensional representation of the object from the information available in the two-dimensional image on the retina. In the previous section, we discussed processes whereby this two-dimensional image could be used as a basis for inferring the distance between the spectator and the various surfaces the image comprises. However, for purposes of object recognition, depth information is not enough: One has to know what the object is like on the "other side" too. That is, one has to have a full three-dimensional representation, not just a sense of those surfaces of the object within one's field of vision. A general theory of how this recognition might be accomplished—indeed, of the extent to which it *could* be accomplished—is lacking at present. However, as noted earlier, Marr and Nishihara have proposed a solution that would account for the recognition of many organic forms, including humans and animals. The details of their scheme are quite technical and will not be described here. For our purposes, the following features are the ones that count:

1. The process of recognition and creation of a full three-dimensional representation is thought to entail the derivation of a *structural* representation of the object in question. This representation indicates the object's principal axes (i.e., the axes of major symmetry of the various parts of the object) and their relative proportions and orientations. This structural representation is thought to serve as the basis for recognition by being matched with structural models stored in memory.

2. The "catalogue" of structural models in memory is thought of as being arranged hierarchically, starting with more general, all-encompassing forms (e.g., a general "primate" form including apes as well as humans) and proceeding downward toward increasing structural differentiation and specificity (e.g., the particular arrangement and proportions of limbs that differentiate humans from apes). Furthermore, it is assumed that the process of recognition may be recursive, starting with tentative structural representations of the percept and more global levels of the internal catalogue of forms and working downward from there to the degree of representational precision and identificational specificity required by the situation.

3. The mental computations involved in this recognition process should be simpler to the extent that foreshortening is absent from the retinal image of the object being identified. (Foreshortening is absent when the major axes of the various parts of the object are perpendicular to the line of sight of the viewer.)

These features of the theory have interesting implications regarding our ability to recognize objects in various kinds of pictures. To begin with, if this theory is correct in assuming that object recognition in the real world is based on structural representations, it could also explain how viewers can understand pictures in which humans and animals are represented in purely structural terms, rather than in terms of realistic appearance. The most obvious example of such a picture is probably that of stick figures, and it is worth noting that stick figure–like drawings occur in a wide variety of cultures with no known relationship to one another. It could be, then, that the reason stick figures can serve as acceptable images is that they satisfy real-world requirements for object recognition by making immediately available an object's structure.

But stick figures are not the only kinds of pictures in which structure is represented without a realistic envelope. It could be argued that any kind of picture, no matter what its surface characteristics happen to be, should be interpretable via the real-world processes we are considering here, as long as the arrangement of the parts of the picture yields an underlying structure that matches the brain's model. This assumption would account for a viewer's ability to interpret "composite" pictures (e.g., the Michelin man, a "human" composed of tires), children's drawings (in which an undifferentiated circle may stand for a torso and another circle for the head), and "bad" drawings (in which no individual detail may match the appearance of the represented object but the overall structure is closer to that of the object than to anything else).

Pictures of this sort do not represent structure explicitly, the way stick figures do, and, as these examples indicate, they may vary tremendously in terms of their surface appearances. However, as a class, they all appear to be capable of yielding implicit structural information equivalent to (although never entirely identical with) that contained in more realistic images. Consequently, such "unrealistic" pictures may satisfy the requirements of real-life visual recognition processes despite their failure to replicate many of the surface features of real objects.

In general, then, what is being argued here is that an image's lack of surface realism is not necessarily an interpretational obstacle for viewers with no prior exposure to the pictorial conventions according to which that image was constructed. Conversely, we would predict that inexperienced viewers *should* have trouble recognizing a pictured object if the *underlying structure* implicit in the picture is different from the structure of the equivalent real object. A good example of this kind of discrepancy between pictorial style and reality is the so-called "split-representational" style, which is found in some Native American art of the Pacific Northwest.

The characteristic feature of this pictorial style is that objects (mostly animals) are represented by a combination of two simultaneous side views branching out from a single part of the object (e.g., the head). What typically confronts the viewer in a split-representational rendition of an animal is a frontal view of the head and thorax combined with two symmetrical side views of the torso and the limbs. To a viewer who tries to interpret such an image according to real-world principles of object recognition, the pictured animal will appear to have an underlying structure very different from the structure of the real-life version of that animal. Depending on exactly how the artist has gone about achieving the split-representational effect, in the eyes of such a viewer the animal may appear to have two symmetrically opposed spines, a great-than-expected number of limbs, and so on. This pictorial style seems to be a clear example, therefore, of the kinds of circumstances in which viewers do need to be familiar with the representational conventions in order to recognize a pictured object as intended by the artist (cf. Layton, 1991, pp. 179–180).

A related situation that may also call for some degree of pictorial literacy occurs in the case of "foreshortened" images—i.e., images in which one or more of the major structural axes of an object are viewed from such an angle as to appear "compressed" relative to the rest of the object. For example, in an extreme-high-angle photograph of a person, the torso and the limbs, whose principal axes will be almost parallel to the camera's line of sight, will appear foreshortened, whereas the diameter of the head and the width of the shoulders will be rendered without any foreshortening. As noted earlier, foreshortening can cause problems in the recognition of real objects because of its potential for creating a misleading impression of an object's underlying structure, but in real-world vision these potential problems can be counteracted by the strong sense of depth the viewer gets from binocular disparity and motion parallax. In still pictures, however, these two depth cues play no role, so the interpretational difficulties created by foreshortening are likely to be considerably greater.

The presence of such difficulties may be one explanation for the fact that, in Western art, at least, the use of extreme foreshortening seems to have evolved gradually from less foreshortened forms. In particular, a series of transitions leading from the rigorous avoidance of foreshortening in the archaic period to its open embrace in Hellenistic times is typically considered one of the defining characteristics of the history of Greek art; a similar development can be traced in the post-Renaissance history of art in various parts of Italy (e.g., in the case of Venice, the evolution from the head-on views characteristic of Giovanni Bellini and his contemporaries to the flamboyantly low angles of G. B. Tiepolo's ceiling frescoes).

The interpretational obstacles posed by foreshortening may also have played a part in shaping the pictorial style of ancient Egypt, which gives the impression of having been deliberately designed to avoid foreshortening. Like archaic Greek painting, which was clearly influenced by it, ancient Egyptian art typically represents the human figure through a combination of a frontal view of the chest and side views of the head, the lower trunk, and the limbs. This "twisting around" of the chest gives the viewer a direct view of its entire width, and a similar twisting occurs with the eye, which is presented in a frontal view even though the rest of the head is in profile. These "distortions" maximize the structural information available to the viewer, but they also have the effect of confronting the viewer with two incompatible points of view. Would the latter feature of Egyptian art and other representational styles of this kind have caused first-time viewers trouble in recognizing these images?

Existing theories of visual object recognition do not lead to any definite answer to this question, nor is there, to my knowledge, any systematic research with a bearing on it (although it may be worth noting that my own students, both graduate and undergraduate, invariably have to be *told* about the unnatural placement of the Egyptian eye before they can see anything "wrong" with it). Relevant research is also lacking on the kinds of visual "distortions" discussed above in connection with split-representational images. However, most of the other major points that have been made in this discussion of concrete (as opposed to abstract) representation can be checked against various kinds of empirical evidence. It is to this evidence that we now turn.

Empirical Evidence

The overall thrust of our discussion thus far has been that a very wide range of representational pictures, including several types that might not appear at first blush to be very realistic, are based on representational conventions that provide the viewer with information similar to that typically used in real-world perception. A viewer's ability to make sense of these pictures, therefore, does not appear to be based on familiarity with a set of arbitrary representational principles, despite the "unrealistic" appearance of some of these types of pictures. Empirical evidence with a direct bearing on these issues is provided by observations of the responses of inexperienced viewers.

Descriptions of people's first encounters with photographs and other kinds of pictures have existed at least since the late nineteenth century, in the form of accounts written by missionaries and other travelers to parts of the world having no access to mass-produced visual images. As it happens, contrary to the hypotheses we have just discussed, several of these accounts describe the inexperienced viewers as having been unable to figure out the subject of the first picture they were shown. For instance, in a relatively recent case of this sort, the anthropologist Melville Herskovits told of an African woman to whom he showed a black-and-white photograph of her own son. The woman turned the photograph in one direction after another but was unable to make sense of it until Herskovits himself pointed out the details to her (see Segall, Campbell, and Herskovits, 1966, pp. 32–34).

Evidence of this sort is sometimes dismissed as being anecdotal. In fact, however, there is no clear reason why these particular accounts, especially those coming from trained observers such as Herskovits, should not be taken as seriously as more systematic data (see Deregowski, 1980, pp. 107–108). The question regarding these accounts should not be how trustworthy they are but rather what exactly it is that they tell us. Should we take them as evidence that the conventions of pictorial representation are arbitrary after all, despite the arguments about their basis in real-world principles of visual perception?

A crucial point to bear in mind in answering this question is the fact that, in the incident described by Herskovits, all it took for the woman to be able to see the face in the picture was a few on-the-spot instructions. Indeed, this is invariably the case with similar reports of first-time viewers' initial difficulties with pictures. Nowhere do we get any evidence of a need for the kind of lengthy, repeated instruction that is a prerequisite for the understanding of a genuinely arbitrary system of signification such as language (Carroll, 1985, pp. 82–83). Furthermore, there is another consideration that should be taken into account in any interpretation of reports such as Herskovits's: For many of the inexperienced viewers in these accounts, their first encounters with the pictures they were shown were also their first encounters with *paper*. As Herskovits himself pointed out, this fact in itself might explain their initial puzzlement regarding what it was they were being shown.

This possibility was tested directly and systematically by Deregowski et al. (1972) in the course of fieldwork with an Ethiopian tribe, the Me'en, most of whose members had no previous experience with pictures. In the initial stage of this study it was found that when these people were presented with a page from a child's coloring book, they tended to subject it to elaborate scrutiny without attending to the picture itself. Rather, they would smell it, taste it, roll it up, and so forth. As a result of these observations, the investigators prepared a set of pictures on material the Me'en were familiar with, namely, a type of cloth. In tests of the Me'en viewers' comprehension of the two types of pictures, it was found that, whereas the typical response elicited by the paper pictures was "I don't know," this response occurred only five times out of a total of sixty-four responses to the cloth pictures.

These results, then, lend weight to the possibility that the initial incomprehension reported in many informal accounts of viewers' first encounters with pictures may have had more to do with the materials or the situation rather than with the representational principles involved in the pictures themselves. At any rate, even those accounts that do describe difficulties typically report rapid periods of adjustment, so only in the most trivial sense can such cases be seen as supporting the claim to which they are typically attached—namely, that the comprehension of pictures rests on familiarity with a set of *arbitrary* conventions.

Formal, systematic studies of inexperienced viewers' responses to pictures have been conducted frequently during the past thirty years, but with a few exceptions, such as the study by Deregowski and his colleagues described above, the lack of experience of the people studied has not been as complete as in the informal accounts. As the products of industrial technology find their way into ever more "remote" parts of the globe, it becomes increasingly difficult to find subjects who have had absolutely no exposure to pictures, not even in the form of designs on sacks of flour or matchbox covers. Consequently, a number of studies have pursued alternatives to the typical cross-cultural approach that most research in this area has tended to take. We will examine two of these studies first.

In a one-of-a-kind experiment by Hochberg and Brooks (1962), a child was raised with limited exposure to pictures and with no opportunity to learn about pictures from other people in his environment. On those few occasions on which he was inadvertently exposed to a picture (e.g., on a billboard or on the label of a jar of food), his parents, who were also the study's authors, were careful to avoid any interaction that would indicate to the child that the picture was to be taken as a representation of some object or scene. When the child was nineteen months old, he was presented with a series of twenty-one pictures of familiar objects (toys, shoes, cars, etc.) and two people: his sister and his mother. Two kinds of pictures were used, black-and-white photographs and simple line drawings without shading; in cases in which a particular object was represented by both kinds of pictures, the line drawing was normally shown first.

The child's responses were tape-recorded, and the parents' scoring of his interpretations was checked against the scores of two judges who were not present while he was shown the pictures—they worked only with the tapes. The results indicated that the child was able to provide correct identifications for seventeen of the twenty-one pictures. In view of the degree of control exercised in this experiment, these results add considerable confidence to the conclusions reached above—namely, that the absence of color in black-and-white photographs and of color and shading in outline drawings should not prevent an inexperienced viewer (or any viewer, for that matter) from applying real-world interpretational processes to these pictures. Judging from the performance of the child in this study, the information contained in outlines can be interpreted successfully by viewers who have never been taught to associate outlines with real-life forms.

This conclusion has been supported by a sizable group of studies in which animals were used as inexperienced viewers. In a typical example of this kind of research by Zimmerman and Hochberg (1970), outline drawings and black-and-white photographs were tested on young monkeys. In the first phase of the study, conditioning procedures were used to teach the monkeys to discriminate between two objects. Subsequently, the monkeys were presented with outline drawings or photographs instead of the objects themselves. Nevertheless, they were able to discriminate successfully without further training. Similar findings have been reported in other studies on animals (see Herrnstein, 1984, for a review), although the more recent research tends to be somewhat less revealing for our purposes than earlier work, such as that of Zimmerman and Hochberg, because the use of color slides as stimuli, as opposed to outline drawings or black-and-white photographs, has now become almost universal in such research.

In general, the use of animals as subjects makes the implications of this body of research particularly compelling; one's confidence that one is dealing with a truly untutored and inexperienced viewer can be absolute. However, cross-cultural studies with humans make it possible to test for recognition of a broader range of representational styles and subject matter, to probe the limits of recognition, and to examine the influence of culture itself.

A particularly extensive investigation of the influence of representational style on inexperienced viewers' pictorial interpretations was carried out in a study by Cook (1981). The study was based on a series of interviews with 423 villagers from several locations in Papua New Guinea. Most of the informants had traditional occupations (e.g., farming), and half of them were literate. Although they were not totally unfamiliar with pictures, their previous experience was limited. The interviews were based on several sets of picture stories produced specifically for the study and dealing with local subjects such as a woman growing and fetching corn or a man building a grass hut. Each story consisted of four drawings, and each set of four drawings was produced in five different styles: stick-figure drawings, rudimentary outline drawings (i.e., outline drawings lacking such details as facial features), detailed outline drawings, detailed drawings with color, and black-and-white photographs.

The informants were required to identify various objects or components of the pictures, as well as to perform several other tasks, such as telling a story based on the pictures and choosing among alternative orderings for the four pictures in each story. The findings indicated that although representational style did affect viewers' preferences, with color scoring highest on that count and stick figures lowest, style was not a source of significant variation in the informants' ability to *recognize* objects in the pictures. Furthermore, percentages of correct recognition were generally high: for human figures, 97 percent; for tools and weapons, 96 percent; for "things in the environment," 89 percent; for "objects on the ground," 77 percent. These percentages provide added support to this chapter's arguments regarding black-and-white photographs and outline drawings, and they support its arguments about stick figures and other superficially "unrealistic" pictures (in this case, the rudimentary outline drawings).

Further evidence on the interpretability of "unrealistic" pictures comes from a study by Kennedy and Ross (1975), whose findings were replicated by Cook. Working with another group of New Guineans (the Songe), Kennedy and Ross examined the relationship between ease of recognition and degree of completeness of a picture. They found that even very sketchy renditions of human figures were recognized almost universally among their informants (see also Kennedy, 1983). Similarly high levels of recognition of black-and-white outline drawings of familiar objects have been reported in research done in the Gambia by Spain (1983) and in Lesotho by Dusenbury (1990). In general, then, the cumulative evidence from the various types of studies cited thus far supports the conclusion that the recognition of *single objects* in pictures is a task that inexperienced viewers should not find incompatible with their real-world perceptual habits. As noted earlier, this general conclusion does not mean that all types of pictorial subjects are recognized with equal ease. However, this aspect of the matter will be discussed in connection with research that goes beyond the recognition of single objects.

Pictorial Depth Perception

The most controversial study of inexperienced viewers' ability to deal with representations of more than one object in a single scene has undoubtedly been Hudson's 1960 investigation of pictorial depth perception in South Africa. This study was based on a set of six pictures, all variations on the following situation: in the foreground, a hunter aiming a spear at an antelope; in the background, an elephant standing under a tree. The hunter is on the left, the antelope is on the right, and the elephant, which is drawn much smaller than the other two, appears between them. The images were designed to contain different combinations of four pictorial depth cues: occlusion, linear perspective, relative size, and height in the visual field. In two of the six pictures, occlusion was incorporated into the basic situation by interposing a series of overlapping landscape contours between the foreground figures and the elephant in the background. In another three pictures, linear perspective was present in the form of two straight lines, representing a road, converging from foreground to background. All pictures conformed to the relative-size depth cue by having the elephant and tree appear smaller than the foreground figures, and the elephant's feet were always shown resting on a higher point in the picture plane than the feet of the hunter and antelope (see Figure 2.1).

Hudson's subjects were black and white residents of South Africa, drawn from a variety of occupations (laborers, clerks, schoolchildren, and teachers) and representing several levels of education (from no formal education to graduate training). They were shown the pictures one by one and asked to identify the various objects in them, to say what the man was doing, and to indicate which was closer to the man, the antelope or the elephant. The basic aim of this test was to ascertain whether the viewer was able to infer

Figure 2.1 The Hudson pictorial depth-perception test. *Source:* W. Hudson, "Pictorial Depth Perception in African Groups," *Journal of Social Psychology*, 52 (1960): 183–208. Reprinted with permission of the Helen Dwight Reid Educational Foundation. Published by Heldref Publications, 1319 10th Street, N.W., Washington, D.C. 20036-1802. Copyright © 1960.

that the elephant was supposed to be in the background and that, despite the fact that the elephant's figure appears between the hunter and the antelope in the picture, it is the antelope that is being hunted. Accordingly, responses that did not identify the antelope as the hunter's quarry were scored as being "two-dimensional," as were those in which the viewer said the elephant was closer to the man than the antelope was.

The subjects' performance on this test varied somewhat with the type of depth cue present in the picture, although these differences were not great. In general, occlusion appears to have been the most effective and relative size the weakest. However, the major finding of this study had to do with differences among the various groups tested. "Three-dimensional" interpretations were more likely for those viewers (black and white) who were attending school than for those who had never attended or who had completed their schooling and were now working elsewhere, either as mine laborers or as mine clerks. Among illiterate mine laborers, three-dimensional interpretations were almost entirely absent, whereas among fifth- and sixth-graders they occurred in frequencies ranging from 75 to 100 percent. Hudson interpreted these findings as an indication that the ability to infer depth from the various cues utilized in these pictures is contingent on pictorial experience—in this case, the frequent exposure to pictures that occurs in the everyday life of people attending school.

Hudson's conclusions have attracted continuing attention, and his method has served as the basis for several studies by other investigators. These studies have involved both direct replication—i.e., use of the same pictures as in Hudson's original study—and variations on Hudson's stimuli and testing procedures. The results of this body of research exhibit an interesting pattern: Direct replications for the most part confirm Hudson's finding of a relatively greater tendency for two-dimensional interpretations among less experienced viewers, but other kinds of pictures and testing procedures turn out to be consistently less likely to evoke such two-dimensional responses. For example, in the study by Cook (1981) described above, subjects were shown a series of four pictures of a man hunting a pig and were asked to pick one picture in which a particular pair of objects (e.g., the man's arrow and the pig) were *close* to each other and one picture in which they were *far* from each other. Although the hunter's arrow overlaps the figure of the pig in the picture in which the two are meant to be far from each other, only 10 percent of Cook's subjects failed at this task—i.e., based their responses on graphic proximity in the picture plane as opposed to distance in three-dimensional space (Cook, 1981, pp. 62–64).

The contrast between Hudson's test and other procedures emerges most clearly from studies in which the two have been paired for a single set of subjects. For example, Deregowski (1968) compared subjects' responses to Hudson's test with their performance on a construction task in which they were given Plasticine and strips of bamboo and asked to copy a set of geometrical drawings. In these drawings, which can conveniently be described as variations on the theme of a transparent rectangular solid, various combinations of occlusion, linear perspective, relative size, and height in the picture plane were available as indications of three-dimensionality. Although these drawings can be considered more abstract and therefore, perhaps, more difficult to interpret than Hudson's, subjects were more likely to perform three-dimensionally on the construction task (i.e., to build three-dimensional models) than on Hudson's test.

Further examples of the relative difficulty of Hudson's test compared to variant procedures will be cited shortly. The presence of a consistent difference in results between Hudson's procedure and the various others allows us to probe for a more precise explanation of the reasons behind the inexperienced viewers' responses to these procedures. A brief review of one of the direct replications of Hudson's procedure will serve as a convenient point of departure for such an exploration. In a study conducted in Uganda, Kilbride and Robbins (1969) elicited interpretations of Hudson's pictures from two sets of subjects: rural residents, with relatively little pictorial experience, and urban residents, with relatively greater experience. For present purposes, the important aspect of the findings has to do with the subjects' identifications of various objects in the pictures. What makes this study very useful as a tool for understanding how inexperienced viewers approach these pictures is that the authors record the *nature* of misidentifications, rather than just their number.

As one would expect from research cited previously, identification of the man, the spear, and the two animals tended to be relatively unproblematic for both sets of respondents. However, there were large differences between the two groups in the frequency of correct identifications of the other four items tested: the tree under which the elephant is standing, the hill on which it is standing, and two versions of the roadway connecting the foreground of the picture with the background. Except for one version of the roadway, these components of the pictures elicited almost no misidentifications from the urban residents, whereas substantial numbers of the rural residents got them wrong. What could have accounted for these errors? Why should the rural residents have interpreted some parts of the pictures correctly and others not?

A clue is contained in the nature of the erroneous responses. Regarding the tree, for example, these included such interpretations as "table," "flower," "boat," "crocodile," and "football cup" (presumably the equivalent of "soccer trophy"). With some imagination, it is possible to see how such interpretations could have been attached to the shape of this particular tree; but what seems much more difficult to account for is how the people who made them could have considered such interpretations compatible with the rest of the scene and, in particular, with the fact that the object they were describing as a flower or a soccer trophy is "clearly" (to an experienced viewer) towering above the elephant standing right next to it. The inescapable conclusion seems to be that the viewers who made such interpretations were not treating the two objects as part of the same scene.

A similar argument can be made about misidentifications of the other "difficult" parts of the pictures. For example, the hill on which the elephant is standing was called a "stone" or a "plate"; one of the roadways was called the "sea" (despite the fact that the man is standing on it); and the other roadway was seen as the letter "A." If such responses are indeed indicative of a failure to see the picture as a single scene, then the difference in frequency of misidentification between the "easy" and "difficult" components of the pictures becomes more understandable: The man, the two animals, and the spear are all instances of objects that fit Marr and Nishihara's criteria (discussed above) for three-dimensional perception and recognition purely on the basis of their own outline. Conversely, the other objects as drawn here (a single curved line for the hill, two converging lines for the roadways, a bundle of vertical lines topped by an ellipse for the tree) are undoubtedly much more dependent upon context for an unambiguous interpretation. If inexperienced viewers were not seeing these objects as part of a single scene and consequently not drawing on context for their interpretation, misidentification of the sort described above should be expected. Such failure of integration might also explain the two-dimensional responses on Hudson's test: A person who was not seeing the scene as a unified whole would have to respond that the elephant was closer to the hunter and might not be able to give a satisfactory answer as to what the hunter was doing.

The next question, then, is why inexperienced viewers should have particular difficulty seeing Hudson's pictures as single scenes. There are at least two possible answers. The reason could be lack of familiarity with Western pictorial conventions. In and of themselves, Hudson's pictures contain few unifying features—a common horizon line, the roadway in some versions, and some degree of occlusion, but no texture or detail to indicate that the man and the animals are inhabiting the same landscape. In contrast, the pictures used in Cook's depth-perception test contain a textured, grassy ground (and were embedded in a narrative context), whereas in the Deregowski study the picture is of a single object. It is reasonable to assume that the tendency to treat a picture as a single scene when the cues for doing so are weak may depend on one's degree of familiarity with a particular representational style. To the extent that the inexperienced subjects in Hudson's study and its replications were indeed less likely to see his pictures as single scenes, the findings of these studies can be seen as confirming the importance of experience for pictorial interpretation—but experience in discerning what is to be treated as a single scene rather than experience with depth cues.

However, there is another possible explanation, one raised by several studies in which the layout of Hudson's pictures was retained but the figures changed so as to make the situation closer to the subjects' familiar environment. For example, in studies performed in various parts of Africa by Omari and McGintie (1974) and by Mshelia and Lapidus (1990), Hudson's antelope and elephant were replaced by domestic animals (a goat and a cow in the former case, a cat and a dog in the latter) and Hudson's traditional hunter became a modern-day rural African; in a study of Arabic-American children by Hamdi et al. (1982), the spatial framework of Hudson's pictures was used as the basis of several variations with Arabic subject matter (i.e., a man in Arabic dress, a camel, and a donkey; a man in Arabic dress, a mosque, and a roadside store; a man and two pieces of Arabic headdress); and in a study done in India by Ohri (1981), the figures in Hudson's pictures were replaced by "familiar characters."

The consistent result of such substitutions is a finding of more frequent three-dimensional responses for the pictures with more familiar subject matter. This effect has been confirmed in research with experienced viewers (U.S. students) by Hagen and Johnson (1977), who compared responses to Hudson's original pictures with responses to pictures in which the man and animals had been replaced by people playing with beach balls; and by Hamdi et al. (1982), who tested several American versions of Hudson's pictures containing such things as a mailbox, a fire hydrant, a candy machine, and a shopping cart. The reason for these findings, one may assume, is that viewers find it easier to integrate the elements of a picture into a three-dimensional percept if they already have a good idea of what the represented scene should look like.

What are the implications of these findings for Hudson's original study and for its replications? At first glance, the situation depicted in Hudson's pictures may seem perfectly appropriate to the various African settings in which these pictures have been tested, and the results of the studies cited immediately above may therefore seem irrelevant. Indeed, Hudson's pictures were clearly designed to be used with an African audience. Nonetheless, their relevance to the actual environment and experiences of that audience should not be taken for granted. The Africa depicted in these pictures—a loincloth-wearing, spear-carrying hunter in a landscape populated by big game—might still have been a reality in some parts of the continent when the research of Hudson and his successors was taking place, but it seems doubtful that the kinds of people who were actually studied in this research—South African mine laborers, Ugandan farmers—would have had much direct contact at all with such situations. On the contrary, it is possible that, for many Africans, familiarity with that particular version of Africa may actually be more likely to occur secondhand—for example, through pictorial media.

Consequently, those subjects who were more experienced with pictures might also have had greater previous experience with the kind of hunting scene depicted in Hudson's pictures, and this familiarity, rather than knowledge of pictorial codes, might account for their superior ability to form an integrated, three-dimensional percept. Data supportive of this possibility occurred in the Kilbride and Robbins study (1969), in which 10 percent of the rural residents accurately identified the picture of the elephant as that of a large animal but were apparently uncertain as to the exact nature of the animal, calling it a hippopotamus, a rhinoceros, and so on. This uncertainty is consistent with the fact that the only large animal likely to be found in their own immediate environment would be a cow.

Taken together, then, the various studies we have reviewed thus far in

connection with Hudson's work suggest that inexperienced viewers' difficulties in seeing depth in pictures may not be as extreme as Hudson's data
would lead one to conclude they are. Nevertheless, even in circumstances
that, according to this body of findings, should have been most favorable to
inexperienced viewers—familiar subject matter combined with strong cues
uniting the various parts of a scene—these viewers' tendency to see depth in
pictures appears to have remained below that of their more experienced
counterparts. It would seem to follow that these findings must be due, at
least in part, to a difference between less experienced and more experienced
viewers in degree of sensitivity toward the depth information available to
them in the various studies we have looked at.

The pictures used in these studies contained various combinations of four
different depth cues: occlusion; linear perspective; relative size; and height
in the visual field. One of these, occlusion, clearly functions as a standard
depth cue in the real world, too, although it must be remembered that
the information it provides is limited: A viewer who was relying solely on
occlusion might be able to tell that one object was closer than another, but
occlusion in and of itself would give no sense of the absolute distance between the two objects. However, when it comes to the other three types of
depth information employed in these studies, there is (as we saw earlier)
some uncertainty regarding their status as real-world depth cues. It is these
latter three depth cues in particular, then—viz., linear perspective, relative
size, and height in the visual field—to which we can point as examples of
types of depth information we would not necessarily expect an inexperienced viewer of pictures to be able to handle adequately. In that sense, the
research we have reviewed suggests that these depth cues may be components of a specifically pictorial literacy in the area of depth perception.

However, it is important to be precise about the nature of this literacy. All
three of these depth cues are based on regularities observable in the real
visual surround: the apparent convergence of receding parallel lines; the inverse relationship between apparent size and distance; the inverse relationship between height in the visual field and distance on a horizontal surface
at which the viewer is looking. These are obviously not arbitrary indicators
of distance. Consequently, the kind of pictorial sophistication with which we
are dealing here consists of a heightened sensitivity to the pictorial use of
types of information that the viewer also regularly encounters in reality. This
sophistication does not involve the learning of a set of arbitrary connections
between symbol and meaning, and in this context, therefore, the term
"literacy" should not be taken to imply anything more than a very loose
analogy to the characteristics of language proper.

3

The Interpretation of Film and Television

In the course of a research project on parent-child discussions about television (Messaris and Sarett, 1981), my coauthor was told the following story by one of our interviewees, the mother of an eight-year-old boy. She and her son were watching an episode of "The Incredible Hulk." The climactic event in this show was the Hulk's rescue of a young woman who had been in danger of drowning. After the rescue, the young woman reexperienced a traumatic memory from her childhood: the death, by drowning, of her older sister. This memory was presented on the screen in the form of a flashback—at which point in the show our interviewee's eight-year-old turned to her and asked: Since the Hulk had rescued the first young woman, why didn't he now also rescue the second one?

This kind of misunderstanding is not unusual in research on children's interpretations of film and television. The findings in this area of research suggest that children may experience difficulties in the interpretation of a variety of editing devices, including reversal of camera angle (Comuntzis, 1987), transitions to subjective shots (Comuntzis-Page, 1991), and instant replays (Rice et al., 1986), as well as flashbacks (Calvert, 1988). Such findings are often taken as evidence that the interpretation of the formal structure of film and television requires visual literacy—i.e., prior experience of structural conventions, such as the well-known but increasingly obsolescent use of a blurred or warped image to signal a transition into a flashback.

In fact, however, research with children is of questionable relevance to the issue of a specifically cinematic literacy. The reason is that it is often hard to tell whether a child's difficulties with a particular cinematic device stem from insufficient exposure to that specific device or, instead, are an inevitable consequence of the child's general level of mental development (see Abelman, 1990; Acker and Tiemens, 1981). Before they have reached a certain stage of cognitive maturation, all children have trouble figuring out how something looks from another person's point of view, or imagining what another person's subjective reality might be like, or conceiving of time as a reversible entity. It seems very likely that it is mental characteristics such as these, rather than any lack of cinematic experience, that may account for the miscomprehension reported in studies of children's film/TV interpretations. At any rate, given the TV viewing patterns of most families in our society, it is probably safe to assume that the children who participate in these studies are already veterans of many an evening spent in front of the tube.

In view of these complications, the discussion that follows will be concerned primarily with adult viewers so that we may concentrate on the effects of visual experience in and of itself. Reference to research with children will be made when appropriate, but this research will play a secondary role in the overall argument. I should also point out that, as in Chapter 2, this discussion will deal mainly with viewers' interpretations of the manifest content of representational films and TV programs. Questions of aesthetic evaluation or the analysis of manipulative devices will be addressed in Chapter 5.

It seems reasonable to begin our discussion of movies with an extrapolation from what we have said about still pictures. Because the representational principles typical of photographs are consistent with many of the requirements of real-world interpretational processes, the same should be true of moving pictures (film or television) *without editing*—i.e., movies in which the action flows without interruption, as it would in reality. In fact, the case for transferability of real-world interpretational processes should be stronger when it comes to movies, not simply because of the greater lifelikeness imparted by motion but also, and more fundamentally, because the presence of motion parallax should make the perception of depth much more compelling.

Suggestive evidence regarding these issues is contained in surviving accounts of audience reactions to the first movies ever made, which typically consisted of single, unedited shots lasting no more than a few minutes. The recurrent theme in most of these accounts is admiration at how true to life the images in these movies appeared to their audiences, and there does not seem to be a single instance of incomprehension or even difficulty of comprehension (see Ramsaye, 1926, pp. 129–130, 196–197, 204–205, 227–228, 240–241; Kauffmann and Henstell, 1972, pp. 3–4). What such accounts cannot tell us, of course, is what role prior experience with other visual media, including photographs and various optical devices, may have played in preparing these early audiences for the acceptance of the new medium (see Fell, 1974; Hollander, 1989).

There is another limitation to the generalizability of these accounts. Almost without exception, early movies did not contain any camera movement. Thus, audience reactions to them cannot tell us about potential interpretational difficulties resulting from the fact that, when viewers look at a shot produced by a moving camera, their visual experience of motion is unaccompanied by the bodily sensations of movement that would ordinarily go along with a shifting visual field in the real world. It has been argued that this discrepancy can sometimes be disorienting even for experienced viewers (Stephenson and Phelps, 1989, p. 78), and there is some informal evidence of less experienced viewers having found camera movement confusing (panning shots were apparently taken as indicating that houses were moving; see Wilson, 1983, p. 32). However, a more systematic investigation of first-time viewers' responses to movies (Hobbs et al., 1988) reported no interpretational problems arising from pans or other camera movements when these movements were embedded in a narrative dealing with events and places from the viewers' own culture. Consequently, although it may be true that viewers need to adjust to the presence of a visual field that moves independently of their own actions, this kind of adjustment is evidently not a major obstacle to interpretation when the subject of the movie is culturally familiar to the viewer.

To a certain extent, camera movement can be seen as posing some of the same interpretational problems as editing. Editing, too, requires of the viewer an acceptance of the possibility of "disembodied" shifts in point of view. Indeed, several kinds of editing can be thought of as having specific types of camera movements as counterparts (most obviously, cutting to a close-up versus moving the camera in). However, almost all editing represents a radical departure from the possibilities of real-world visual experience, whereas camera movement typically does not. In that sense, the potential problems posed by editing are qualitatively different from anything we have discussed thus far. These problems will be our main concern in the remainder of this chapter.

My analysis of editing is centered on the transitions between shots. The basic questions I am concerned with are these: What kinds of information are typically provided to the viewer as guides for the interpretation of any particular transition? What kinds of prior knowledge and cognitive skills must a viewer have in order to be able to make sense of these informational cues? The category of information that is of primary concern for our purposes is that of formal visual conventions.

Any editing transition is a potential point of discontinuity in the events represented by a movie. Discontinuity can occur in the *location* of these events; in the flow of *time;* and in these events' *relationship to reality* (e.g., a transition from "reality" to dream, from ongoing reality to the remembered reality of a flashback, or from reality observed directly to the reported reality of the narrated flashback). As the case of flashbacks illustrates, these types of discontinuity are not mutually exclusive. A convenient starting point for a discussion of editing is the distinction between editing that does entail discontinuity in one or more of the senses listed above and editing that does not. The latter kind of editing, in which location, time frame, and relationship to reality do not change, is by far the more frequent, and it is with this that we shall begin the discussion.

Point-of-View Editing

Editing that does not disrupt the continuity of location, time, or reality typically occurs within a single scene rather than across scenes, but this correspondence is not exact. Nor is it easy to give a definition of "scene" that would not be circular in our terms. Therefore, the only label I shall use for this kind of editing is "point-of-view editing." This label refers to a shift in camera position within a single location, a single time frame, and a single stream of reality. This kind of editing can have several functions, but perhaps the most basic of these is to enable the viewer to derive a sense of a coherent space-time continuum from a series of fragmentary images. What principles do viewers follow in performing this interpretational process? Is there a set of medium-specific conventions, a "grammar," that editors and viewers have to follow?

Many people who write about film and television make it clear that they believe in the existence of such a grammar, not just for this aspect of editing but for editing in general. Yet with a few notable exceptions (e.g., Bordwell et al., 1985, pp. 42–69, 194–230; Metz, 1974, pp. 108–146), contemporary film and television scholars appear somewhat reluctant to attempt any systematic account of what such a grammar might look like—i.e., what set of formal principles might be the basis on which viewers arrive at appropriate interpretations of the events represented in edited sequences. It is worth considering for a moment a possible reason for the general lack of such accounts in recent scholarly literature.

In a popular textbook on film "language," the author, in the course of pointing out that film is only "like" a language, makes the claim that it is impossible to be "ungrammatical" in film (Monaco, 1981, p. 121). If this statement were literally true, its implication would be that no matter how a filmmaker put a film together, audiences would be able to infer the meaning intended—in other words, that interpretation is independent of the structure of the message. However, it seems unlikely that this is what the author meant to say. A more likely reading of his claim might be that certain well-known formulas of Hollywood-style editing (as described, for instance, in Reisz and Millar, 1968) can apparently be violated with no great loss of understanding on the part of the audience.

The standard examples regarding this point are the films of the French New Wave directors, especially Jean-Luc Godard, in which such "mistakes"

as jump cuts were introduced without major consequences for viewers' comprehension. (At least, this is the generally accepted version of these events.
One problem with using self-consciously rule-defying movies as one's
test case is that people who complain that they *don't* understand them can
readily be dismissed as artistic reactionaries.) Of course, one could say that
all these films demonstrate is that the traditional Hollywood editing formulas were too restrictive or too slow to change with the times. It seems to
me, however, that there is a more general point here about the nature of the
interpretational process the audience brings to bear on the formal structure
of a film or television program. To illustrate this point, I want to consider
two specific instances of point-of-view editing that have been singled out in
scholarly analyses as breaking movie conventions.

The first example is from Alfred Hitchcock's *The Birds* (1963). The editing "mistake" occurs in a scene in which the film's protagonist is sitting in a
schoolyard, waiting for a class taught by a friend of hers to be dismissed. As
she waits, killer birds begin to gather on the bars of a jungle gym some
distance behind her. They are shown flying down one at a time, and these
shots are intercut with shots of the woman impatiently smoking a cigarette.
When she finally happens to turn around and look at the jungle gym, it is
completely covered with birds.

In the course of an exceptionally thorough discussion of the applicability
of linguistic concepts such as grammaticality to movies, John Carroll (1980)
has pointed out that the editing of this sequence violates what he considers
to be a firm rule—namely, that, if a character is shown looking out of the
frame of a shot, the following shot will be taken by the audience as an indication of what that character is looking at. In this sequence, however, shots
of the woman looking out of the frame are followed by shots of the birds
congregating on the jungle gym, but this juxtaposition is clearly *not* meant
to imply that the woman is looking at the birds; it is only at the end of the
sequence that she turns around and sees them. If Carroll's description of
the expected meaning of this kind of editing is correct, and if such "grammatical rules" do matter, then viewers should be confused by the sequence.
Are they?

In an informal test with a class of students who had not yet discussed the
issues involved here, it became clear that at least some of them did indeed
experience uncertainty or discombobulation at the point in this sequence at
which the violation of convention occurs. However, this uncertainty was
only momentary, and in no case did it result in a wrong interpretation. The
reason may be evident even to someone who hasn't seen this movie. Because
the woman's facial expression in the shots intercut with the shots of the
birds doesn't contain anything that can be construed as a reaction to them
(she already knows that birds have been attacking people in this area),
she obviously can't be looking at them. Rather, she must just be gazing

abstractedly into the distance. This interpretation is reinforced by the fact that, when she finally does turn around, she is clearly horrified. In other words, the reason this violation of convention doesn't lead to lasting misinterpretation is that the implications of such a misinterpretation are implausible. (Actually, there is a second reason: A long shot at the beginning of this sequence shows that the woman is facing away from the jungle gym.)

Does this argument mean that Carroll is wrong in calling this sequence "ungrammatical"? Judging from the results of the informal experiment described above, I would say that he is clearly correct, both in his assessment of this particular sequence and more generally in his identification of this rule of movie grammar. However, the fact that this violation turns out not to matter very much seems to me to illustrate an important principle about the way mainstream narrative films and television programs work: The role of formal conventions in conveying a movie's meaning is generally subordinate to conventional standards of plausibility or probability ("conventional" in the sense that the filmmaker must be able to assume them of the audience). In other words, the viewer's interpretation of edited sequences is largely a matter of cross-referencing possible interpretations against a broader context (i.e., the larger story in the movie itself, together with corresponding situations from real life and other movies) rather than a matter of "decoding" formal devices (e.g., an off-screen look followed by a cut to a new shot). To put this more compactly: Interpretation is driven by the narrative *context*, not the *code*.

I shall now turn to a second example of an edited sequence that has been described by writers as a violation of a rule of Hollywood-style editing. This sequence comes from a noncommercial film called *The Spirit of the Navajo* by Maxine and Mary Jane Tsosie. The film was produced as part of Sol Worth and John Adair's ground-breaking study of the relationship between culture and visual syntax (Worth and Adair, 1972), in which several Navajos with little film-related experience were taught how to use 16mm film equipment and encouraged to make films on subjects of their own choosing. Worth and Adair were hoping to use these films as data on how cinematic codes are shaped by culture. *The Spirit of the Navajo* is a twenty-minute film that shows a Navajo *yataalii* (singer, i.e., medicine man) performing a traditional curing ceremony.

The sequence that concerns us here occurs during a part of the film in which the medicine man is shown gathering certain plants for use during the ceremony itself. The sequence consists of a series of shots of the man snipping at plants or walking about in an open landscape. In their analysis of the films, Worth and Adair use this sequence as evidence that the well-known Hollywood rule for cutting on motion is a culture-specific convention that the Navajos see no reason to follow. According to this rule, when an action is broken up by editing, each new shot should pick up the action at exactly the point at which the previous shot left off. If this rule is violated and some of the action is left out, the result is considered an error and is called a jump-cut.

In the eyes of Worth and Adair, the plant-gathering sequence from *The Spirit of the Navajo* is full of jump-cuts (e.g., a shot of the man kneeling is followed by a shot of him standing, with no transition between the two positions) and, therefore, evidence in favor of their argument about the cultural specificity of Hollywood editing. This argument was also supported by direct questioning of the filmmakers, who clearly did not see anything wrong with this way of showing things (Worth and Adair, 1972, p. 172). However, when I saw this film for the first time, before having read Worth and Adair's analysis, my response to this sequence was rather different. Rather than seeing an "error," I found myself altogether unable to judge the sequence and unable to tell whether it looked "right" or "wrong."

More specifically, it appeared to me that there were two possibilities. On the one hand, the filmmakers could have intended the representation of a continuous action, in which case their editing style would be judged by Hollywood standards to contain jump-cuts. On the other hand, it was also possible that continuous action was in fact not implied, that the various shots corresponded to representative fragments of a larger process, in which case the editing would not be considered inappropriate by Hollywood standards. In retrospect, it seems to me that the reasons for this difference between my own response and that of the study's authors have a lot to do with the way viewers in general go about making sense of films.

Worth and Adair, who had both worked extensively with the Navajos and had very full knowledge of the subject matter of this film, in particular, knew what the intended real-life equivalent of this sequence would have been (namely, a continuous action) and therefore could judge whether the editing conformed to the way a Hollywood filmmaker would have done it. However, at the time I first saw this film, I could have been considered a substantially naive viewer. Not only was I unfamiliar with the "code," I also knew next to nothing about the traditional healing ceremony that is the film's subject. Because I had no idea what the plant-gathering sequence would have looked like in real life, I had no way of judging the appropriateness (by Hollywood standards) of the editing.

What we have here is, in a sense, the converse of the situation we encountered in the example from *The Birds*. In that situation, the viewer's contextual knowledge (about the woman's previous encounters with the birds and her probable response to seeing them again) overruled the misleading information resulting from the editing error. Here, my lack of contextual knowledge left me incapable of making a firm interpretation or judging the plausibility of alternative readings (since the editing would have looked quite appropriate, by Hollywood standards, if the intent were merely to show snippets of a larger event).

Once again, therefore, the general principle seems to be that, in the interpretational habits of Hollywood-trained viewers, narrative context comes before code. I would emphasize that this principle should be taken as a characteristic of mainstream commercial cinema only, rather than as an inherent property of the medium. It is interesting to note, however, that when the makers of *The Spirit of the Navajo* were questioned about the sequence discussed above, the reasoning they gave for their editing was precisely an appeal to contextually determined plausibility: We know the man is walking from here to here, so, if we just show parts of it, the viewer should be able to fill in the rest. (For another example of a broader application of the principle of contextual primacy, see Bordwell, 1985, p. 128.)

If my reasoning about the role of narrative context in viewers' interpretation of Hollywood-style movies is correct, it might also explain why actual descriptions of the interpretational rules for editing have not been attempted more often in recent scholarly literature: The primacy of context gives codes a marginal quality and allows them to fluctuate with relative impunity, thus making the task of the analyst that much more unrewarding and uncertain. Nevertheless, as I have already said, I think it would be wrong to conclude that "anything goes" as far as editing is concerned. Although exceptions and violations of rules may be frequent, in the case of point-of-view editing at least there are still certain anchoring conventions that can reasonably be thought of as constituting a "code."

We have already encountered two elements of this code—viz., the prohibition against jump cuts and the rule that an off-screen glance triggers a shot of what is being looked at. Neither rule is inviolate, but both are adhered to with considerable consistency in mainstream commercial cinema and television. However, the most prominent structural feature of point-of-view editing in mainstream media is an overarching principle that encompasses a broad variety of more specific formulas. Ignoring some of the finer points (cf. Mamet, 1985, p. ix), the overall thrust of these formulas can be summarized quite succinctly: Their main goal is to keep the spectator consistently on one side of an unfolding action or interaction. For example, in a conversation scene that begins with one character on the left side of the screen and the other character on the right side, this relative orientation should be maintained from shot to shot; if two people having a conversation are shot in individual close-ups, their lines of sight should intersect (i.e., one should look left, the other right); in an action sequence, a movement that unfolds from left to right in one shot should preserve this direction in the next shot. A particularly clear illustration of the second formula occurs in a scene from Mario Van Peebles's *New Jack City* (Figures 3.1 and 3.2), in

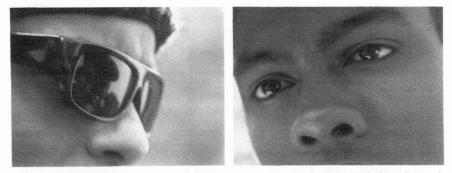

Figures 3.1 and 3.2 Eye-line match links the close-ups. *Source: New Jack City* (directed by Mario Van Peebles). Copyright © 1991 Warner Bros., Inc. All rights reserved.

which the intersecting eye-lines are the only visual cues tying the two shots together.

These formulas are sometimes referred to as the 180-degree-line rule; eye-line matching; and the rule of continuity of screen direction, respectively. It should be evident that all of them stem from the same basic principle. As with the off-screen glance and anti–jump cut rules, this general principle is certainly not immune from violation, but it is probably stable enough to be a legitimate example of a cinematic code, and it will be the primary reference point in our discussion of whether the ability to comprehend point-of-view editing rests on a cinematic "literacy." However, we shall begin this discussion with a brief look at off-screen glances and jump cuts.

According to a researcher who works with children, "Learning to decode the symbols of film and television is something like learning to read" (Greenfield, 1984, p. 10). Taken literally, such a statement implies that the informational cues of film and television are arbitrary, a matter of "pure" convention. Let us examine the validity of this claim with respect to the convention of an off-screen glance as a cue for a shot of what a character is looking at. A specific analogy between this kind of convention and language has been proposed by Pier Paolo Pasolini, who, in addition to being a filmmaker, was also a (usually) very astute writer about film. According to Pasolini, this device serves the same function as the use of "he said . . . " or "she said . . . " in verbal narration (Pasolini, 1962, p. 368). Although this argument does not necessarily imply that the device is an arbitrary convention (in the sense in which the words are), it is a convenient point of departure for thinking about the convention's origins.

To me, Pasolini's analogy seems too loose. The shot that follows an off-screen glance typically depicts a person or situation with whom or with which the "glancer" is interacting or is about to interact. By contrast, the linguistic construction that follows "he/she said . . . " is typically the speaker's own contribution to an interaction, and it is only when someone else responds to his or her statements that we get any kind of equivalence to the off-screen-glance/object-of-glance construction. A more plausible analogue of this cinematic construction seems to me to be readily available in everyday visual experience.

I don't think I am making a novel observation when I say that there is an element of "contagiousness" in human visual attention. When we see someone looking at something, we tend to respond by following that person's line of sight if her or his facial expression or the general situation suggests that what is being looked at may be interesting. A good argument could probably be made in favor of a genetic explanation of this tendency: It is easy to imagine how the behavior in question might confer an evolutionary advantage on any social animal. However, such an assumption is not necessary for the point I want to make, nor would it really strengthen this point to any appreciable extent.

With regard to the basic question we are examining here, what emerges from these observations is this: If the process of visual attention in the real world is indeed characterized by the tendency I have described above, then the cinematic convention of using an off-screen glance to link a character with what she or he is looking at reproduces a visual sequence that even the most inexperienced viewer of film or television will have experienced often in real life. In that sense, therefore, this convention is anything but arbitrary.

Let us now examine the same issue with regard to the convention of avoiding jump-cuts in the editing of characters' movements. As we have seen, Worth and Adair found several violations of this convention in a film made by two of the participants in their study of Navajo filmmakers. Although the Navajo filmmakers' own explanation of the jump-cuts was essentially an invocation of the capacity of narrative context to bridge gaps in action, Worth and Adair also argued that the jump-cuts might have been a reflection of certain aspects of Navajo verbal grammar (Worth and Adair, 1972). In other words, they see the Navajo jump-cuts as an example of cross-cultural differences in conventions of cinematic structure; and, where there is a cross-cultural difference in representational conventions, there is always the possibility—although by no means a certitude—that one or the other culture's conventions, or perhaps both, may be arbitrary. Is this the case here?

If the Worth-Adair assumption that the Navajo jump-cuts reproduce some feature of Navajo grammar is true, then in that respect and in that context the jump-cuts are indeed arbitrary—that is, they are isomorphic with an element in an arbitrary system of representation. But in this case, arbitrariness might not necessarily mean that a first-time viewer would have trouble understanding the convention. A speaker of Navajo, no matter how inexperienced with respect to movies, might be able to interpret the jump-cut on the basis of its analogue in the Navajo language. However, what about the Hollywood convention that says jump-cuts are to be avoided? If we agree that Navajo jump-cuts are arbitrary, must we also conclude that Hollywood's non–jump-cut editing is arbitrary?

I have occasionally encountered among my colleagues and students the well-intentioned belief that it is ethnocentric to assume that Western representational conventions can be any closer to visual reality than the conventions of other cultures. If "their" images are arbitrary, this argument goes, so must "ours" be—it's just that we're used to the arbitrariness and are no longer aware of it. This is an admirable principle, both in its ethical premises and in its skeptical approach to that which is taken for granted. Nevertheless, I assume that it will be clear upon reflection that as a fixed rule, this principle is illogical. There is no necessary connection between a finding of arbitrary conventions in one culture and the conclusion that another culture's conventions are also arbitrary. So we ask again: Is the Hollywood practice of editing motion without substantial gaps a convention that first-time viewers have to learn to understand?

I would say that, if anything, the exact opposite is true: This is a convention deliberately designed so that viewers would *not* have to master an arbitrary interpretational principle. Because the essence of this convention is the preservation of a complete record of characters' motions, what the convention effectively accomplishes is the elimination of any need for codification of that aspect of the information in the image. By definition, this representational convention is not arbitrary.

This brings us, then, to the more crucial issue in this discussion of point-of-view editing—namely, the general principle that the camera should be kept on one side of the action. Here, however, the conclusions are not as self-evident as in the case of jump cuts. The various specific formulas (the 180-degree-line rule and so forth) encompassed by this general principle were designed to make it easier for the viewer to arrive at a coherent sense of spatial relationships on the basis of a succession of partial images. This, it may be argued, is the central interpretational demand that point-of-view editing imposes on the viewer. Do these formulas have the intended effect? Or, to ask a narrower question: Do they free the viewer from having to learn a specifically cinematic set of interpretational rules? The answer to this question depends on what one conceives the viewer's real-world skills of spatial perception to be.

We know that in real-world vision people derive a coherent mental representation of their surroundings from a series of disconnected partial views. The eyes fixate on a certain spot in the visual surround, register that view, and then move on rapidly—and imperceptibly—to another fixation point, which may be far removed, in terms of visual angle, from the previous one. These momentary impressions are then synthesized by the brain in an ongoing process of internal modeling of what is "out there."

The essential feature of this process, for our purposes, is that it involves a series of discrete images and the possibility of a substantial difference in point of view between one image and the next. In these respects the process appears to be analogous to the task demanded of the viewer by point-of-view editing. It is tempting to conclude that the former is in fact the basis for the latter and, consequently, that the 180-degree-line rule and related formulas are means of ensuring that the viewer's cinematic experience does not depart too drastically from the possibilities of real-world perception.

This view certainly appears to have been a working premise among the filmmakers who were most immediately involved in the development of the Hollywood style of editing. For example, in the following statement, D. W. Griffith draws a direct parallel between point-of-view editing and the process of everyday vision: "Looking at real things, the human vision fastens itself upon a quick succession of small comprehensible incidents; and we form our eventual impressions, like a mosaic, out of such detail. . . . The director counterfeits the operation of the eye with his lens." (Griffith, 1926, quoted in Jesionowski, 1987, p. 46) Somewhat more recently, John Huston told an interviewer the following:

> All the things we have laboriously learned to do with film, were already part of the physiological and psychological experience of man before film was invented. . . . Let me make an experiment—maybe you will understand better what I mean. Move your eyes, quickly, from an object on one side of the room to an object on the other side. In a film you would use the cut. Watch! There—you did exactly what I expected: in moving your head from one side of the room to the other, you briefly closed your eyes. Try it again, in the other direction. There! You see, you do it automatically. Once you know the distance between the two objects, you blink instinctively. That's a cut. . . . In the same way, almost all the devices of film have a physiological counterpart. (excerpted from Bachmann, 1965; see Sarris, 1967, p. 270)

Strictly speaking, however, there is only one kind of point-of-view editing that has an exact real-world equivalent: changes in point of view from a stationary camera position. It should be obvious that this situation is quite rare; editing almost invariably involves a change in the position of the camera. Consequently, logical deduction alone cannot answer the question of whether there is enough similarity between real-world perception and the more routine forms of point-of-view editing to enable a viewer to bridge the two automatically, without prior adaptation to the specific visual experience of movies.

However, there is some empirical evidence with a direct bearing on this question. This evidence comes from a study by Renée Hobbs and her associates (Hobbs et al., 1988). The study was conducted in Kenya, in an area in which the local population had very limited experience with modern mass media and no experience at all with film or television, except for a single exposure to a government-sponsored development film, which had been seen by some 40 percent of the study's subjects. Hobbs's study was based on two versions of a videotape that was made expressly for the purposes of this research. Both versions presented a story based on local circumstances: A boy takes his family's sheep and goats out to pasture, falls asleep, allowing the animals to be stolen by a thief, and is then reprimanded severely by his father.

One version of the videotape was done in a continuous long-shot with limited camera movement. The other version involved point-of-view editing in the form of shifts in magnification and in angle of view, as well as a single cut to a subjective shot of the father, seen from the perspective of the boy. Despite the fact that the tapes were viewed under relatively unfavorable circumstances (through the eyepiece of a black-and-white video camera) and despite the fact that the researchers used a relatively demanding measure of comprehension—viz., unaided recall of the story's key incidents—the subjects were able to follow the story quite readily. Most crucial, there were no significant differences in comprehension between the two versions of the tape. In other words, even for first-time or second-time viewers, point-of-view editing appears to be close enough to everyday visual experience so as not to be an obstacle to interpretation.

This conclusion has also received indirect support from a pair of experiments by Georgette Comuntzis-Page on children's interpretations of reverse-angle editing (Comuntzis, 1987; Comuntzis-Page, 1991). Earlier research had found that, although some forms of editing within a single place and time frame appear to pose no interpretational obstacle even to three-year-olds (see Smith et al., 1985), problems in comprehension do arise when the editing involves a shift from the subjective perspective of one character to that of another (see Messaris, 1982, for a review of these findings). At first blush, the latter finding may seem to contradict the contention that the comprehension of point-of-view editing does not require previous experience with film or television. However, as I pointed out at the beginning of this chapter, a child's inability to understand a particular editing convention does not necessarily mean that the child is lacking in media experience. Rather, the difficulty may have to do with the child's general cognitive development. Even if the interpretational process required by the convention is a perfect analogue of adult viewers' real-world cognitive skills, children who have not yet developed those real-world skills may be unable to make sense of the convention no matter how many times they have encountered it before.

The kind of convention that concerns us here has been explored in the work of Comuntzis-Page. Her experiments, which were performed with children between the ages of three and seven, tested the subjects' ability to understand the spatial relationships in two short videos involving reverse-angle editing (e.g., cutting back and forth between matching over-the-shoulder shots of two people playing chess). The experiments also tested children's real-world perspective-taking ability through a variant of the well-known Piagetian three-mountain test (in which the child is asked to guess how a certain three-dimensional display would appear to viewers positioned at various points along its perimeter; see Chapter 4). In both experiments, it turned out that children's successful performance on the video-interpretation task was contingent on real-world perspective-taking ability as measured by the Piaget-based test. However, no relationship was found between video comprehension and level of previous TV viewing. As with the Hobbs study, then, these findings support the notion that the mental capacity to integrate the successive partial views in an edited sequence may be a derivative of real-world cognitive skills and may not depend on previous experience with visual media.

It is also worth noting that, although the introduction of point-of-view editing into the films of the first decade of this century (in place of the single-take, theaterlike scenes of the very first movies) was apparently undertaken with some hesitation by the film pioneers of the day, there is no record of audience difficulty with it or protest against it. We have already seen that D. W. Griffith considered point-of-view editing an extension of the principles of real-life vision, and, although Griffith liked to boast about resistance to the various innovations in film structure with which he credited himself, he appears not to have encountered any obstacles in his initial moves to break scenes down into shots (beginning with *For Love of Gold* in 1908; see Jacobs, 1968).

What these facts do not tell us, of course, is what, if any, the limits of an inexperienced viewer's adaptability to point-of-view editing might be. If the purpose of the Hollywood conventions for point-of-view editing is to stay within the bounds of the inexperienced (adult) viewer's interpretational capacities, the findings we have reviewed are certainly consistent with the conclusion that this purpose has been achieved. It does not follow, however, that violations of these conventions would necessarily cause an inexperienced viewer to misinterpret the editing. The Navajo filmmakers' assumption—that if one is familiar with the situation portrayed in a film, one should be able to compensate mentally for the gaps created by jump-cuts—may be valid for the other point-of-view conventions as well. In fact, violations of the other conventions are considerably more frequent than jump cuts in mass-market movies and TV programs; if anything, then, the principle that contextual knowledge can overrule code violations may be even more applicable to these other conventions.

The potential primacy of narrative context over code is a possibility we shall encounter again in later sections of this chapter, when we examine forms of editing beyond point-of-view. However, there is an important distinction between the way narrative context operates in point-of-view editing, on the one hand, and its function in these latter forms of editing, on the other. As we have already seen in the case of Pasolini and Worth, several film theorists have argued that various aspects of the editing structure of movies may be analogues or even derivatives of linguistic structures. (Similar points have been made about the relationship between film narrative and oral traditions in Africa [Diawara, 1988] and Australia [Michaels, 1986].) As far as the larger structural elements of a narrative film or TV program are concerned—i.e., such things as parallel editing or scene changes—I do think there is some validity to such arguments. When we discuss these forms of editing, I shall pursue this point further.

However, as I have already argued in reference to Pasolini and Worth, when it comes to point-of-view editing I think the search for structural analogues in language is misguided. The characteristic tasks with which point-of-view editing confronts a viewer (viz., integrating a succession of images into a coherent conception of action, interaction, and space) are fundamentally *visual* operations, based on mental processes that are routinely involved in the act of vision in everyday life. Therefore, when we say that a viewer's interpretation of point-of-view editing can be guided by contextual knowledge, it should be understood that the knowledge in question has to do with the visual aspects of motion and space, not with linguistic structures.

Finally, before we move on to other issues, one more difference between point-of-view editing and the various other kinds of editing is worth emphasizing. In the typical Hollywood-style fiction film or TV program, point-of-view editing accounts for the vast majority of the transitions between shots. To get a sense of what the actual proportions might be, I did an analysis of all the shot changes in a sample of nine fictional TV programs for the Fall 1986 broadcast season. This sample included three soap operas ("General Hospital," "Guiding Light," "Days of Our Lives"); three sitcoms ("Growing Pains," "Bob Newhart Show," "The Cosby Show"); and three crime dramas ("MacGyver," "Magnum, P.I.," and "Miami Vice").

The shot-transition counts for these three genres were as follows: for the soap operas, 559 per episode; for the sitcoms, 250 per episode; and for the crime dramas, 398 per episode. These shot transitions were classified into five categories, four of which had to do with aspects of editing that we shall consider in later sections of this chapter (e.g., flashbacks). The fifth category was the one that concerns us here: point-of-view editing. This was by far the most frequent type of transition, amounting to fully 95 percent of the transitions in the three soap operas, 96 percent in the sitcoms, and 94 percent in the crime dramas. Therefore, by accounting for the process by which viewers interpret point-of-view editing, one has gone a long way toward explaining the interpretation of editing as a whole. The arguments developed above have attempted to explain what I see as the core problem of point-of-view editing. However, there are certain other aspects to this kind of editing I have not examined yet and to which I shall turn my attention in the next section of this chapter.

Editing as an Indicator of Thoughts and Emotions

The creation of a coherent space/time continuum out of the fragments presented in a movie or TV program is one of the central intellectual tasks these media demand of their viewers. As I have just indicated, this task is a recurring component of the interpretation of fictional narrative editing. It should be evident that this task also confronts the viewer of a variety of other genres, such as news, sports, and game shows. Regardless of genre, however, the function of point-of-view editing is obviously not confined to linking motions, interactions, and fragments of space. Accordingly, the present section will consider other aspects of this kind of editing and the interpretational skills corresponding to them.

To begin with, let us consider what, other than space/time/action linkages, might be involved in point-of-view editing as applied to a purely fictional sequence of images. A convenient example of a scene in which other types of linkages are clearly present occurs in the film *Sabotage* (1936) by Alfred Hitchcock. The film deals with a man who recklessly involves his wife's young brother in an act of intended sabotage during which the boy, an unwitting participant, is killed. The scene that concerns us here follows this incident and takes place in the dining room of the couple's home. The man is seated at the table, preparing to eat, while the woman uses various utensils—including a carving knife—to serve the food. Although the man has tried to conceal the facts about her brother's death, the woman has discovered the truth, and as the scene progresses it becomes apparent—first to the attentive viewer, then to the man himself—that she is thinking of using the knife as an instrument of vengeance.

Neither the woman's thoughts nor the man's are expressed in words. Furthermore, in line with Hitchcock's intentions, the actors' facial expressions are unrevealing. Instead, the unfolding drama—the woman's growing desire for revenge, the man's sudden awareness of her thoughts—is developed by means of editing. The editing principles applied to this scene have been described in detail by Hitchcock (Truffaut, 1967, pp. 77–80), but they are quite clear even without this authorial explanation. The progression of the woman's thoughts is conveyed through two kinds of juxtapositions: first, between shots of her and shots of various reminders of her dead brother (e.g., his empty place at the table); second, between shots of her and shots of the knife, in close-up. Such juxtapositions, together with the interactions among them, create an unequivocal sense of what is on the woman's mind and what she is thinking of doing about it.

The man's awakening to her intentions is signaled in similar fashion, by a cut from the knife to his face. An additional element indicates that the tension in the scene is reaching a high point: The man's face is in a much tighter close-up than it had been in before. Both of the editing devices Hitchcock has used here—i.e., the juxtaposition of a person in thought with the object of those thoughts and the move in for a close-up to heighten the drama—are standard components of narrative editing style in Hollywood movies and elsewhere. However, the questions they pose to the interpreter are quite different from those considered in the previous section of this chapter. From our current perspective, the relevant questions are no longer "Where is the knife relative to the woman?" or "What happened to the rest of the man's body?" Rather, what concerns us now is how these sequences of images can serve as the basis for inferences about characters' thoughts and for assessments of the flow of dramatic interest.

The possibility that editing can be used to convey a sense of characters' thoughts is one of the earliest discoveries in the history of explicit theorizing about the movies. The formulation of this possibility is usually associated with Lev Kuleshov and other filmmakers working during the early years of Soviet cinema. In its best-known incarnation, the so-called "Kuleshov effect" is illustrated in Kuleshov's experiment involving an "expressionless" close-up of the actor Mozhukhin juxtaposed with a variety of other scenes, including a plate of soup on a table, a corpse in a coffin, and a little girl playing with a toy bear. According to Kuleshov's colleague V. I. Pudovkin, to whom we owe the best-known description of this experiment, viewers who saw these sequences without having been told about the editing responded with enthusiastic praise for Mozhukhin's acting. In other words, the editing led these viewers to see subtle changes in expression, from thoughts of food to deep sorrow to a "light, happy smile," where in fact there were no such expressions (Pudovkin, 1958, p. 168; but see Holland, 1989; Polan, 1986; Prince and Hensley, 1992, for skeptical interpretations of this account).

A more recent experiment by Kessler (1970) is less dramatic, in that perceived changes in overt expression were not at issue, but it is nonetheless supportive of the general principle behind this kind of editing. In this experiment, viewers were shown a brief film in which shots of a young woman were juxtaposed with shots of various sports (e.g., hockey, archery). Although the woman was never shown participating in any of the sports, these juxtapositions in themselves were sufficient to create a sense of the woman's involvement with them. Furthermore, it was found that viewers' inferences about the woman's interest in each of the sports depended on the amount of screen time devoted to any one of them.

The kinds of juxtapositions explored in these experiments are firmly established features of film and TV editing, occurring most commonly, perhaps, in the conventional reaction-shot sequence, in which shots of a speaker or other object of interest are intercut with shots of a listener or observer. Such sequences are a typical ingredient of dialogue scenes in fiction films, as well as of nonfictional dialogues in talk shows and other TV programs. However, the potential role of image juxtaposition as an indicator of characters' thoughts or reactions is probably most evident in the absence of dialogue (e.g., in scenes in which one character is secretly following the doings of another) and in those nonfictional cases in which a certain sequence of events is rearranged through editing (as in the many instances in which an interviewer's reactions are inserted into a TV interview after the fact). Assuming, as the evidence suggests, that viewers typically do use the juxtaposition of images—rather than just the facial expressions in them—as clues to what lies beneath the surface of characters' faces, we are confronted with an interpretational skill that is evidently quite different from those considered earlier in this chapter. What might account for viewers' ability to make these kinds of inferences?

Although the precise visual sequence with which the viewer is confronted on the screen—i.e., a view of a character juxtaposed with a view of some object or situation of interest to that character—may not have an exact parallel in reality, the basic inferential task the viewer has to perform is similar to an extremely common real-world task, that of judging other people's intentions from the context of their facial expressions and behavior. The degree to which this process is central to interpersonal communication bears some emphasis. As researchers in the areas of nonverbal communication and person perception have noted, people's appearance, expressions, and actions are frequently ambiguous or even completely opaque in the absence of information about the objects or situations to which they are addressed. Indeed, Birdwhistell (1970) has argued that no facial expression or gesture has a determinate meaning out of context. The ability to take context into account in inferring thoughts and assessing intentions is consequently a vital component of any mature person's social skills. It is conceivable, therefore, that this ability, rather than any direct experience with editing conventions, may serve as the basis of the interpretational competence called for by the kinds of editing we are concerned with here.

The notion that the Kuleshov effect and related cinematic devices are derivatives of the real-world dependence of expressive meaning on context is consistent with the implications of another, less widely known experiment described by the Soviet filmmaker. In this experiment, Kuleshov filmed an actor in two roles: first, in a jail cell as a famished prisoner being offered a bowl of soup; second, as a prisoner released from jail and taken out into the open air. The actor was invited to use every means at his disposal to express the sentiments appropriate to these two situations: on the one hand, craving for the soup; on the other, delight at the sight of birds, clouds, the sun.

Then Kuleshov produced various versions of the two scenes, in some of which the shots of the actor were transposed from one scene to the other.

By his own account, regardless of how the scenes were scrambled, viewers were unable to detect any discrepancy in the actor's performance (Kuleshov, 1974, p. 54). Despite the fact that the actor had a clear and distinct sentiment in mind in each case, his facial expressions in themselves were apparently incapable of conveying a specific enough sense of his thoughts, and the viewers' ultimate interpretations were evidently fixed by the overall context (cf. Mamet, 1991, pp. 68–71). This is essentially the point investigators of real-life social perception have made about the information available in facial expressions and other overt indicators of thought and intention. Unlike the more famous Kuleshov experiment mentioned earlier, in which the use of an unvarying, neutral expression might be seen as somewhat artificial, this one is based on a closer approximation of real-life conditions, in the sense that the actor's performance was allowed to vary with the situation. It therefore makes the potential parallel between real life and this aspect of movie-viewing clearer.

As this discussion suggests, then, both reality and exposure to film or television are potential avenues to the kind of visual literacy we have been considering. One possibility does not necessarily exclude the other, of course. It is conceivable that these two sources of interpretational competence might work together, either by reinforcing each other or by interacting in a more complex fashion. For example, previous exposure to editing might teach a viewer which juxtapositions of images to look at, whereas real-life social experience might guide the actual inferences drawn from those juxtapositions. In the absence of research aimed specifically at disentangling these two threads (for example, a study of inexperienced adult viewers' susceptibility to the Kuleshov effect), it is unclear that one can be more specific about either the necessary preconditions for this aspect of visual literacy or the typical mix of experiences leading to it. However, the essential point for our purposes is that, far from being a purely arbitrary convention, "Kuleshov-style" editing appears to be based on a conjunction of informational cues that are a routine aspect of real-world person perception.

The Modulation of Emphasis and Viewer Involvement

The second aspect of editing illustrated by the dinner scene from *Sabotage* has to do with dramatic emphasis and flow, i.e., with the degree of intensity that formal structure can impart to the events on the screen. In the example from *Sabotage,* this structural modulation of intensity is illustrated in what is probably its most common form: a move to a tighter close-up. Variations in shot tightness can serve a variety of purposes, of course—for example, they can be used for essentially informational reasons or, as we will see in Chapter 5, to manipulate viewers' identification with the people on the screen—but it is probably safe to say that regulation of intensity is one of their primary functions.

The use of close-ups for emphasis, as in the scene from *Sabotage,* is too common a convention to need further illustration, and the opposite usage (i.e., drawing the camera back to reduce intensity) is no rarity either, as it occurs of necessity every time a scene continues past a close-up climax. The interpretation of these conventional devices is presumably a routine matter for any competent viewer. But what is the source of this interpretational ability? To take the specific case of the dinner scene in *Sabotage:* What previous knowledge or ability must the viewer have in order to be able to tell that the move to a close-up signifies that the scene is reaching its climax?

As in the case of the Kuleshov effect, this question could have more than one possible answer. Before the alternatives are spelled out, though, it will be useful to examine the notion of structural modulation of intensity a little further. It should be obvious that changes in the tightness of shots are not the only means by which editing may be linked to intensity. Two other devices that are commonly used in this way are the manipulation of shot duration and the choice of transitional mechanism (e.g., cut, fade, or dissolve). Although it is probably true that neither of these devices is associated with variations in dramatic intensity as frequently as shot tightness is, modulation of intensity is nonetheless a standard feature of both.

The manipulation of shot duration as a means of modulating dramatic flow has been experimented with at least since the days of Kuleshov and Eisenstein (1957, p. 72ff). It is encountered routinely today in such places as commercials, music videos, and action movies, in which accelerated editing is used to create a sense of excitement or dynamism. Evidence that this kind of manipulation works—i.e., that audiences do indeed perceive a heightening of intensity as a result of it—comes from an experiment by Penn (1971) involving several variations on the basic editing device of cross-cutting between two objects. The experimental films were of three different kinds of objects—rectangles, cars, and humans—filmed at rest and in motion; the editing speeds tested ranged from 7.5 seconds per shot to 0.5 seconds per shot and included accelerating and decelerating modes. The central finding was that higher editing speeds led viewers to give the films higher ratings on the semantic-differential scales of "potency" and "activity."

The use of transitional mechanisms in connection with variations in emphasis or intensity is not a common feature of contemporary films and TV programs; the current tendency in fictional editing is to rely on a single transitional device, the straight cut, in all circumstances. In other visual genres, however, a broader range of transitional mechanisms is still very much in evidence, and instances of the kind of usage we are examining here are more typical. Not surprisingly, a study of TV commercials furnishes one of the more prominent examples. This study, by Welch and her colleagues (1979), entailed an analysis of formal characteristics of commercials aimed at children. In particular, the researchers were interested in differences between commercials aimed at boys and commercials aimed at girls. In terms of editing, the sharpest difference observed involved transitional mechanisms: The boys' commercials (which, as one might expect, contained much more activity, aggression, and noise than the girls') were characterized by a significantly higher frequency of straight cuts and a significantly lower frequency of fades and dissolves.

As these examples suggest, then, there seem to be a number of ways in which editing can be used as an "intensifier" of content, and it is worth noting that the devices we have examined often occur together. For instance, the Welch study found that the predominance of straight cuts in boys' commercials was paralleled by a higher rate of scene changes. With this background in mind, we return to the central question of this discussion: On what basis are viewers able to make sense of the kinds of devices we have examined?

Although the three devices considered here have all been discussed under a single general heading, it should be clear that there are differences in the nuances of meaning entailed by each. There may be instances in which their meanings seem to overlap, but these devices are never interchangeable. Nonetheless, despite the fact that the precise meaning associated with any one of these devices is inevitably peculiar to that one device, it can be argued that there is a common principle in the way in which those meanings arise. It was because of this possibility that these devices were discussed together.

Each of these devices can be said to acquire its meaning by approximating some feature of real-world experience. In the case of shot tightness being used as an intensifier, the aspect of experience being replicated is surely the greater involvement that comes with increased proximity to people and objects, whereas both editing rate and transitional speed can be seen as deriving their significance from a real-world association between speed and intensity. In none of these cases do the meanings appear to derive from a purely arbitrary convention (as, for example, in a numerical scale of intensity, in which the visual appearance of the symbols bears no relationship to the magnitudes that are symbolized). This conclusion does not mean, of course, that the meanings are not conventional at all. But the conventions appear to be based on analogy rather than invented out of the blue. In fact, this may be one of the reasons for their effectiveness: In the presence of these devices, the spectator is put through a vicarious experience in which intensity is actually simulated, not simply referred to.

If the argument up to this point is correct, then, the analogical element in the devices we have been discussing could be a common route to their interpretation. Rather than having to learn the meaning of each device individually through repeated exposure and the development of association (or, less likely, through explicit instruction), viewers might be able to rely in all cases on a single principle, that of analogy. Even if a viewer had never encountered a particular device before, the presence of the analogy could serve as a guide to an adequate response. Of course, it is possible that sensitivity to the kinds of analogies we are concerned with here may vary both with general intelligence and with degree of exposure to visual media. Therefore, the argument that has just been made does not imply that experience with film or television is totally irrelevant to the understanding of close-ups, editing tempo, and so on. However, what is being argued is that the intellectual skills needed for the interpretation of these devices are not qualitatively different from certain mental processes that all viewers should have in their everyday experience.

The overall conclusion from what has been said about editing so far is that the intellectual skills required for the interpretation of point-of-view changes are derived largely from preexisting real-world mental processes rather than being developed solely in conjunction with film or TV viewing. We have examined three types of meaning that may arise from editing in which point of view changes within a single location and time frame: first, the sense of a coherent space encompassing the more limited views provided by the individual shots in a sequence; second, interpretations of the significance of characters' facial expressions; and third, perceptions of dramatic intensity. This list does not exhaust the possibilities, of course, especially as far as the more artistic or "poetic" uses of film and video are concerned. However, I do think that these three types of meaning give a fair representation of the more mainstream uses of single-location/single-time-frame editing, whose basic functions are typically the presentation of character, action, and setting, and the inflection of narrative.

With regard to these basic functions, then, I am arguing that the interpretation of point-of-view transitions does not require a specifically cinematic literacy, in the sense of familiarity with a set of movie-specific visual codes. Because point-of-view transitions constitute the vast majority of the editing transitions in a typical fiction film as well as in many other types of film or TV fare (e.g., talk shows, game shows, most kinds of sports programs), this argument in and of itself constitutes a major step toward a comprehensive account of the issue of editing as a whole. All the same, no discussion of the interpretation of editing would be complete without a look at scene changes and at certain "rhetorical" juxtapositions of images that are usually associated with Eisensteinian montage but nowadays are most likely to occur in advertising. These aspects of editing will be the topic of the remainder of this chapter.

Beyond Point-of-View Editing

In discussing editing in which the images brought together are from different locations and/or time frames, it may be useful to begin with a distinction between two fairly different types or aspects of this overall category: on the one hand, editing in which the main purpose is to carry forward a narrative; on the other hand, editing that juxtaposes images in order to indicate an analogy or contrast, to imply a generalization, and so forth. Examples of the former would be a flashback or, indeed, any scene change, where the primary function of the editing is to weave together the spatiotemporal strands of an unfolding story. As for the latter, a canonical example is the famous scene from Eisenstein's *Strike* (1925) in which striking workers being killed by government troops are juxtaposed with brief interpolated shots of cattle being butchered in a slaughterhouse.

Of course, these two kinds of editing are not mutually exclusive. A narrative connection can also contain elements of analogy or contrast, as, for example, in the transition from a prehuman primate throwing a bone in the air to a spaceship preparing to dock at a space station in *2001: A Space Odyssey* (1968). Despite the possibility of overlap between narrative and what might be termed rhetorical editing, from an analytical perspective the demands these types of editing make on the viewer seem quite different. In one case, the viewer is called upon to integrate a sequence of events into a coherent sense of spatial and temporal relationships. In the other case, the viewer must be able to grasp the point of a visual "comment" (such as a comparison or contrast). Accordingly, the distinction between these two aspects of editing will be retained in the discussion that follows.

A convenient approach to the analysis of narrative transitions is to break this kind of editing down further according to what it is that changes from one shot to the next. We can distinguish among four possibilities:

1. a change both in location and in time frame—e.g., the scene change from *2001* mentioned above, or, in a news program, the transition from a weather forecaster to a satellite picture taken earlier in the day;
2. a change in location only—e.g., the transition between a news anchorperson and a live report from the scene of a story or, in a fictional film, suspense-sequence cross-cutting between a person in danger and a would-be rescuer;
3. a change in time frame only—e.g., an instant replay in a sports telecast or, in a movie, a shot of a couple beginning to make love followed by a shot of a postcoital embrace;
4. a change in the type of reality depicted on the screen, e.g., a scene in which a character goes into a hallucination (a transition from staged reality to staged fantasy) or, in a talk show, switching from the host and guest to a video clip of the guest's latest movie (a transition from "real reality" to fiction).

As these examples may suggest, when these transitions occur in the context of a nonfictional format (e.g., TV news broadcast, sports program, talk show), they are typically accompanied by verbal narration that explains what is happening (e.g., "Here's how things looked from the satellite this afternoon"). Probably the only major exception to this rule is the instant replay, which often occurs without a verbal introduction (although subsequent voiceover commentary spelling out the action is still the norm). Because our concern here is mainly with the visual aspects of the information available to the viewer, our primary focus will be on editing in the various fictional genres.

Changes in Both Location and Time Frame

In my analysis of shot changes in the sample of nine fictional TV programs described earlier in this chapter, the four kinds of transitions we are dealing with now added up to approximately 5 percent of the total number of shot changes—180 out of a total of 3,621. Within this relatively tiny grouping, changes in both location and time occupied a prominent position; this category and the one other appreciably frequent category, changes in location only, accounted for the bulk of that figure of 180. As for the formal characteristics of this kind of transition, a director of both films and TV advertisements, John Frankenheimer, is quoted as saying: "No longer do movies use the fade to black and the slow dissolve the way they used to" (quoted in Miller, 1990, p. 50). Commenting on this statement, critic Mark Crispin Miller argues that fades and dissolves have been dropped from movies in favor of direct cuts because the pace of these earlier devices was too slow for an audience used to the rhythms of TV ads.

The notion that scene changes in movies have become more abrupt is certainly correct, and if systematic evidence is necessary on such a point, it is available from a study by Carey (1982). This study was concerned with editing transitions involving either a combined location/time-frame change or a change in only one of these elements. The study was based on a sample of ten commercial feature films (all U.S.-made) for each decade from the 1920s through the 1970s. The basic point of Carey's analysis was to find out how the conventions for indicating a location/time-frame transition had changed over this span of time. The most telling part of his findings was that there had been a marked decrease in the sheer amount of on-screen time devoted to signaling these transitions. In particular, the average duration of a transition went from over six seconds in the films of the 1920s to less than half a second in the films of the 1960s and 1970s. The reason for this decline was not only a decrease in the frequency of fades and dissolves but also the abandonment of what Carey calls "multiple-element" transitions—verbal captions, images of clocks, calendar pages, and the like—inserted between the end of one scene and the beginning of the next. In

Carey's sample of films, there was a trend from heavy use of fades in the 1920s and 1930s to their replacement by dissolves in the 1940s and 1950s and, finally, the emergence of the straight cut as the dominant transitional device in the 1960s and 1970s. At the same time, the proportion of transitions using multiple elements declined from about two-thirds in the 1920s to a quarter in the next three decades to less than 5 percent in the 1960s and 1970s.

Carey interprets these findings as an indication that audiences have become increasingly fluent at performing the mental tasks of spatiotemporal integration posed by this kind of editing. In other words, he assumes that these changes in editing conventions were driven by changes in the audience's level of interpretational sophistication. This is a somewhat different assumption from the view of such people as Frankenheimer or Miller, who see the trend toward briefer transitions as an indication that audiences' tastes have been shaped by advertising, but both of these assumptions have in common a focus on the viewer as the source of the cinematic trends we are concerned with. These assumptions are certainly reasonable, and they both tend to occur spontaneously and quite readily to my students when I describe Carey's study in class. However, I am not sure that these assumptions tell the whole story, or even a major part of the story, of why editing transitions have developed in the manner in which they have.

Although there may be some truth to the assumption that feature-film editing mirrors what happens in TV advertising, this notion by itself cannot be more than a partial explanation of the trends observed in Carey's study, because these trends began well before the introduction of television as a mass medium and, as Carey notes, they were steady (rather than accelerating). Carey's own interpretation of these trends assumes that for early film audiences, and by implication for all inexperienced viewers, location/timeframe transitions would have been unclear or confusing without the titles, clocks, fades, and other cues. There can be little doubt that many early filmmakers were indeed operating on such an assumption—the mere presence of these devices suggests as much—but the degree to which this assumption accurately reflects inexperienced audiences' actual interpretational capacities is another matter.

Until a short time ago, it was very difficult to say with any certainty just what inexperienced viewers of film or television are really capable of. Accounts of such viewers' responses to movies were few, were not based on systematic observation, and tended to contradict one another. This situation has changed, however, as a result of Renée Hobbs and other investigators' ongoing research with members of the Pokot tribe in Kenya. In the first phase of this research (described earlier in this chapter), Hobbs and her colleagues tested their informants' responses to point-of-view editing. The second phase was concerned with the kind of editing we are examining now.

Once again, the researchers created videotaped stories based on the local culture and showed this material to viewers who hadn't seen movies or television before (Hobbs and Frost, 1989). The results indicated that when viewers were dealing with familiar content—i.e., incidents that were typical of their own daily lives—transitional editing involving location/time-frame changes was not an obstacle to interpretation, not even with respect to flashbacks.

The likelihood that previous experience with visual media is not a primary prerequisite for making sense of space/time transitions has also been supported by some recent research with children. In contrast to Hobbs and Frost's finding that first-time adult viewers were able to interpret a flashback without difficulty, a study by Calvert (1988) had found that the meaning of flashbacks was unclear to preschool children. Furthermore, in a study by Smith et al. (1985), younger children (four-year-olds) were also found to have difficulty in interpreting parallel editing (i.e., cross-cutting between two lines of action developing simultaneously). However, the results of subsequent research suggest that the reason for these findings is unlikely to have been any lack of television experience on the part of the young children. Rather, it seems that here too, as with same-place/same-time editing transitions, general cognitive development may have been the determining variable.

This conclusion emerges from two recent experiments with similar designs, one dealing with a flashback in an animated cartoon (Gabbadon, 1992), the other with parallel editing in excerpts from children's movies (Bell, 1992). In both studies, a child's understanding of the editing devices in question was found to depend on the level of the child's cognitive development. (With regard to flashbacks, the critical cognitive-development factor was the child's performance on a Piagetian liquid-conservation test; in the case of parallel editing, it was the child's capacity for decentered thought, as measured by means of the Matrix Test of Referential Communication.) However, both studies found that the children's ability to comprehend the editing devices was unrelated to the level of their previous television consumption, and it is this finding that speaks most directly to our present concerns.

As with the results of Hobbs and Frost's study, these findings encompass what might seem to be a particularly "difficult" transition: the flashback. Taken together, then, the results of these three studies raise doubts about the assumption that the reason for the longer duration of location/time-frame transitions in early cinema was that inexperienced viewers found such editing difficult to understand and therefore needed to have it explained. It follows, too, that the reason for the subsequent speeding-up of these transitions is unlikely to have been a simple matter of greater interpretational fluency on the part of viewers (as even first-time viewers seem to be sufficiently fluent as far as this aspect of film/TV interpretation is concerned). Rather, it seems to me that an adequate understanding of what has happened, and is still happening, to scene-change editing requires that we look at this issue from the filmmaker's perspective, not just from the perspective of the viewer.

From the point of view of a filmmaker working within the Hollywood tradition, a device whose only function is to explain the spatiotemporal connection between two scenes without participating in the narrative progression (action or character development) of the scenes themselves is likely to be viewed as a contradiction of two related stylistic imperatives: the notion that narration should be self-effacing (i.e., should conform to an "invisible style," encouraging the illusion of reality) and the notion that a film should "show it, not tell it" (cf. Kozloff, 1988, pp. 12–16). An extreme version of this point of view is exemplified by Howard Hawks's avoidance of flashbacks on the grounds that they were an artificial substitute for information that a good filmmaker should be able to convey through the unbroken forward flow of the narrative. As he put it in an interview with Joseph McBride, "If you're not good enough to tell a story without having flashbacks, why the hell do you try to tell them?" (McBride, 1982, pp. 75–76).

Hawks aside, these tendencies of Hollywood filmmakers obviously do not preclude the possibility that such devices as slow dissolves, wipes, pages flipping off a calendar, spinning train wheels, or transitional landmarks such as the Statue of Liberty or the Eiffel Tower might be incorporated into a film for their own sake—i.e., for their intrinsic aesthetic value rather than for their utility in helping the audience to understand a transition. But I do think it is fair to say that, to the extent that the latter function is the main reason for the use of one of these devices, resorting to it is commonly viewed—by filmmakers themselves—as something of a cop-out.

So, for example, in Alfred Hitchcock's *North by Northwest* (1959), when the hero goes from Chicago to what the script calls "Prairie Stop on Highway Forty-One" (scene of the celebrated attack by a crop-dusting plane), the transition involves a lengthy panoramic shot of the bus arriving at its destination, dropping the hero off, and driving away. Although the audience has already been told at the end of the previous scene where the hero is going and why he is going there, the lengthy introduction to the new scene was needed, according to Hitchcock, in order to make it clear how vast and empty and out of the way the new location is (Truffaut, 1967, p. 193). Earlier in the film, however, when the action shifts completely unexpectedly from New York to the headquarters of a government agency in Washington, D.C., the only indication that we are now in the seat of government—information of some significance to the theme of the film—is a reflection of the Capitol dome in the agency's nameplate, a device designed to make the use of this familiar transitional symbol as unobtrusive as possible.

A similar aesthetic principle also appears to be at work in fictional television. For instance, in an episode of the long-defunct sitcom *Mr. Smith,* I was surprised to encounter an extraordinarily lengthy example of the "multiple-element" transition style, which according to Carey's data had all but disappeared from movies more than two decades earlier. This transition included no fewer than six separate shots: a panoramic shot of Atlantic City (site of the new scene); a long-shot of the outside of a casino; a long-shot of the inside of the casino; a shot of the scene's two protagonists entering the casino; a shot of a sign advertising an all-ape jazz band (the show's plot is too baroque to bear synopsis); and a shot of the ape band itself, after which the two human protagonists are shown in the audience and the scene's dialogue begins. My first assumption was that all of these transitional images, during which no new plot information is imparted, had been designed with a juvenile audience in mind.

However, the very next transition, in which a person takes a briefcase full of money from one hotel room to another, was handled with a straight cut from the closing of the briefcase in the first room to a close-up of its opening in the second, with no indication of elapsed time or of the difference in location; and, as a further example, to be discussed presently, will demonstrate, this absence of transitional information was characteristic of the rest of the show. In retrospect, therefore, it seems to me that the multiple shots of the protagonists' arrival at the casino and progress through it were there not for whatever value they might have had in helping younger viewers to follow the story but because of the assumption that viewers of all ages would probably enjoy a visual tour of a gambling spot. Even in a show like this, then, in which the needs of a younger audience must be catered to at some level, the modal approach toward location/time-frame transitions appears to be not simply a speeding up but also the actual avoidance of any devices, such as establishing shots, whose main function would be to explain the transition to the viewer.

If TV producers and film directors do indeed tend to avoid explaining transitions through the use of explicit transitional devices, how is the viewer supposed to make sense of this aspect of editing? The answer, as I have already suggested, is that the necessary information is supposed to come from the development of the narrative—which means that it will typically come mostly from dialogue rather than the image. A case in point is David Lean's much-admired straight cut from a man holding a burning match to a red-hot desert sunrise in *Lawrence of Arabia* (1962). Lean, who was himself an editor before he became a director, had spoken rather proudly of the fact that this transition goes from an interior scene in Cairo to the Arabian desert without any interpolated explanatory material (or even a dissolve, which the original script had called for; see Morris and Raskin, 1992, p. 141). But the reason he (and the film's editor, Anne Coates) could get away with this is that a perfectly sufficient explanation of the transition is already there in the dialogue that takes place right before the transition, in which T. E. Lawrence discusses his impending involvement in the Arab-Ottoman conflict.

In other words, even though fictional editing may superficially appear to operate on very different principles from the verbally narrated transitions typical of such nonfictional forms as news and sports programs, in fact there is considerable similarity between these two areas, in the sense that fictional transitions are also heavily reliant on verbal "set-ups." It must be emphasized, however, that these verbal transitional cues, which are embedded in dialogue, differ in a crucial sense from such traditional, and largely obsolete, transitional devices as intertitles or captions: Verbal cues are typically made to seem as if they arise spontaneously from the story itself, whereas the latter devices typically serve no other function than to explain the transition.

More generally, what we have here is another manifestation of the same principle we encountered in our examination of point-of-view editing—viz., the primacy of narrative context over code as the basis of cinematic intelligibility. In the case of point-of-view editing, this principle seems to be one of the reasons—although certainly not the only reason—for the relative impunity with which filmmakers have been able to break some of the traditional Hollywood rules for creating continuity within a scene. In the case of scene-change editing of the kind we are considering now, the explanatory role of this general principle in accounting for the trends we have examined seems even greater. In fact, this principle seems to be at work in all four of the categories of spatial and/or temporal transitions we will be looking at. I will point to further instances of the principle below.

However, before we leave the topic of combined location/time-frame transitions behind us, I want to make one final observation. Carey argues (and in this he echoes a frequently voiced opinion on this matter) that the various traditional scene-change devices were something akin to linguistic conventions that viewers understood only because they had grown accustomed to them. I would argue that, quite to the contrary, these conventions (train wheels, calendar leaves, even fades and dissolves) were meant to make sense immediately, on first viewing, and in that respect were quite unlike the arbitrary conventions of language.

Changes in Location Only

From the point of view of the film director or TV producer, the problem of creating an intelligible transition when location is the only thing that changes hinges on the following question: How does one make it clear to the viewer that time frame is *not* changing—i.e., that time is flowing uninterruptedly from one location to the next? An obvious solution would be to link the two locations with clocks showing the same time, or with some other indicator of time, such as the position of the sun. However, I can't remember the last time I saw anything such as this in a movie, and my impression is that, even in the early years of narrative cinema, such explicitness in the signaling of continuous time flow was rare.

The reason this type of device is not used more often, I think, is that when simultaneity of time frames is a crucial feature of narrative development, the narrative itself will tend to contain information that makes this point clear to the viewer. When a character in a movie says, "May my mother drop dead if I'm lying," and the next thing we see is an elderly woman clutching her chest and keeling over (as in François Truffaut's *Shoot the Piano Player* [1960]), the implication that the second event came immediately after the first is part and parcel of the narrative logic of the situation, and in this context the idea that a viewer might need an extranarrative informational cue about the time relationship between the two shots seems quite absurd.

Over and above the role of narrative, however, there is also another element in this little scene from *Shoot the Piano Player* that may, by itself, serve as an additional indicator of the nature of time flow across the scene's edits. After the brief shot of the dying mother, the narrative goes back to the original location and time frame. This kind of bracketing of one scene by another may, under certain circumstances, imply continuous time flow across the scenes. I have in mind situations in which we leave the first location at a certain point in time, go to the second location for a time interval of whatever length, and then pick up the action at the first location with a time lapse equal to that same interval. If the narrative content of the two scenes that are being linked in this way already implies simultaneity (for example: a person in danger in one scene; someone coming to the rescue in the other), then I suspect that a match between the duration of the intervening scene and the implied time lapse upon resumption of action in the first strengthens the viewer's sense of an uninterrupted time flow between them.

Of course, such an effect, if it does exist, might be nothing more than the result of viewers' accumulated experience of suspense-sequence parallel editing, which is probably the kind of situation in which location-only transitions are most likely to occur. It would be interesting to know, therefore, how the earliest film audiences responded to this kind of editing, which became a regular feature of movies as early as 1907 with such films as *The Mill Girl* (Bowser, 1983, p. 335; see also Gaudreault, 1979). Although I am not aware of any surviving accounts that would tell us about the more typical viewers of the day, the interpretation of parallel editing is addressed at some length in a professional film review of 1908, and the reviewer's comments suggest that there may indeed be some kind of inherent logic to the bracketing of scenes that would make them carry time-flow implications even for a relatively inexperienced viewer.

The review in question is of a 1908 film called *The Blue and the Grey,* from the *New York Dramatic Mirror* of June 20, 1908. This film contains a transition from a scene in which the hero is brought before a firing squad to be shot to a scene in which his girlfriend manages to secure a letter of pardon and then hurries back to save him. What is involved here, in other words, is a shift backward in time when the location changes, whereas the kind of bracketing we have been discussing preserves the natural flow of time and would have required cross-cutting between the two scenes to begin before the hero was brought to the firing squad in order for the two actions to climax simultaneously without any violations in the continuity of the time frame.

In the eyes of the critic of 1908, the film's backward time shift was a case of "faulty story construction," and his comments imply that he thinks viewers in general would normally associate this kind of editing with an unbroken forward flow of time. As he puts it, "The spectator is then asked to imagine the firing squad suspending the fatal discharge while the girl rides from Washington to the Union camp" (quoted in Kauffmann and Henstell, 1972, p. 7). Because the editing conventions of 1908 were still relatively fluid, this reviewer was probably not objecting to the violation of an established filmmaking code; thus, this response seems to suggest that the bracketing of scenes in a story involving simultaneous actions implies unbroken forward time flow even for an inexperienced viewer, perhaps because of the naturalness of uninterrupted time progression. However, it is entirely possible that this reviewer represents an atypical perspective or that, even as early as 1908, the weight of precedent had already given viewers' assumptions about parallel editing the shape we now take for granted.

Whatever the truth may be about early viewers' responses to the specific situation of bracketing, the more general principle that location-only changes do not require any explanation other than the information contained in the narrative itself clearly goes back to some of the earliest experiments in the development of narrative editing. A revealing incident regarding this issue is Linda Arvidson's description of the experience of her husband, D. W. Griffith, in making the film *After Many Years* (1908). In this film, Griffith used a direct transition, without intertitles or other explanatory devices, to go from the film's hero, who has been cast away on a desert island and is looking fondly at a locket with his wife's picture in it, to the wife herself, standing on the porch of their house (this sequence is reproduced and discussed in Jesionowski, 1987, pp. 40, 42).

According to Arvidson, Griffith's colleagues objected strongly to what they thought would be a confusing piece of editing, but audiences had no trouble understanding what was happening (Mrs. D. W. Griffith, 1975, p. 66). Apparently, Griffith's confidence that direct transitions of this kind would work was based on an analogy with literature. He assumed that audiences would have been primed by novels for the possibility of going directly from one scene to another and would not have any trouble applying their experience with verbal storytelling to the new medium.

Other filmmakers (notably Eisenstein) have shared this belief, and, indeed, at this level of structure—i.e., the temporal and spatial organization of the scenes in a narrative—analogies between movies and literature are probably at their most convincing. However, regardless of the validity of the analogy, Arvidson's account of the making and reception of *After Many Years* clearly suggests that even the earliest film audiences were capable of understanding direct, "unexplained" transitions. Griffith's role in this episode is a good example of an attitude to which I referred earlier—viz., filmmakers' deliberate avoidance of interpolated explanatory material.

Changes in Time Frame Only

Transitions in which the time frame changes but location remains the same have traditionally obeyed rather different rules depending on whether the jump in time was into the future or into the past. Because flashbacks typically entail a switch from ongoing reality to remembered reality, it may be more appropriate to discuss them under our next and final subheading, that of changes in type of reality. Indeed, as we shall see, the conventions for indicating a flashback have traditionally resembled the conventions for transitions into dreams or hallucinations much more than they have resembled the conventions for showing a forward time lapse, although this situation is changing with the general atrophying of transitional markers. Our main topic in this section, then, will be situations in which time skips forward within a single location.

This type of transition is encountered much less frequently than the two types discussed above; in fact, in my analysis of the shot changes in nine TV programs, it turned out to be the rarest category of all, occurring just four times out of a total of 3,621 shot changes (whereas there were thirteen changes in type of reality). Because of this rareness, it can be argued that a potential interpretational problem associated with such transitions is that they might be confused with the vastly more frequent category of simple point-of-view changes, as in both cases location remains the same from one shot to the next.

Perhaps in response to this possibility, forward time lapses have traditionally been presented through some combination of the following three devices, each of which can be seen as averting the kind of confusion I have just described: first, and most simply, a dissolve, fade, or other relatively slow transitional device (as opposed to the straight cut), which would be extremely unlikely to occur between two shots in point-of-view editing; second, maintenance of the same point of view on either side of the dissolve or other means of punctuation, a practice that is by definition incompatible with point-of-view editing (defined as *change* in point of view); and, third, the use of an explicit "before-after" contrast, as in the old cliché of an empty ashtray dissolving to an overflowing mass of stubs, or, somewhat more subtly, a view of daylight outside the window dissolving to darkness.

A notable example of the combined use of all three of these devices occurs at the conclusion of Satyajit Ray's *The Home and the World* (1984). The film's central character, a woman who has unthinkingly put her husband in a very dangerous position, is waiting anxiously to find out what fate has befallen him. She is shown head-on, in a lengthy medium-shot. There is a dissolve, and she is still in the same position. Another dissolve follows, and again there is no change. This happens several more times, and then, after one more dissolve, we find the woman with her hair cut short and dressed in mourning.

This example, from a recent film, illustrates one of the trends in the evolution of this kind of editing. As one would have predicted from the general tendencies discussed above in connection with the other types of transitions, signaling a time-frame change through a before-after contrast with no other function in the narrative has become passé, if not completely obsolete. Before-after contrasts as such are still very common, but when they are used they now invariably emerge from an essential component of the narrative, as in the final two shots of Ray's film. However, I have noticed a device in some recent films that may be a vestigial remnant of the "old-style" before-after contrast and that, moreover, may be a genuine example of a movie convention whose correct interpretation does depend on prior moviegoing experience.

Two examples of this device: In *Mad Max* (1979), a woman who has just taken a swim in the sea lies down on the beach and falls asleep; there is a shot of the sun; the woman is now awake again. In the episode of "Mr. Smith" discussed above, an orangutan is being taught to play blackjack (he has a very high IQ); there is a cut to the chandelier above the table; the lesson is now over. In both cases, what would traditionally have been the basis of a contrast (the sun high in the sky, then lower; the chandelier off, then on) is now presented as a single element with no inherent indication of a passage of time. It is possible that, in this new guise, this device is meant to function simply as a "wedge" keeping the two shots apart (although in that case *any* cutaway should be capable of serving this function, which I doubt is true). Alternatively, and in my view more likely, this device may represent an incomplete attempt to get away from the more traditional use of suns and lights and clocks and windows as indicators of the passage of time. If this assumption is correct, and if viewers can only interpret the new version of the device by implicitly linking it to the old, then this is one instance of the kind of "visual literacy" that many writers, such as Carey, assume to be a typical prerequisite for cinematic interpretation as a whole—but which I am arguing is not.

With the above possible exception, the general evolution of time-frame-change conventions provides us with yet another set of variations on the theme that narrative context supersedes specific codes as a source of transitional information. At the same time that extranarrative before-after contrasts have become obsolescent, filmmakers have also been eliminating the use of dissolves, fades, and so on when these are redundant with other means of signaling the passage of time. An up-to-the-minute, stripped-down time-frame change is likely to work as follows: If the narrative itself contains a significant contrast, that contrast will become the main indicator of the passage of time (as in the conclusion of Stanley Kubrick's *The Shining,* in which a straight cut takes us from a nighttime shot of a dying man to a daytime shot of his corpse). Otherwise, a dissolve will be used (as in all the transitions except the final one in the sequence from *The Home and the World* described above). In either case, the camera's point of view will probably remain constant across the transitions, perhaps, as noted above, to avert confusion with other kinds of transitions.

There is also another respect in which the case of time-frame changes illustrates the interpretational primacy of narrative over code. Although the association between this kind of editing and the use of dissolves in particular has come to be quite regular and even predictable, it should nevertheless be clear that the interpretation "dissolve equals passage of time" is completely dependent on the narrative context. If the context so dictates, a dissolve is capable of having the exact opposite meaning—i.e., that time has *not* passed.

A good example of this effect occurs in Alfred Hitchcock's *The Wrong Man* (1956), in which the unjustly imprisoned protagonist, a victim of a case of mistaken identity, prays to Jesus for deliverance. The scene switches to the real villain, about to commit the crime that will lead to his apprehension and the release of his innocent look-alike, and here Hitchcock wanted to make it clear that the first event leads immediately to the second. The dissolve that links these two scenes presumably does make this point clear to viewers who share, or at least understand, the religious framework from which this narrative sequence draws its assumptions. In other words, as long as a viewer is guided by the same assumptions, it should be easy to tell that, in this context, a dissolve must signify temporal blending rather than separation.

Changes in Type of Reality

A similar point can be made about the conventions associated with flashbacks, hallucinations, and other transitions from ordinary reality to memory, fantasy or dream. As I have already indicated, my reason for classifying flashbacks with these kinds of transitions, rather than with location/time-frame changes or simple time-frame changes, is that flashbacks and hallucinations have historically shared a central transitional convention: the blurring or warping of the image at the point of the transition. This device has been used to mark a transition into and sometimes out of subjectively experienced memory, recounted memory, dream, hallucination, and even divine revelation.

There are many ways in which this blurring of the image can occur, but I do not think there is any systematic variation according to the specific type of transition for which it is used. It is also worth noting that all of the types of transitions in the above list have traditionally been associated with another common convention as well—viz., a move towards a closer view of the character who is about to experience the memory, dream, or what have you. Furthermore, the likelihood that we are dealing with a single family of transitions here is strengthened by the fact that flashbacks and dream sequences apparently share a common ancestry, having both originated in the form of "thought balloons" in the films of the silent era (Salt, 1983, p. 292; Turim, 1989, p. 28).

These commonalities of form suggest that the filmmakers who developed these conventions were operating on the assumption that there is some common principle at work in the various types of transitions listed above. That common principle is presumably embodied in the symbolic device of the blurred or warped image. As I see it, this device was clearly conceived as an analogical representation of mental disorientation, which is evidently the shared element that Hollywood filmmakers have perceived in the processes of slipping into a dream, succumbing to a hallucination, or being overcome by a powerful memory. My guess is that, as an analogical symbol, the blurred image probably made sense even to its first viewers, assuming that they shared this perception of the processes in question or that the film itself made this perception understandable.

Despite its analogical basis, however, this device would obviously make no sense to a viewer who for whatever reason (perhaps cultural difference) was unable to conceive of the transition to a dream, hallucination, or gripping memory as a mentally disorienting experience. Furthermore, even viewers for whom the analogy was indeed persuasive could not possibly be expected to make sense of this device by itself. Because many different experiences can entail mental disorientation and because many meanings other than mental disorientation could plausibly be associated with a warped or blurred image, it follows that the viewer must be "told," through the development of the narrative itself, how exactly to read this transitional device. Here is one more instance, then, of the primacy of narrative context: Even when there is a conventional code, it may not be very informative without the narrative. (Conversely, the narrative can function adequately without this conventional device, as we shall see shortly.)

This example also illustrates another general principle, the multivalent nature of many analogical devices. A similar multiplicity of possible meanings—and consequent dependence on narrative context to fix the meaning actually intended—is characteristic of both fades and dissolves (hence the dissolve's capacity to serve either as a link or, by contrast to the straight cut, as a wedge between time frames). I would argue that this principle also accounts for the range of meanings associated with the variable of camera-to-subject distance. (For a more extensive discussion of the double character of dissolves, including its putative psychoanalytic implications, see Metz, 1982, ch. 23.)

The ultimate consequence of the primacy of context has been the same for reality transitions as for the other transitional devices we have looked at in this section. Someone who had followed this discussion, even someone who had not seen a movie in twenty years, would already know what anyone who does watch film or television knows—that blurred images as signs of reality transitions are a thing of the past. Although this loss has been compensated to a certain extent by the use of contrasting visual styles (e.g., black-and-white flashbacks in Joseph Ruben's color film *True Believer* [1989] or a green tint for a Freudian dream about jealousy in Robert Benton's *Still of the Night* [1982]), the predominant tendency, as everything we have seen so far would have led us to predict, is toward transitions that stand alone, unaccompanied by any explanatory devices other than whatever information is present in the narrative.

What the logical end point of this trend might look like is exemplified by a scene from Marco Bellocchio's *Devil in the Flesh* (1986). A crucial element of this scene is that it consists of a single, continuous shot, with no editing. The setting is a psychiatrist's office. In the center is a couch, with its back to the viewer. The psychiatrist himself is sitting in a chair to one side of the screen. A patient enters, greets the psychiatrist, and, as he takes his place on the couch, casually mentions having seen the psychiatrist's son with a certain young woman. Then the patient lies down, disappearing from view behind the back of the couch. The psychiatrist has obviously been stunned by what he has just heard. He appears to be struggling to control powerful emotions. Then, with no interruption in this scene's single, continuous long-shot, the young woman whom the patient had mentioned rises into view from behind the back of the couch. She is naked, and, from the interaction that ensues, the viewer can infer that this is a flashback: The woman had been a patient of the psychiatrist's, and had made an attempt to seduce him. Here, then, is what the ultimate working out of the trend toward narrative primacy might lead to: not only the elimination of extranarrative transitional conventions but also the disappearance of editing itself.

Propositional Editing

In my preliminary remarks about types of editing involving something other than a point-of-view change, I proposed a distinction between two general categories or aspects: narrative editing, which we have just examined, and editing in which two or more images are brought together for the purpose of making a comment (for example, to suggest an analogy or contrast between two objects or situations). This latter kind of editing, which I would like to examine now, is often associated in film scholars' minds with the films of Eisenstein and with his writing about montage, but I think the most appropriate label for the specific devices I want to consider here may be the term "propositional editing."

In order to give a fuller illustration of what this kind of editing entails and of my reasons for using this term, I would like to begin by looking at an example of propositional editing in the form in which it is probably most likely to be encountered in today's mass media. This example is from a much-discussed political campaign film used in Ronald Reagan's 1984 re-election campaign. (For a book-length analysis of this film, see Morreale, 1991.)

In this film's first scene, the only part that will concern us here, the oath-of-office ceremony from Reagan's first-term inauguration in 1981 is intercut with a number of early-morning images of U.S. citizens going to work. The specific sequence of images is as follows: a tractor setting out across a field of wheat; a truck driving off from a farmhouse; the oath-of-office ceremony; a cowboy shooing a horse out of a corral; a hard-hatted construction worker guiding a crane; the oath-of-office ceremony; workers arriving at the gates of a factory; a commuter joining a carpool; the oath-of-office ceremony. The intended theme of this sequence, stated verbally in voiceover by Ronald Reagan himself at the sequence's conclusion, was "a new beginning": literally, in the sense of America going back to work, and more metaphorically, perhaps, in the sense of spiritual renewal.

The interpretational tasks confronting the viewer of this sequence are quite different from those we have been examining in connection with narrative editing. Here the issue is no longer one of working out the temporal or spatial interconnections of an evolving story line. A viewer might perhaps wonder if the farmer and the cowboy and the various other industrious citizens were actually doing what they were doing at the same time that Ronald Reagan was being sworn in, but any answer to such a question would be irrelevant—the basic point of this sequence's editing structure has nothing to do with any "literal" connection between the inauguration and the other scenes.

Instead, a viewer must be able to do the following two things in order to come up with an interpretation of this sequence that would fit the one intended by its producers: first, extract from the individual images of American workers a more general sense of "America going back to work" or "the nation doing well again"; second, derive from the juxtaposition of the inauguration and the workers a sense of how the inauguration is related to these general phenomena—e.g., "Because of Reagan's inauguration, America is going back to work" (a causal connection), or "Reagan's inauguration is like a new beginning for the nation as a whole" (an analogy or comparison).

The purpose of this sequence, then, is not simply to present a set of events (the president being inaugurated, people going to work) but rather to make various comments or propositions about the events themselves as well as about aspects of reality not represented directly in this film (i.e., the economy, U.S. citizens in general). The distinction between presentational and propositional forms of communication is a crucial issue in discussions of the nature of visual communication, and it is for this reason that I have chosen the label "propositional editing" for the kind of editing exemplified by this film.

It is a widely held belief among theorists of visual communication that the capacity to make propositions is actually alien to the intrinsic nature of images. Gombrich (1972), Worth (1982), and others have argued that the essence of images is to present an event or situation but not to comment explicitly about whether it is true or not, how it is related to events or situations not shown, or what larger events or circumstances it is a part of. It is certainly the case that images lack the extensive set of explicit symbols and syntactic devices that verbal language possesses for conveying such meanings—e.g., the distinction between declarative, interrogative, and imperative modes; such words as "not," "never," "always," "like," "similar," "different"; or the syntactic constructs of hypothesis, conditionality, and contingency. However, as the existence of the Reagan campaign film and other examples mentioned earlier in this chapter makes clear, filmmakers do attempt to create propositional structures in visual form, and there is a real question as to what conventions such structures tend to follow and what viewers are able to make of these conventions.

As I have indicated, the kind of editing which I am labeling "propositional" is often thought of as being especially characteristic of the films of Eisenstein, but its use was in fact quite widespread during the era of silent cinema. After the coming of sound, however, the more explicit forms of this kind of editing quickly became a rarity in fiction films, perhaps because, as André Bazin (1967) argued, it was seen as being incompatible with Hollywood filmmakers' increasing tendency toward unobtrusive narration (the so-called "invisible style" of Hollywood cinema). For example, the blatant analogy suggested by the juxtaposition of kissing lovers and exploding fireworks in a notorious scene from Hitchcock's *To Catch a Thief* (Figures 3.3 and 3.4) was certainly an anachronism when the film appeared in 1955. But propositional editing has found a new place for itself in advertising (see Prince, 1990), both commercial and political, and it is in this connection that we will examine it here.

Figures 3.3 and 3.4　Propositional editing: implied analogy. *Source: To Catch a Thief* (directed by Alfred Hitchcock, Paramount, 1955).

Some sense of the range of meanings typically evoked through propositional editing is suggested by our discussion of the Reagan campaign film. More precisely, I would distinguish among the following four possibilities: (1) comparison or analogy; (2) contrast; (3) causality; and (4) generalization. This list is not intended to be exhaustive, but I do think that it encompasses the most frequent uses of propositional editing in the mass media. (See Clifton, 1983; Dyer, 1989, ch. 8; and Kaplan, 1990, 1992, for alternative classification schemes, partially overlapping this one.)

As a prelude to considering how viewers make sense of this type of editing, two points need to be stressed. To begin with, the four kinds of propositional editing described above are typically not very easy to tell apart on a purely formal basis. Editing for the purpose of implying a generalization, which usually entails the concatenation of a number of related images, may be relatively distinct from the other three varieties, but within that group of three I do not think it is possible to make any reliable formal distinction. All three typically involve cross-cutting between two different images or two different categories of images, which we could term the "subject image/category" and the "object image/category," and it is up to the viewer (assisted, perhaps, by a voiceover narration, a printed slogan, or some other verbal device) to figure out whether the content of the juxtaposed images is consistent with an interpretation of analogy, contrast, or causality. Furthermore, as the Reagan campaign film demonstrates, a single propositional sequence may readily combine two or more of the four kinds of editing strategies on our list (not to mention other possibilities I have not considered here), making the formal boundaries between them even less distinct.

A second important point about propositional editing as it is usually practiced in the mass media is that the basis on which images are brought together in such editing is very rarely visual. In other words, what links the "subject image" to the "object image" is most often a conceptual similarity or difference rather than a visual one. (This distinction is obviously less meaningful in the case of cause/effect editing than for the other three varieties.) Indeed, I can think of very few recent ads in which visual form was the principal basis for the image juxtaposition, as in one case in which a string of pearls is compared to the lights of the Brooklyn Bridge.

Both of these properties of propositional editing suggest that a major prerequisite for its interpretation must be the capacity to discern the presence of conceptual relationships between the objects or situations portrayed in a sequence of images—and to do so very swiftly in most cases, as the pacing of propositional editing in TV ads is typically quite rapid. Take the case of a Xerox ad used during the 1988 Winter Olympics, in which the Xerox logo was intercut with images of a champion ice skater. In and of itself, the kind of rapid cross-cutting employed in this ad doesn't tell us whether what is intended is an analogy, a contrast, or a causal connection. This information has to come from the actual content of the images, which means that the viewer must be able to intuit some conceptual link between them: perhaps analogy (the technical perfection of the copier compared with the perfect artistry of the skater); perhaps causality (i.e., the inference that Xerox helped make possible the skater's championship performance because Xerox equipment was used by Olympic Games officials, a fact noted in the commercial's soundtrack); or possibly both of these interpretations at the same time—they are obviously not incompatible, and advertising often relies on precisely this kind of "overdetermination" of the meaning of product-image juxtapositions.

What kinds of prior experience, if any, might be required for one to make the kind of interpretation illustrated in this example? To a certain extent, the answer depends on the degree of abstractness or complexity of the conceptual relationships implied in the editing. Some juxtapositions may be so obvious or compelling—or crude—that even the most untutored intelligence should be able to grasp them. Much of the propositional editing of the silent cinema and the early sound era is of this sort, and I suspect that it is this overobviousness (e.g., the juxtaposition of gossiping housewives and hissing cats in Richard Boleslavski's *Theodora Goes Wild* [1936]), not simply an incompatibility with Hollywood conventions, that led to the decline of propositional editing in fiction film. However, in its reincarnation as an advertising tool, propositional editing is often considerably more complex than in these early fiction-film examples. This greater complexity suggests that perhaps not all viewers are equally adept at grasping the intended meanings of these latter-day forms of propositional editing.

More specifically, in view of the significant conceptual (as opposed to perceptual/visual) element in the interpretation of this kind of editing, it seems reasonable to assume that general educational level might make some difference in a viewer's interpretational abilities. Does this assumption mean that specifically visual experience is irrelevant in this case? The answer to this question depends in large part on how the formal structures of propositional editing would appear to a visually inexperienced viewer. To my eyes, it seems very clear that these formal structures must have originated in attempts to mimic the structures of verbal syntax—to wit, the juxtaposition of subject and object in simile, contrast, or cause/effect propositions, and the concatenation of individual instances in rhetorical reiteration. However, I am not at all sure that any vestige of this ancestry would be apparent to a first-time viewer, especially in the case of repeated visual cross-cutting, in which both "subject" and "object" occur more than once (as opposed to their single occurrence in the equivalent linguistic constructions). It seems more than likely, therefore, that some degree of specific experience with propositional editing may be required for a viewer to be able to recognize its characteristic patterns of juxtaposition and iteration as frameworks for the conceptual integration of images.

Ideally, an empirical examination of these questions would have to involve research with viewers who had never seen movies before, or at least had no previous exposure to this kind of editing. Such research has yet to be done in the case of propositional editing, but some suggestive findings have come from a study Nielsen and I conducted on interpretational differences between professional TV production personnel, "ordinary" viewers with college education, and "ordinary" viewers with less than college education (Messaris and Nielsen, 1989). This study was based on two relatively complex instances of propositional editing: the Reagan campaign film described above and a commercial for fruit preserves. In the latter ad, images of fruit and of the final product (jars of preserves) are intercut with images of nature and life on the farm (a valley with mountains in the background; children climbing over a picket fence), suggesting the purity and wholesomeness with which such scenery is traditionally associated in U.S. culture. Although these images are accompanied by a soundtrack, the words spoken are allusive and abstract, and there is no direct verbal translation of the relationships among the images.

Each of these ads was shown to one viewer at a time, and each screening was followed by a detailed interview on the viewer's interpretation of the ad's message. The interviews were designed to probe for whatever connections the viewer might have seen among the ad's images, described in whatever vocabulary the viewer might choose to employ. The object of our analysis of these interviews was to determine whether a respondent had seen the ad as an implied proposition of some sort (e.g., "It's an attempt to relate Ronald Reagan with down-home American values") as opposed to interpreting it primarily as a narrative or a visual demonstration of the product (e.g., "The commercial brings out the different fruits [this brand] puts in their jellies").

The frequencies of propositional interpretations for the three groups of viewers were as follows: among the TV professionals, 87 percent in the case of the Reagan campaign film and 100 percent in the case of the fruit-preserve commercial; among the more educated "ordinary" viewers, 59 percent in the case of the Reagan film and 100 percent in the case of the commercial; and, among the less-educated viewers, 22 percent in the case of the Reagan film and 50 percent in the case of the commercial. It would appear, then, that the capacity to discern a propositional statement in editing of this sort should not be taken for granted among all viewers. Both formal education and specifically visual experience appear to contribute significantly to a viewer's development of this form of interpretational skill, and in this area we may indeed be justified in speaking of a need for visual literacy—but also for literacy in its more traditional sense.

Does this conclusion also mean that propositional editing in advertising is wasted upon substantial segments of the mass audience? Not necessarily. Ads are made to be shown—and seen—more than once, and repetition may enhance effectiveness in not one but two ways: First, it may make the propositional element in an ad more evident; second, it may bring about an *unconscious* association between product and image even for those viewers who were never consciously aware of the intended proposition. This "Pavlovian" effect has been shown to work with images (see Zuckerman, 1990), and, to the extent that awareness of its working might diminish its power, one might be tempted to conclude that, for the *advertiser,* the relative opacity of propositional editing is by no means an unambiguous defect.

4

General Cognitive Consequences of Visual Literacy

Now that we have examined in some detail the cognitive skills that viewers use in making sense of visual media, we are ready to turn our attention to possible broader consequences of possessing those skills. More specifically, we will now ask the following question: Beyond its immediate effects on our ability to comprehend pictorial material, what else—if anything—does visual "literacy" do for us? In this chapter, we look at the potential impact of visual literacy on a viewer's general cognitive skills. We will be concerned with the following questions: What kinds of intellectual tools for dealing with everyday, nonmediated reality does one acquire by virtue of being proficient in the interpretation of visual media? How, if at all, does visual literacy enhance one's capacity for understanding the world?

Propositionality Revisited

Discussions of these questions inevitably lead to comparisons between pictorial and linguistic representations of reality. Anyone who teaches visual communication, as I do, has probably had more than one encounter with a student wanting to turn in a film or a video or a photo essay instead of a written exam or term paper or thesis. Implicit in many requests of this sort is a complaint: How can someone who takes pictures seriously insist on the use of verbal forms of analysis? Isn't such an insistence the result of an unthinking adherence to the prevalent verbal bias of academic scholarship? These are reasonable concerns. Addressing them must involve a detailed examination of the extent to which the use of pictures can replicate the intellectual operations made possible by words.

Let's say the student who wants to turn in a visual work instead of a verbal paper has received permission to do so, with the added stipulation that the work should make its point exclusively through pictures, with no verbal assistance in the form of voiceover narration, dialogue, captions, and the like. Of the various kinds of information a typical work of verbal scholarship might be expected to contain, is there anything the student would not be able to incorporate visually?

One self-evident "deficiency" of images in comparison with language is that they are incapable of representing nonvisual experience (e.g., a "loud sound," a "pungent aroma") or abstract entities (e.g., "argument," "conclusion"), although they can of course evoke the former or portray a concrete instance of the latter. Let us assume, then, that the student's topic is both visual and concrete. In what ways would the analysis of this topic suffer as a result of being deprived of words? A good place to begin exploring this issue is the point made by Sol Worth (1982) in a well-known paper, "Pictures Can't Say Ain't"—viz., that pictures cannot explicitly indicate that something isn't true. As we will see shortly, this point is just the tip of the iceberg when it comes to things that pictures cannot do, but it is worth taking a moment to look at it closely before expanding our view.

In its narrowest interpretation, Worth's argument is that pictures contain no equivalent of the linguistic vocabulary of negation: "no," "not," "never." To this there are at least two possible objections. One objection is that the ubiquitous "do not" sign (a red circle with a diagonal slash through it) is an obvious exception to Worth's claim. If we are willing to accept this sign as a picture—rather than a specialized symbol of the same order as traffic lights—we can agree to this exception, although we may still question whether its scope is equivalent to the range of meanings covered by the various forms of verbal negation.

The second objection is more revealing. In a discussion of the possibility of conveying negation through visual images, Branigan (1986, p. 10) cites a scene from Alfred Hitchcock's *Vertigo* (1958): A private investigator who has been following a mysterious woman sees her park her car, go into a building, and, a short while later, draw the blind in one of the windows. But when he goes into the building after her, he finds the room where the blind was drawn empty, and, looking out the window, he sees a vacant space where her car was parked. Branigan argues that these are examples of pictorial negation: The images convey the information that the woman is *not* in the room and that the car is *not* where she had left it. Because this is obviously not a unique instance, we might want to conclude that images *can* express negation after all.

Nevertheless, there is an important difference between this form of negation and its verbal counterpart. "The woman is not there" expresses negation explicitly, through the use of the word "not"; that is, in language the capacity for negation is built into the *code*. However, the images of the empty room and vacant parking space can be taken as signifying negation only by virtue of their juxtaposition with the previous images of the woman's presence. Here, then, as Branigan points out, negation is purely a matter of *context*. Juxtaposed with a different set of images (e.g., the private investigator looking for a place to park), the same shot of the vacant space could acquire a different kind of meaning; in fact, the implication of the entire original juxtaposition (woman's car present versus woman's car absent) could undergo a reversal of sorts under suitable contextual conditions ("There's *no* place left to park" versus "Now there *is* a place to park").

As we have already seen, the dependence of meaning on context rather than on code is a characteristic of pictures that goes beyond the expression of negation. This premise brings us to a more general point and to the crux of this comparison between pictures and words. It should already be evident, on the basis of the concluding section of Chapter 3, that the absence of a pictorial code for negation is merely a corollary of the more fundamental point that pictures have no explicit means of expressing *affirmation*. What we are dealing with here is the more general principle that pictures lack a systematic set of symbols and syntactic devices for making propositions. As we have seen, this lack has not prevented filmmakers from trying to generate implicit propositions through editing, and there is a history of attempts at propositional editing both in the cinema and, more recently, in TV advertising. However, the existence of the examples of this form of editing examined in Chapter 3 should not be mistaken as evidence that editors can simply use appropriate visual juxtapositions to get around the problem of the lack of a propositional apparatus. For one thing, as the research on this subject indicates (Messaris and Nielsen, 1989; see also Messaris, 1981), a conscious understanding of the point of propositional editing may be problematic even for experienced viewers. More important, however, even if viewer comprehension were not a problem, there is a crucial aspect of linguistic propositionality for which it is very hard to imagine any visual equivalent. Let me illustrate this feature of language through a concrete example from a National Geographic wildlife documentary.

One of my reasons for choosing a TV nature documentary as an example of differences between pictures and words is that here, more than anywhere else, perhaps, we are likely to get what may appear to be considerable redundancy between these two modes. Because the visual images in nature documentaries often seem to be essentially aimed at illustrating the verbal narrative, this form of television may be the closest thing we can get to a natural experiment on the question of how well visual structure can approximate the propositional syntax of language. At any rate, the particular example I have chosen, a brief segment of a program on wild horses, is a good illustration of the crucial aspect of propositionality to which I want to draw attention.

The segment in question is preceded by a description of the social organization of wild horses, in the course of which the narrator points out that horses typically congregate in bands under the leadership of a dominant stallion. Then comes the relevant section. On the soundtrack, we are told the following: "The band is generally peaceful, so long as the stallion's leadership remains uncontested. But trouble inevitably begins when another stallion seeks to intrude." The images that accompany these words are: (1) a band of peaceful horses; (2) the dominant stallion; (3) an intruder. This sequence is followed by a fight between the two stallions, which is shown through a series of seven shots, during which the verbal narration is replaced by dramatic music. The fight ends with the victory of the dominant stallion, at which point the verbal narration resumes and we get the following concluding statement: "Unless the stallion is old or weak, his defense is usually successful. The challenger will continue his search for mares, while the victorious stallion leads his harem swiftly away." The images that go along with this are: (1) the dominant stallion with his band; (2) the intruder galloping away; (3) the dominant stallion with his band.

In the two sequences that are accompanied by verbal narration, the timing of the editing of the images coincides exactly with syntactic transitions in the narrator's words; at first glance, it may appear that the match between visual and verbal information in these sequences is quite precise. When the narrator refers to the band of horses, we see them on the screen; when he talks about the dominant stallion, there is an immediate cut to a picture of that animal; and when the intruder enters the verbal narrative, its image simultaneously replaces that of the other horse.

However, on the basis of the brief description of this segment, a moment's reflection should make it clear that there are certain elements in the verbal narrative that this particular sequence of images does not capture. There are, for example, those two generalizations—"*generally* peaceful"; "*usually* successful"—for which an editor might perhaps attempt to devise equivalents following the principles discussed in Chapter 3 but for which there is certainly no equivalent in the present set of images. However, in my view the elements of the verbal narration that most sharply illustrate the lack of propositionality in the accompanying images are the following three: first, the conditional construction in the first sentence ("generally peaceful, *so long as*"); second, the hypothetical construction that follows it ("trouble *inevitably* begins *when* another stallion"); third, the exception expressed at the beginning of the final sentence ("*unless* the stallion is old or weak . . . his defense is *usually* . . .").

There is a common theme here: What all of these linguistic constructions exemplify is the capacity of language to delimit the circumstances within which a certain state of affairs is true. The differences in phrasing and in meaning among these three examples are a small indication of the extraordinary range and precision of the linguistic apparatus for dealing with this issue. Do the images that accompany these words contain any trace of this aspect of their meaning? If not, is it possible to conceive of some other set of images that would?

It seems to me that there is a fundamental difference between what we see on the screen and what the words are referring to in these sections of the narrative. The visuals depict a single, concrete instance of the kinds of events that this documentary is about. The words, however, are expressions of rules governing the entire class of these events. A viewer might perhaps be led to infer some of these rules from the images. For example, the sequence of peaceful horses—lead stallion—intruder—fight can be seen as implying causality. But would someone who saw the sequence without the accompanying words know that the particular chain of events portrayed was "inevitable" (as the words indicate)?

In order to make that point or, indeed, to express any of the degrees of qualification contained in the soundtrack's linguistic constructions, the visuals would have to be able to go beyond the representation of a single instance of these events. We might imagine, for example, ten different scenes of an intruder stallion challenging the leader, with each intrusion culminating in a fight, to make the point about the "inevitable" relationship between these two events. To illustrate the verbal narration's statement that the leader usually wins except when he is old or weak, the visuals could show (1) a young, healthy horse winning a fight, (2) an old horse losing, and (3) a weak horse losing. But even if we overlook the absurd cumbersomeness of these devices, it should be clear that they would still fall short of doing what the equivalent verbal constructions do, for two reasons.

First, it would still be up to the viewer to make a leap from the individual instances presented in the visuals to the general rule expressed in the words. Second—and this brings us back to our earlier discussion of negation and assertion in pictures—it would still be up to the viewer to decide whether these images should be taken as assertions of fact about some aspect of reality. It is the first of these two problems that concerns us here. Ultimately, the only way the images could fully overcome this problem—i.e., the only way they could precisely match this aspect of the information contained in the words—would be for them to replicate the entire range of individual instances encompassed by the propositions expressed in the words. To put it differently, the only way for images to achieve a literal match for this aspect of propositionality would be for them to regurgitate the entire mass of specifics encapsulated in any one of the verbal constructions we have examined. It goes without saying, I think, that what we have arrived at is not merely a difference in degree between the properties of words and pictures but, rather, a fundamental difference in kind.

The implications of this difference are considerable. The ability to make explicit conditional statements about the reality of a particular situation is an essential component of the analytical (as opposed to the descriptive) function of communication. Therefore, if I am correct in arguing that images lack this ability, it must also be true that images are "deficient" in a more general sense as vehicles of analytical communication. It is because of this "deficiency" that the purely pictorial transmission of information would be an impracticable goal in any intellectual discipline other than a purely descriptive one (e.g., some forms of ethnography). It follows, too, that whatever resistance against pictorial term papers and theses may still exist in the academic world is not simply a result of insufficient scholarly concern for visual literacy.

The more general point is that advocacy for visual literacy should not be based on the false assumption that what is to be gained is another tool for analytical communication. When it comes to descriptive communication, pictures are indeed capable of extraordinary range and subtlety, as Tufte (1990) has shown. But despite the history of propositional editing, examined in Chapter 3, it seems appropriate to think of images as being primarily a *presentational* mode of communication, a system for *representing* events rather than making propositions about them. Accordingly, the search for potential broader cognitive consequences of visual literacy should be focused on the presentational function of images.

Representational Categories and World Views

Here, too, it may be useful to begin our investigation with a look at language, in particular with the following question: What are the more general cognitive consequences of the linguistic system of representing reality? To acquire a language is to gain access to an extraordinarily comprehensive, shared system for the representation of experience. But the symbols this system comprises are not simply a set of labels for preexisting categories in the "real world." Rather, language is, to a significant extent, a creative force that carves out its own categories of representation and, in so doing, gives form to its own reality. In this sense, then, the acquisition of a language is also the acquisition of a cognitive framework or, in more popular terms, a "worldview."

An example of this process is the area of color terminology. Although the apparatus of color perception is the same in all fully functional human eyes—which means that the colors of the spectrum are objectively real for human vision—languages differ with regard to the color categories for which they provide names. According to a systematic study of this phenomenon by Berlin and Kay (1969), the number of basic color terms appears to range from as low as two in some languages to a high of eleven or twelve. (Basic color terms, as defined by Berlin and Kay, are those that are not subsumed under some broader, more inclusive term.) In other words, a language's "picture" of the color spectrum is not simply a passive record of physical fact.

This is not to say, of course, that language is completely *independent* of physical fact. As Berlin and Kay have shown, the *number* of distinctions within the color spectrum may differ from one language to another, but the *types* of distinctions made are very similar. Thus, all languages contain terms for light and dark (in some languages, these are the only color terms in the vocabulary); all languages with three or more colors have a term for red; all languages with five or more colors have terms for yellow and green; and so forth. Perhaps the most accurate way of describing the classificatory function of language, therefore, is to say that language selects, from among the infinite variety of possible distinctions provided by external reality, a subset of distinctions that will find recognition in vocabulary and syntax. These selections may sometimes seem arbitrary or haphazard to an outsider, but it is probably safe to assume that they reflect historical, if not current, needs of the users of the language. In the case of color terminology, for example, Berlin and Kay found that the extensiveness of a society's color vocabulary was related to social complexity—an indication, perhaps, that expansion in color vocabulary follows the increases in technological sophistication that go along with societal diversification. (However, see Baines, 1985, for a contrary view.)

More generally, we might say that language is shaped by social imperatives. In turn, however, language appears to shape the cognitive frameworks of the new members of a society, as they become habituated to the distinctions made by its vocabulary and syntax. This possibility (which was first envisioned by Humboldt [1836] but has come to be associated with the names of Sapir [1921] and Whorf [1956]) has been tested with respect to color terminology by Kay and Kempton (1984).

The method employed by these researchers was based on the fact that Tarahumara, a Native American language, does not have separate words for the colors green and blue. Because English does make such a terminological distinction, Kay and Kempton hypothesized that speakers of English would be more sensitive than speakers of Tarahumara to color differences in the green-blue range of the spectrum. This assumption was tested through a series of sorting tasks, the results of which consistently supported the hypothesis: English speakers were able to make finer green-blue range discriminations than their Tarahumara-speaking counterparts. To the extent that the results of this experiment and a few others like it are typical of a broader linguistic process, we may say that language shapes cognition by "fine-tuning" a person's set of conceptual distinctions in one direction or another. (For further discussion of these issues, see Bloom, 1981; Cooper et al., 1991; Lakoff, 1987; Lucy, 1992a, 1992b; and, with reference to written language, Scribner and Cole, 1981.)

It should be emphasized that the potential role of language in shaping cognition is not simply a matter of a few cross-cultural differences in terminology or syntax. Language is the most comprehensive system of human communication, the one that comes closest, in principle, to encompassing all of human experience, both the tangible world of objects and events and the intangible world of forces that animate them. It gives structure to its users' conceptions of time and space, causality and contingency—hence the central role it is typically accorded in discussions of the role of communication in creating social reality. It is important to keep this point in mind as we turn to the mode of communication that most concerns us: visual images. To what extent might the cognitive consequences of images parallel those of language in this area? Like language, images are a comprehensive system for the representation of experience. Indeed, these two are the only modes of communication of which such a claim may be made. (Mathematical systems and the various "nonverbal" modes—e.g., facial expression, gesture, interpersonal space—are all quite limited in their domains of reference, whereas much of music can be argued to be altogether nonreferential.) Images may lack language's capacity for abstraction and for reference to intangible concepts, but the full sweep of the visible world lies within their compass.

However, there is a crucial difference between images and language that raises considerable doubt about whether images can be said to shape cognitive frameworks to the same extent as the linguistic representational system does. As Ferdinand de Saussure (1966) pointed out, the property of language on which we have been focusing—viz., its classificatory or distinction-making character—stems from another property that is fundamental to its nature: the arbitrariness of the linguistic sign. With the exception of onomatopoeic words, the elements of language are related to their referents by virtue of purely arbitrary convention. It follows that learning the meaning of a term must always entail the learning of boundaries and distinctions beyond which the term does not apply. For example, children who have just learned a new word will sometimes point to a variety of objects, repeating, in each case, the same question: "Is this an X?" "Is *this* an X?" The fact that linguistic meaning is based on such distinctions—X versus not X—has led to its conventional (although not, of course, universally accepted) designation as a digital system of communication, by analogy with the binary codification of digital computers. Both of these aspects of language, its arbitrariness and its consequent "digitality," differ sharply from the corresponding characteristics of images.

Images are fundamentally an analogic, rather than digital, mode of communication, which means two things. First, as we have already seen, their ability to make sense to viewers is based to a great extent on the imitation of perceptual cues that people use in their interpretations of raw, unmediated reality. Second—and this is the important point for present purposes—images are capable, in principle, of representing the full range of gradations of the phenomena of the visible world; therefore, unlike words, they are not forced to deal in categories (cf. Bateson, 1972, pp. 372–374). For example, many kinds of images, including color photographs and oil paintings, are capable of rendering an infinite number of intermediate positions between any two colors of the spectrum, whereas all languages are limited to a finite set of distinctions and a corresponding set of fixed categories. Words divide the world into black and white (and, in some languages, gray), large and small, strong and weak, good and bad. Images, however, can represent *shades* of gray, *ranges* of size, and *degrees* of those external attributes that viewers use in making inferences about power and morality.

Of course, the fact that images *can,* in principle, represent reality without reducing it to set categories doesn't mean that they always do so in practice. Both literally and metaphorically, a particular pictorial style may operate within the confines of a limited palette. For example, there is a type of high-contrast black-and-white photograph, sometimes referred to (not entirely accurately) as a "solarized" print, that collapses all shades of gray into the two extremes of jet black and stark white; comparable reductions to basic categories can also be found in the pictorial styles of other cultures and past historical periods—e.g., the "black figure" style of ancient Greek vase painting. However, in a pictorial environment saturated by photography and color television, examples such as these are bound to be increasingly marginal, and it is hard to imagine them having much of an effect on anyone's conceptions of reality.

Furthermore, even if we could go back in time for a look at categorical representation in instances in which it was a dominant feature of a particular pictorial culture, there would still be reason to doubt whether images could have an effect comparable to that of language on people's cognitive categories. Language is a mode of communication that virtually all adult members of a society (including most people with impaired hearing or vocalization abilities) participate in actively, not only as recipients of messages but also as producers. With regard to images, most people in most societies are mostly confined to the role of spectator of other people's productions. One's participation in the linguistic scheme for classifying reality is therefore compulsory in a manner—and to an extent—rarely characteristic of one's involvement with images. In general, then, the case for an effect of images on most viewers' systems of cognitive classification does not seem particularly compelling, either in terms of historical fact or in terms of current possibility.

Empirical research on the cognitive consequences of visual literacy has typically dealt with specific intellectual skills, rather than with general mental frameworks. However, a study we have already examined, Worth and Adair's experiment on Navajo filmmaking, does have a bearing on the kinds of consequences we are concerned with here. The study was premised on the idea that images might play a similar role to that of language in structuring the worldview of a society. As already noted, a group of Navajo informants who had been taught the technical rudiments of filmmaking but who had had little or no exposure to commercial cinema produced a number of short films (16mm, black-and-white, silent) on various aspects of Navajo life (e.g., the work of a silversmith, a curing ceremony, the construction of a well). These films were analyzed by the study's authors, a communications researcher (with professional filmmaking experience) and an anthropologist, with the intention of exploring the relationship between the films' visual structure and the conceptual framework of traditional Navajo culture. Ironically, however, whereas the study had begun with the premise that it might be appropriate to extend to images the "Whorfian" assumptions which are traditionally applied only to language, i.e., the view of communication as a shaper of cognitive frameworks, the actual analysis of the data concludes by affirming the centrality of linguistic structure as a source of Navajos' worldviews.

Worth and Adair describe three major structural patterns that stood out in their analysis of the Navajo films: with regard to shot composition, an almost complete absence of facial close-ups; with regard to editing, the frequent use of what a Hollywood-habituated viewer would see as jump cuts; and with regard to overall narrative structure, a disproportionately large amount of screen time (again, by Hollywood standards) devoted to transitional walking (i.e., a character going from one "scene" to the next). The authors deal with these patterns as manifestations of the Navajo view of reality, and a major aim of the analysis is to trace each pattern back to its roots in Navajo culture. Significantly, in none of the three cases does this search for roots lead back to any element of Navajo visual arts whereas in two of the three cases the authors argue that there are clear linguistic sources for the observed patterns.

In particular, both the jump cuts and the transitional walking are seen as reflecting basic features of Navajo language and oral tradition: in the former case, the way in which Navajo syntax deals with motion; in the latter, the attention paid to walking by Navajo stories and poems. Only in the case of the Navajo films' lack of close-ups does the analysis lead to a nonlinguistic source, but even then the source turns out to be an aspect of Navajo traditional interpersonal behavior—the avoidance of too-direct face-to-face encounters—rather than some facet of Navajo visual imagery. (Perhaps it should be mentioned, incidentally, that Navajos have a refined tradition of two-dimensional visual art, both representational and abstract, and that accomplished artists and their work were actually featured in some of the films made for this study.) If anything, then, these findings reinforce the notion of the primacy of language as a framer of a culture's worldview but lend scant support to an analogous view of the role of images. (See Willemen, 1983, for a theory of cinematic structure whose implications parallel Worth and Adair's conclusions on the priority of verbal language.)

Spatial Intelligence

Up to this point in our discussion of cognitive consequences of visual literacy, we have examined the issue in global terms, in relation to the structuring of thought as a whole. We now turn to the relationship between visual literacy and more specific intellectual skills. As we have seen in Chapters 2 and 3, it can be argued that the interpretation of images, both still and moving, is based on a variety of cognitive abilities that all people develop in the process of learning to make sense of everyday, unmediated reality. Some of these abilities (e.g., identifying objects on the basis of outlines) appear to be directly applicable to the perception of images, whereas others (e.g., depth perception) may require considerable extension or modification. In either case, it is conceivable that the development of "literacy" in visual media may lead to an overall enhancement of these abilities, not only with regard to the interpretation of images but also as far as their real-life applications are concerned.

This possibility was envisioned very clearly by film theorist Béla Balázs. Balázs was impressed by the tremendous magnification that large-screen close-ups can give to the smallest nuances of facial expression. As a result of this phenomenon, he argued, movie audiences would have to become more adept at "reading" the human face, whose meanings had receded from view during the era of the printed word (Balázs, 1952, p. 39–45). A similar point could be made about the cognitive skill of "reading" facial expressions in relation to their contexts, a real-life ability that appears to be crucial to the Kuleshov effect. Whatever their merits, both of these examples illustrate the potential reciprocal effect of visual literacy on real-life skills of *social* perception. In what follows, however, the emphasis will be on cognitive skills involved in making sense of the *physical* environment.

In our review of the process of interpretation of still pictures (Chapter 2), it was noted that several "unrealistic" pictorial conventions are readily interpretable on the basis of real-life visual skills, despite the fact that pictures containing these conventions may look very different from everyday, unmediated reality. In other words, conventions of this sort do not seem to "stretch" the ordinary interpretational abilities that a typical viewer might be expected to develop independently of any prior experience with pictorial media. The most notable exception to this pattern is the set of conventions involved in the depiction of the third dimension—i.e., depth or distance "into" the picture. As we saw in Chapter 2, two crucial indicators of depth in real-life perception (viz., binocular disparity and motion parallax) cannot be reproduced in still pictures. Accordingly, we would expect viewers who were unfamiliar with pictures to have some trouble seeing depth in them, an expectation borne out by the research results reviewed in Chapter 2.

These research results suggest that experienced viewers of pictures become particularly sensitive to certain sources of information that may not play a major role in the process of seeing depth in everyday reality. Three informational sources of this kind were discussed in Chapter 2, on the basis of the research evidence: (1) an object's height on the picture plane, which can serve as a cue to depth (the higher the object, the farther the distance) in some kinds of situations (for example, if all the objects in the picture are standing on a flat surface viewed at eye-level); (2) the relative apparent size of objects (a reliable depth cue if the viewer has prior knowledge of the objects' *actual* sizes relative to one another); and (3) "linear perspective" in the form of two converging lines (such as, for example, railroad tracks or the edges of a wall). (As indicated in Chapter 2, in real-world perception we need a repeated *pattern* of convergence or increasing density, e.g., the railroad *ties* or the *bricks* in the wall, in order for this form of perspective to satisfy the requirements of the standard texture-gradient depth cue.) These three kinds of information about the third dimension have played various roles in the pictorial conventions of the different cultures that have attempted to portray three-dimensional space on a flat surface, but all three of them appear frequently in photographs and in many other kinds of images in the post-Renaissance Western tradition.

As noted in Chapter 2, and as should be quite obvious in any case, these kinds of information are also present in nonmediated visual reality. Pictorial styles that incorporate them can thus be said to be realistic in that respect. However, it is unclear to what extent these three kinds of information actually serve as automatic depth cues in real-world vision: As we have seen, pictorially inexperienced viewers do not seem to find them very useful when they appear in pictures. Therefore, because experienced viewers of pictures evidently *do* use this information with ease in making sense of pictorial space, perhaps this is an area in which experience with pictures also enhances real-world cognitive abilities. In other words, if there is any carryover from pictures to reality in one's ability to make use of these three depth cues, then depth perception would be a good example of a cognitive skill that could be enhanced by experience with pictorial media.

As far as I know, there is no empirical evidence of such a connection. But let us assume that the necessary evidence did exist. What would the broader import of this evidence be? The answer depends, I think, on how modular a skill one believes depth perception to be. Although precise depth perception in itself is highly critical in some occupations (such as race-car driving in Western culture, or hunting in many traditional cultures), most of the kinds of activities that individuals of the modern world are likely to engage in are probably served quite adequately by the baseline levels of depth-perception ability that most human beings acquire automatically. However, perhaps this is too narrow a view of the matter. It is conceivable that the enhancement of depth-perception abilities might lead to a more general stimulation of one's capacity for perceiving and thinking about three-dimensional space, and in that case we would be dealing with a type of cognitive activity that plays a very important role in general intelligence (see Edgerton, 1991).

This general realm of cognitive activity has been labeled "spatial intelligence" by Gardner (1983). In Gardner's view, it is a relatively distinct sphere of intelligence, entailing the ability to form accurate mental representations of spatial relationships and, perhaps more important, to envision the consequences of transformations in these relationships. Gardner points out that this kind of intelligence is central not only to the visual arts but also to many areas of science. To the extent that the enhancement of depth-perception abilities does indeed lead to a stimulation of spatial intelligence as a whole, we have one line of reasoning suggesting a potential wider cognitive consequence of pictorial literacy.

As I have indicated, to my knowledge the specific connections outlined above (i.e., between spatial intelligence and pictorial depth perception) have not been tested empirically. However, the more general proposition that is in question here—viz., that experience with visual media might have a positive impact on spatial intelligence—has been addressed by several studies of children. The common focus of these studies is on the ability of motion pictures, including television, to represent different points of view in succession (e.g., to switch from a frontal view of a person to a side view). It was argued in Chapter 3 that the viewer's ability to produce a coherent mental representation of on-screen space from such a succession of views is an extension of the real-world cognitive skill involved in producing an integrated conception of our surroundings from the partial evidence of our successive glances. Because this real-world cognitive skill must be stretched somewhat—often quite considerably—to fit the demands of film and television, it seems reasonable to assume that this may be another area in which enhanced literacy in visual media might entail a reciprocal enhancement of spatial intelligence.

One piece of evidence with a bearing on this proposition is a study by Comuntzis (1987) that found a positive relationship between children's scores on spatial-intelligence tasks and their ability to make sense of editing involving successive over-the-shoulder shots. Although Comuntzis was concerned with spatial intelligence as the causal agent rather than as the effect, it is conceivable that her findings may be the result of reciprocal influences. However, other studies in this area have dealt directly with the causal direction we are concerned with here.

In a widely cited experiment by Salomon (1979), children were shown images of familiar objects presented in a variety of ways. One group of children saw a movie in which the camera gradually swings around from the initial point of view to a reverse angle. In a second experimental situation, the reversal of angle was accomplished by switching from one still image to another. After repeated exposure to one of the presentational modes, the ability to perform the angle reversal mentally was tested for each child. The test employed was a variant of one of the standard tests of spatial intelligence: the Piagetian three-mountain test, in which children are shown a picture of a person looking at a mountainous landscape and then asked to pick out, from a variety of alternatives, the view of the landscape that most accurately corresponds to what that person sees. In Salomon's version of this test, the pictures involved an interaction between two people rather than a view of a landscape (see Figure 4.1).

In Salomon's study, the children in the moving-camera group did better on this test than did the children in the two-image group. Salomon bases his explanation of this finding on the notion that the former situation "models" the cognitive process required of the subjects in the three-mountain test, whereas the latter situation "short-circuits" it. He also contrasts these two possibilities with a third, which he labels "activation," represented in his study by an experimental condition in which children were shown only a single image of the initial view of the object. Children in this third group did somewhat better on the three-mountain test than did the children who saw the two different images, and Salomon indicates that this finding is accounted for by superior performance among those children in the single-image group who were already relatively high in spatial intelligence. For these children, Salomon argues, the single image served as an activator of abilities that were high enough not to require the more complete treatment of the modeling condition.

The implications of all these results for the process of TV viewing outside the experimental laboratory are unclear. On the one hand, it could be argued that, because most types of television programming typically present space through editing—i.e., as shown in Salomon's two-image condition—rather than in a single static shot or through continuous camera movement, the viewer's processes of spatial cognition are being continually short-circuited and might actually be expected to atrophy in the case of heavy TV exposure. On the other hand, however, it is possible that the short-circuiting condition in Salomon's experiment failed to match the results of the others not because it was too weak a stimulus but rather because it was too challenging—i.e., the instantaneous reversal of camera angle in the two-image condition might have been too demanding for the children in this study, all of whom were second-graders. The attendant confusion might have prevented the children who saw this version from benefiting as much as their counterparts in the other two groups. This interpretation is consistent

Imagine that you are the girl sitting on the window sill. How would you see the painter?

Figure 4.1 Salomon's version of the three-mountain test. Reprinted with permission of Gavriel Salomon.

with Salomon's observation that a few children whose spatial-intelligence abilities were relatively high to begin with did seem to benefit from seeing the two-image presentation.

These issues have also been explored in a more natural setting in a study by Forbes and Lonner (1980; see also Forbes et al., 1984; Lonner et al., 1985). This study was conducted at the time of the introduction of satellite TV programming to certain parts of Alaska that had previously not had any regular television service. By testing children in these areas and comparing their performance to that of matched samples in places where television had not yet arrived, the researchers were able to get a sense of the effects of the new medium. The study employed several standard tests of cognitive abilities, focusing both on visual and on linguistic skills. Unfortunately, however, the results that most directly concern us here were inconsistent. Although the children from the areas with satellite reception tended to do worse than the other children on tests of spatial intelligence, a different analysis of the children's scores, with individual exposure to television as the independent variable, yielded an opposite pattern of findings. The reason for this disparity in the results is unclear, so this study does little to modify the picture with which Salomon's research left us.

One final set of findings should be mentioned briefly before we conclude our examination of this area. In an informal study of the impact of television on spatial intelligence, Wachtel (1984) examined the historical trends in Swiss children's scores on the three-mountain test in relation to the introduction of television to Switzerland. He found that there had been a pronounced *decrease* in these scores over the period during which television became an established medium in that country.

Of course, as Wachtel himself acknowledges, it is impossible to infer a causal connection from data of this kind, especially given the fact that the testing procedures were not stable over time. However, his discussion of these findings contains a pair of interesting observations that amplify and extend Salomon's point about short-circuiting. He notes that (1) television editing does not provide the full range of visual and kinesthetic experience that real-world changes in point of view provide, and (2) the TV viewer is confronted with a preorganized sequence of points of view, rather than a space that can be actively explored.

The latter argument is particularly significant. There is a well-known body of research in developmental psychology that has demonstrated that the early development of visual skills goes hand-in-hand with the active, physical exploration of the environment and is severely stunted in the absence of such exploration (e.g., see Gregory, 1990; see also Olson, 1974). It is conceivable, of course, that once the initial foundation of spatial intelligence has been laid, subsequent development might be less dependent on self-directed, physical movement through a real three-dimensional environment. Salomon's findings in the modeling condition would certainly suggest as much. Nevertheless, on balance it seems fair to say that neither the empirical evidence we have reviewed nor the theoretical arguments we have considered build a particularly strong case in favor of the idea that experience as a spectator of still pictures or film and television is a significant contributor to general spatial intelligence.

From Concrete to Abstract to Analogy

Up to this point, our search for broader cognitive consequences of visual literacy has not been especially fruitful, but there is one more possibility that remains to be explored. We began by looking at images in comparison to language, then went on to examine them in terms of the specifically visual area of spatial intelligence. We will now return to matters related to language once again, but this time our focus will be on the interplay between words and images rather than on their unique characteristics and separate functions.

It has already been noted that when visuals are combined with verbal narration, the sequencing of the images is often governed by what the words are doing. This situation is especially prevalent in informational films and TV programs (e.g., news shows and documentaries), where it is indeed the norm. In such cases the main function of the images is to portray the people, places, and events referred to in the verbal narrative, and the interpretational process called for by the visuals is arguably only an extension of the real-life act of understanding a spoken narrative accompanied by pointing, physical imitation, and other forms of visual illustration. Furthermore, research on people's responses to TV news has found that when the visuals do not match the verbal narrative closely enough, they tend to be dropped from the viewer's mental processing of incoming information (Grimes, 1989).

All of these observations suggest that the interaction between words and images in the typical news program or documentary is probably not much of a stimulus for the development of cognitive skills beyond those involved in following a verbal description. In fact, one could even argue that the presence of the visuals in these kinds of situations actually impedes the development of audience members' mental abilities: There is considerable evidence that the addition of pictures to a verbal story suppresses the listener's imaginative reconstruction of the events referred to in the narrative (Greenfield and Beagles-Roos, 1988; Meringoff et al., 1983; see also Williams and Harrison, 1986).

However, not all combinations of words and images follow the pattern with which we have been concerned up to this point—i.e., a "literal" match between the visual illustration and the subject of the verbal narration. Even in typical informational genres, the visual-verbal connection is sometimes quite abstract, and in such cases the possibilities for broader cognitive involvement on the viewer's part become more pronounced. As an example of these possibilities, let us take a brief look at the structure of a widely aired commercial for Smucker's fruit preserves.

This thirty-second commercial begins with a brief opening shot of a picturesque landscape accompanied by soft music that keeps playing as the commercial continues. Over this musical background, a man's voice goes through a list of what it takes to produce a product as good as this particular brand of preserves. Each of the ingredients he mentions is paired to an image on the screen. In the following rendition of the voice-over soundtrack, the image that accompanies each item is listed after the line that mentions it: "If you could taste time" (man walking across a wide expanse of cultivated land), "caring" (man tending a fruit tree), "dedication" (man carefully stacking one crate of fruit above another); "if you could taste the sun" (cherries sparkling in sunlight), "rain" (berries moist from rain), "fresh air" (a farmyard scene: children clambering over a fence, horses in background); "if you could taste tradition" (an older farmer talking to a younger one) "and pride" (plump strawberries); "this is what it would taste like every time" (display of the preserves).

It should be obvious from the very first line spoken by the narrator that the relationship between images and words in this commercial is quite different from the one discussed earlier in this chapter in our examination of the wild-horses documentary. There we were concerned with images that were direct representations of concrete things mentioned in the narration, a particular object or action. In the commercial, the narration itself makes it clear that one should not expect concrete correlatives in the images. "If you could taste time, care, dedication," the narrator says, but obviously one cannot—not just because these things aren't edible but because they aren't concrete objects at all. With the exception of rain and the sun, all the "ingredients" referred to in the soundtrack are abstractions.

In and of itself, this abstractness virtually eliminates any possibility of a direct relationship between the words and the accompanying visuals. Visuals of the kind we are dealing with here—i.e., pictures produced by a camera rather than by hand—are almost inevitably images of concrete, particular objects and events. A camera has to record whatever is in front of the lens when the button is pressed, and what is in front of the lens must be some specific slice of concrete reality. It is true, of course, that specificity and concreteness can be obscured through manipulations of focus or other such means, and it is always possible to produce a camera image of abstract graphics—although even then it is not clear that one could obtain a direct match with a verbal abstraction. But the typical photographic image, in commercial television at least, is of the kind used in this commercial: a picture of a particular scene that existed in reality at a particular time and place (even if that place was a studio). It follows, then, that this commercial's visuals cannot correspond directly to the abstractions of the verbal soundtrack. Consequently, in place of the kind of redundancy between words and pictures that we often get in news stories, this commercial confronts us with a very different order of relationship.

The general principle behind this relationship is fairly straightforward: For every abstraction mentioned on the soundtrack, we get an image of a concrete situation exemplifying that abstraction. Thus, when the speaker refers to "time" as something that goes into making the preserves, we see a concrete instance of a time-consuming activity (walking across a wide field); when the speaker mentions "tradition," we see a specific example of the sort of incident out of which a tradition emerges (an older man passing knowledge on to a younger one); and so forth.

Interestingly enough, this general principle seems to be in evidence even in two cases, the references to "the sun" and "rain," in which the words could have been interpreted at a concrete level and visualized directly—as is done, in fact, with the words "fresh air," which are paired to a shot of just that (framed by the farmyard setting, which testifies to the air's purity). Instead of such a direct approach, what we get in the case of "the sun" is an image (sunshine playing off fruit) that encourages a more abstract interpretation of what is being implied—not literally the sun but rather its effect on fruit. The same goes for the image corresponding to rain (fruit dripping with moisture).

With regard to word-image relationships, then, the basic interpretive task confronting the viewer in this commercial is that of bridging two levels of representation, the abstractions in the soundtrack and the concrete representations of the visuals. How might we account for a viewer's ability to perform such a task, and what cognitive skills might the demands of this situation bring into play?

On the one hand, the interpretive process demanded by this type of editing could be viewed as being largely a matter of experience with visual media. Although the typical pattern of much informational programming is probably the one we discussed in connection with the wild-horses documentary, in which the images were paired with concrete verbal referents, there are several uses of verbal narration that are more likely to involve abstractions. For example, a nature documentary might accompany footage of wolves hunting caribou with a verbal disquisition on ecological balance; a children's program might use a skit featuring popular puppet characters to reinforce verbal exhortations about the importance of sharing; and a political advertisement for an incumbent president might pair images of happy and industrious citizens with a verbal paean to the spirit of renewal achieved during his or her first term in office. It can also be argued that there is a parallel between these kinds of situations and certain uses of labels, captions, or other accompanying text in the case of still pictures—as, for example, when the label "American Gothic" (which, technically speaking, describes a style of Midwestern architecture), is attached to a painting of a somber-faced rural couple.

On the other hand, however, it is possible that the intellectual skills that are brought into play in such circumstances, whether with moving pictures or still images, are not confined to these circumstances alone. Rather, it may be the case that these skills are related to aptitude for abstract reasoning in a more general sense, and it is further conceivable that the act of interpreting visual-verbal juxtapositions of this sort serves to *extend* the interpreter's abstract thinking abilities rather than merely drawing on them passively.

In this connection, it is worth noting that aside from these visual-verbal juxtapositions, there is at least one other type of cinematic construction in whose interpretation the capacity to "see" abstract qualities in concrete images undoubtedly plays a major role. What I have in mind here is exemplified rather elegantly in a brief sequence from Kon Ichikawa's *The Makioka Sisters* (1983). Close to the end of this film, there is a scene in which an unmarried woman, who has endured a series of disappointing attempts at third-party matchmaking, finally meets a suitor she finds attractive. As she faces this man for the first time, Ichikawa's camera travels from a shot of her to a shot of wind-ruffled foliage—with red colors prominent—in the window behind her. In order to interpret this juxtaposition in the manner the director presumably intended, the viewer must be able to perceive in each of the two images a cluster of abstract qualities—e.g., invigoration, warmth—both have in common. The ability to perceive these abstract qualities forms the basis for seeing an analogy between the two images.

Analogical constructions of this sort are clearly an important element of some forms of purely propositional editing (such as the series of Exxon commercials in which speeding cars are intercut with charging tigers, a device whose sole intent is to imply an analogy), but they may also be present in situations in which propositionality is a less obvious feature of the editing (such as the sequence in *2001* in which a prehuman primate who has just learned to use tools throws a bone in the air and the scene switches to a spaceship and space-station spinning in the void).

Furthermore, as the example from *2001* may suggest, the kind of mental operation that these analogical constructions demand of the viewer is obviously a very significant ingredient of everyday or real-world intelligence, as opposed to specifically cinematic literacy. The frame of mind that can see the wealth of similarities between an ape-man's bone/axe and a space station is an integral part of both the poetic and the scientific process. In fact, it can be argued that analogical thinking of this order is a prime mover of intellectual advances, as it allows for the lessons learned in one context to be expanded to another (cf. Whittock, 1990).

At least in principle, then, an argument can be made in favor of the notion that some aspects of visual interpretation may have a parallel in viewers' *more general* skills of abstraction and analogical thinking. But is there any good reason to suppose that experience in the former actually enhances the latter? Some empirical evidence with a possible bearing, although not a direct one, on this supposition comes from a study in which I asked undergraduate students with varying degrees of film-related experience to interpret a ten-minute fiction film (Messaris, 1981).

In one of the scenes of this film, the protagonist, a fashionably dressed young woman, is shown walking into a clothing store, but the shot of her going through the door (which was taken from outside the store) is followed immediately, via match-cutting, by a shot of her entering a church. When I was designing this study, it had seemed to me that no viewer could possibly miss the far-from-subtle implications of this analogical construction. However, to my considerable surprise, it turned out that only among students who had taken film courses or had actually made films themselves was there any significant level of awareness of the analogy. Among the other students, the most frequent interpretation of this sequence was purely narrative—i.e., the transition was seen as a simple scene change from one location to another. I will describe these responses in further detail in Chapter 5. For the moment, the important point is that here we have evidence that viewers with special film-related experience may be more sensitive to analogy and its attendant abstractions than are "ordinary" viewers.

The problem with this finding, of course, is that the viewers were interpreting a ready-made analogy in a movie rather than situations encountered in reality. It is conceivable that the differences between the ordinary viewers and the viewers with film experience were caused primarily by differential sensitivity to the implications of match-cutting rather than differential awareness of the analogy itself. More important, even if we do decide that awareness of the analogy itself was the deciding factor in this case, we might still want to question whether this intellectual aptitude would extend to the world outside of movies. Here our earlier discussion of spatial intelligence might be of some relevance.

As I pointed out in connection with the research of Salomon and Wachtel, it is a standard assumption in the area of developmental psychology that active exploration of reality is necessary for the development of mental skills. When a viewer is faced with an analogical construction in a film, determining the basis of the analogy may be a challenge, but the initial work of bringing together the two terms of the analogy has already been done by someone else. The same goes for the kinds of visual-verbal constructions discussed earlier: The pairing of an abstract narration or caption with a concrete image may stimulate viewers to see an abstraction where they would otherwise not have been aware of one, but the nature of that abstraction has already been set by the words. Given these considerations, the idea that a connection may exist between cinematic or pictorial experience and extra-cinematic or extrapictorial abstractive/analogical skills must remain a very tentative hypothesis.

5

Awareness of Artistry and Manipulation

The interpretational processes examined in Chapters 2 and 3 cover several aspects of the meaning of still and moving images, including: the identity of the objects depicted in an image; the spatial relationships among these objects, whether in a single image or in a succession of several images; the psychological and dramatic implications of the juxtapositions of images; the nature of narrative flow across image transitions; and so forth. I have argued that, for the most part, the cognitive skills required for the interpretation of these aspects of meaning cannot, strictly speaking, be called a form of "literacy," if by this term we mean medium-specific interpretational expertise that can be acquired only through experience in that medium.

Nevertheless, it is probably fair to say that most people who see visual literacy as something to be encouraged and cultivated would consider the level of interpretational ability discussed thus far to be inadequate. The additional element that is typically held to be a prerequisite of mature interpretational ability—if not, in fact, its defining component—can be characterized, in the most general terms, as some degree of explicit awareness about the processes by which meaning is created through the visual media. In other words, what is expected of sophisticated viewers is some degree of self-consciousness about their role as interpreters. The issues involved in this approach to visual literacy are best introduced through a concrete illustration.

In Brian De Palma's *Dressed to Kill* (1980), there is a scene in which a woman is trapped in an elevator by a razor-wielding psychopath. As the victim cringes in terror, the villain is shown advancing on her, with the razor pointing at her face. This shot is presented from the point of view of the woman: The razor, in sharp focus, is in the foreground of the shot, with the villain's face relegated to the out-of-focus background (Figures 5.1 and

5.2). With respect to the kinds of interpretational problems discussed in Chapters 2 and 3, this shot is certainly not without interest. For example, it confronts the viewer with the necessity of integrating a very restricted, subjective view into a broader conception of the space in which the action occurs. However, some significant things about this shot would be quite opaque to a viewer whose level of interpretational expertise went no further than what has been discussed thus far. These additional layers of meaning would be available only to a viewer who was self-conscious about the process of visual communication and therefore explicitly concerned with the filmmaker's manipulation of his material.

What would such a viewer get out of this shot? To begin with, the viewer might realize that the lack of sharp focus in the background of the shot was highly unlikely to have been an accident. At this point in the film, the villain's identity is supposed to be a mystery to the audience. Therefore, there can be little doubt that the narrow depth of field in this shot was a deliberate device for obscuring the villain's facial features, a device someone who was attentive to the workings of the filmmaker would be likely to spot. Such an awareness of the means of audience "manipulation" would obviously prevent the viewer from experiencing whatever vicarious pleasure audiences derive from the murder-mystery elements of films such as *Dressed to Kill*. However, this awareness might give a viewer a very different kind of pleasure—namely, admiration for the filmmaker's relatively subtle solution to the problem of how to conceal the villain's identity in a full-face, head-on shot of some duration.

This admiration—which, it can be argued, is the essence of the aesthetic response to works of art (see Gross, 1973a; Dondis, 1973)—might be particularly keen if the viewer had some familiarity with other filmmakers' ways of handling similar problems. For example, the obvious and most relevant precedents for this film's elevator scene are the two murder scenes in *Psycho*

Figures 5.1 and 5.2   Concealment of identity in a subjective shot. *Source: Dressed to Kill* (directed by Brian De Palma, Filmways, 1980).

(1960), on which *Dressed to Kill* is explicitly based. In the shower scene in *Psycho,* the murderer's face is always shot against an overbright background, so that it is consistently obscured by underexposure—but, as in the razor shot of *Dressed to Kill,* it is shown head-on. In *Psycho's* second murder scene, Hitchcock resorts to the more straightforward device of not showing the villain's face at all: The action begins with a direct overhead shot, in which killer and victim are shown from above, and continues with a quite lengthy shot of the victim as he recoils from a stab to the head and falls backwards down a flight of stairs. The fact that the camera stays with him during his fall and that he himself looks back into it suggests that this shot is to be taken as a subjective view through the eyes of the killer, who is following the victim down the stairs to finish him off. Indeed, the next and last shot in this sequence is a brief side-view of this final stabbing, with the villain's face obscured by the arm holding the knife.

The use of a subjective shot from the villain's point of view as a means of concealing the villain's identity has become a staple of the many "slasher" films that have followed *Psycho* (see Dika, 1990). Indeed, the elevator scene in *Dressed to Kill* is prefaced by precisely this kind of shot. A viewer of *Dressed to Kill* who knew about this tradition might therefore be particularly appreciative of the way in which, a little later in the elevator scene, in the shot with which we began this discussion, De Palma manages to show the villain's face head-on by means of a device that blurs that person's features "legitimately" (because the narrow focus on the razor can be said to be an accurate rendition of the way in which the victim would see things). However, a viewer who knew this much might quite likely also be aware of another aspect of the significance of this shot.

In the eyes of many critics of the visual media, the point of view from which a scene is presented can be a matter of considerable ideological consequence. For example, in an often-cited discussion of the Western post-Renaissance tradition of pictorial representation, Berger (1972) argues that the male perspective typically assumed in this tradition (most significantly, perhaps, in images of women) is a manifestation of power. Similar theories have been based on the pervasive assumption of a male spectator in Hollywood movies (e.g., see Mulvey, 1975, 1989; and, for a different perspective, Lesser, 1991). In the more specific case of subjective shots used for concealing the identity of slasher-movie villains, the following argument can be made: Because the slasher is typically male whereas the "slashee" is traditionally female, and because the subjective shot can be seen as a device for heightening identification with the character through whose eyes one is seeing, subjective shots through the slasher's eyes are an invitation to the audience to participate vicariously in the aggression of a male against a female.

Against this background, an analytical viewer of *Dressed to Kill* might be surprised to find Brian De Palma, the filmmaker who has received probably the harshest criticism for the treatment of women in his films (see MacKinnon, 1990, for a summary and counterargument), giving his audience the female victim's perspective in the elevator scene. More to the point, however, it seems reasonable to assume that the analytical spectator who was aware of the ideological significance of point of view (or any other device) would, as a result of this awareness, be immune to whatever negative influence this device might normally be expected to have. This presumed immunity is the major justification of many of the arguments in favor of education in visual literacy.

As this example from *Dressed to Kill* has indicated, the kind of visual literacy with which this chapter is concerned—namely, the explicit awareness of how visual meaning is created—may involve several relatively distinct, although not unrelated, components, including some understanding of production techniques (in this instance, depth of field as a variable controlled by the filmmaker); some knowledge of relevant precedents (here, the ways in which previous filmmakers dealt with the problem of concealing the villain's face); and some familiarity with relevant critical commentary (whether ideologically oriented, as in this example, or more concerned with aesthetic evaluation).

This kind of visual literacy can be said to have both aesthetic and ideological ramifications. With regard to aesthetics, it provides the viewer with a basis on which to make judgments about quality of execution. With regard to ideological matters, it equips the viewer for drawing inferences about the broader social implications of images, and it can also be assumed to make one less vulnerable to their influence (to the extent, of course, that that influence depends on an unreflecting audience). Regardless of which of these directions a viewer takes, however, the starting point for the interpretive processes this kind of visual literacy makes possible is the judgment that a particular image, feature of an image, or juxtaposition of images should be taken as a deliberate expression of an intended meaning.

The Detection of Artifice

Generic Labels

The ability to make a competent judgment about the presence of intentionality can be considered, in and of itself, a mark of sophistication on the part of the viewer. What kinds of evidence are available for making this judgment, and what must a viewer know in order to do the job competently? Perhaps the most obvious indicator of how much and what kind of intentionality is to be read into some types of images is the presence of a conventional label, such as "photojournalism" or "advertisement." In the case of the standard fictional genres in film and television, labels may indeed be relatively definitive. In other words, a viewer who sits down to watch a "situation comedy" or a "crime drama" or a "soap opera" probably will not have to spend much time figuring out what is staged and what is not.

Even in the case of acknowledged fiction, however, there are exceptions, as, for example, when an actress's hesitation in a soap opera leads the viewer to wonder whether the cause is faulty reading or scripted naturalism. Furthermore, when it comes to those types of films or aspects of TV programming that are not ordinarily included in the general category of fictional entertainment, standard labels are even less likely to serve as definitive a priori indicators of the presence of staging or other kinds of manipulation. For example, such labels cannot inform a viewer ahead of time about the degree of rehearsal that might have gone into a talk show or game show; the extent to which a news program's or documentary's version of events corresponds to that which an on-the-scene viewer would have obtained; or the number of retakes that might have been inserted into a concert program or music video ostensibly taped "live."

Of course, even when a label cannot predetermine the presence of intentionality, it is not devoid of information. To return to the example of the soap-opera actress's hesitation: The reason its intepretation can be in doubt is precisely the fact that the context is a soap opera. The identical hesitation occurring in a mini-series—i.e., a program without the relentless production schedule soap operas typically face—would presumably be much less likely to lead a knowledgeable viewer to question whether it had been intended. In this case, then, the knowledge embodied in the viewer's use of these labels is not simply a matter of having learned that some programs are fictional and others not; and what was true of this situation is probably true, more often than not, of labels in general. For example, a viewer watching an interview on a live talk show might speculate about the extent to which guest and host had prearranged a particular bit of repartée, but would be unlikely to spend much time assessing the creativity of the show's editing, whereas in one's assessment of an interview labeled "investigative reporting," the presence of creative editing (in the euphemistic sense) might become a paramount concern.

In short, the competent use of generic labels is likely to be a matter of some complexity, and one would expect the mastery of such labels and of the generic distinctions they entail to require considerable experience. Although there is no systematic research on this issue with adult viewers, relevant studies with children and adolescents do provide some useful information. A three-year project by Jaglom and Gardner (1981) traced the evolution of preschoolers' conceptions of TV program categories (see also Gardner [with Jaglom], 1985). The findings indicate that the development of a category system involves numerous steps (e.g., distinguishing commercials from the rest of what appears on TV; distinguishing cartoons from programs featuring "real" people); that these steps take time; and—most important, perhaps, for our purposes—that the formation of categories based on producers' intentions (e.g., to teach or to entertain) is a task that, for these children (aged five at the end of the study), is still in the future (Jaglom and Gardner, 1981, p. 46).

In a study by Messaris (1987), it was found that even adolescents were often unclear about the presence of fabrication in TV programs and were therefore dependent on clarification by their parents—which is not to say, of course, that the typical adult viewer is necessarily a master of all the possible intricacies that can be involved in these matters. This study's findings also suggest that in this area of visual literacy, explicit parental teaching may be an important mechanism through which younger viewers acquire the necessary knowledge. This process is illustrated in the following excerpt from a mother's reminiscences about TV-related discussions with her two boys, who were aged two to three and six to seven at the time of this particular incident:

> I remember during the Vietnam War getting very upset: We were watching television, the news, while we were eating dinner. And they were showing the children and women dead in the village and I—I started crying, and I couldn't eat my dinner. And the kids got very upset. It wasn't the thing to watch at dinnertime, actually. . . . I explained to them that everything that you see on television isn't make-believe. The news is real. And . . . it hit cold to them that this was real that they were looking at. And it upset them terribly. [quoted in Messaris, 1987, p. 99]

This incident is a dramatic illustration of the potential significance of labels. It is also a useful point of departure for a consideration of the other elements involved in the experienced viewer's assessment of intentionality. The mother's account of this incident makes it fairly clear that she knew beforehand that the war footage she and her family were watching was part of the news. But let us assume she hadn't known this—as would have been the case, for instance, if she had come across it while changing channels in search of another program. Despite the fact that she would now have no previous information about the type of program in which this war footage was appearing, it seems perfectly plausible to assume that she would not have much difficulty in classifying the footage as unstaged. Of course, the context of these scenes might not be immediately obvious—several alternatives might suggest themselves, including even the possibility of a fictional war film that had incorporated documentary footage into its battle scenes. But even in the absence of context, one would not ordinarily expect an experienced viewer to have trouble making an accurate assessment once the structure of the scene had become apparent.

Staged Behavior

Despite the absence of a generic label, then, the content of an image may in itself be a sufficient indicator of the degree and type of control that went into producing that image, as any experienced viewer who has flipped a TV dial surely knows. In the case of fictional material, this is especially likely to be true of the more conventional varieties of Hollywood films or TV programs, whose actual "look"—the physical appearance of the actors and settings, the fluency of action, the quality of the cinematography—proclaims their ficticity in an instant to the experienced eye. But even in the case of fictional varieties that deliberately attempt a more naturalistic appearance, evidence of ficticity is typically unambiguous: Few creators of fiction in any medium are so strongly committed to realism as to substitute the relative amorphousness of reality for the purposeful structure of narrative. Or, to put it differently: It is quite difficult to conceive of a narrative sequence of actions that could plausibly pass *both* as a fiction film *and* as a documentary.

However, it is not difficult at all to conceive of staged material posing *only* as nonfiction—or, more generally, to conceive of a photograph or a scene in a TV program or a commercial attempting to conceal the degree or type of control that went into its creation. It is in the presence of this kind of attempted deception—which is not always ill-intentioned, of course—that a viewer's ability to decipher intentionality is most likely to become a conscious preoccupation. As a concrete illustration of the considerations that are likely to come into play in these circumstances, let us examine a political advertisement that attracted considerable attention at the time it was made and is still considered among the more creative examples of the political spot.

In 1972, Jay Rockefeller, who had previously been a resident of New York, was running against Arch Moore for governor of West Virginia. In an attempt to depict Rockefeller as an outsider, Moore's campaign used the following ad. The opening image is a brief shot of a Manhattan skyscraper. We hear an off-camera voice: "Excuse me, what do you think about a West Virginian running for governor of New York?" Simultaneously, the camera tilts down to ground level and dissolves to a "man in the street," to whom this question is being posed. The man's answer is dismissive: "That's like— is that a question, or is that a statement? It don't make no sense neither way." We now go to another man in the street, who responds with great amusement (the question isn't repeated): "I think it's preposterous. I think it's ridiculous." The next man in the street seems overwhelmed by the absurdity of the suggestion: "Crazy," he says, in tones of disbelief. "It's crazy. I mean really—I mean—" He is left fumbling for words, and we go on to a quick shot of a man laughing heartily, adding: "You gotta be kidding." As the next man in the street appears, the off-camera voice is heard once again: "A West Virginian for governor of New York?" The man waves the camera away impatiently, and we now go to the final interviewee—a woman this time—while the off-camera voice continues: "How about it?" "That makes as much sense to me," the woman replies, "as having the next governor of West Virginia be a New Yorker."

Although this ad was presumably designed to create an impression of spontaneity, the people who appear in it were all paid actors or campaign aides. The ad is therefore instructive both with regard to the mechanisms by which an appearance of reality is achieved and with regard to the ways in which staging may inadvertently reveal itself. Among the former, the most important may be the ad's format. The random series of "man in the street" interviews is a conventional form for the presentation of public opinion on television, as well as in other mass media, and it could reasonably be expected to connote spontaneity to a TV audience. The significance of this aspect of the ad bears emphasis: The appropriation of preexisting, conventional formats for the presentation of reality, rather than the creation of new formats, seems to be the standard strategy of staged films or TV programs attempting to pass as "real" (cf. McGinnis, 1969; Mitchell, 1988).

In addition to its adoption of a conventional overall framework, the Arch Moore ad deserves mention for at least two other "realistic" strategies it employs. One such strategy is the introduction of errors, rough spots, or lapses in fluency. The ad contains several of these, mostly hesitations on the part of the speakers, but also the "failed" interview (the man who waves the camera away) and the interview that is cut off by the editor while the interviewee is apparently still searching for words. The other notable strategy through which this ad imitates reality has to do with the look (and the sound) of the interviewees. It is obvious that these people were chosen to personify the special flavor of the New Yorker (see Figure 5.3). In their clothes, in their bearing, in their accents, and even in their physical appearance they are quite distinct from the representatives of the citizenry in other ads of this kind. Ironically, it is this attempt at authenticity that may constitute one of the major cues to the fact that the ad was actually staged.

According to Robert Goodman, the media manager who was running the campaign in which this ad was used, the people in the ad "were all from New York" (quoted in Diamond and Bates, 1984, p. 332). Nevertheless, some of them were professional actors, and all of them, professionals and amateurs alike, were playing a part. As one watches the ad, one quickly realizes that the parts they have ended up playing are not those of real New Yorkers (i.e., themselves) but rather a TV advertiser's idea of what non–New Yorkers imagine New Yorkers to be like. Not surprisingly, this turns out to be very similar to any number of fiction-film portrayals of "colorful New York types." Thus, the ad's attempted naturalism has been done

Figure 5.3 Staged spontaneity: a cigarillo-smoking, Brooklynese-speaking "man-in-the-street." *Source:* Arch Moore gubernatorial campaign ad, West Virginia, 1972.

in by a difficulty that all attempts to recreate reality must face, that of breaking away from fictional stereotypes of what reality is like. This incongruity is one major cue exposing the ad's inauthenticity.

A second, closely related cue has to do with the performances of the people in the ad. Here, too, the attempt to appear natural runs into the problem of overcoming fictional conceptions of what natural behavior looks like. As Metz (1974, pp. 235–252) has suggested, actions that are in fact quite stylized may appear perfectly true-to-life in the context of a fictional movie, but even slight discrepancies become very noticeable when the context is reality itself. Although all the performers in the Moore ad are perfectly proficient, the false note of stylization is there in more than one case, and the viewer thus has one more indication that the ad was staged.

These kinds of discrepancies between staged versions of reality and reality itself—discrepancies in behavior, discrepancies in the appearance of things and people—may be the primary indicators that most audience members use in detecting the presence of concealed staging. The competent recognition of these indicators undoubtedly requires quite sophisticated perceptual skills. However, if the essence of these skills is a sensitivity to departures from natural, unstaged appearance or behavior, it seems likely that their primary source is everyday social interaction rather than experience with visual media. Consequently, we might not want to call the possession of such skills a form of visual literacy, in the sense in which we have been using that term.

Editing

There is, however, another way in which the Moore ad reveals itself for what it is, and the ability to discern this kind of evidence of artifice is much more clearly a matter of familiarity with the workings of the visual media. In two different places, the ad uses an editing device that is inconsistent with the notion that what the audience is getting is an exact copy of the image and sound recorded during the (supposedly unstaged) interviews. The first use of this device occurs at the very beginning of the ad: We see a shot of a tall building and hear the "interviewer" asking his question. Then the image dissolves to the first man in the street giving his answer. Because it is virtually inconceivable that a news- or documentary-style production such as this one would have taken two cameras on location, it is clear that the opening image of the building has been grafted onto the interviewer's words after the fact. The same thing happens later in the ad, in the transition between the man who waves the camera away and the woman who delivers the clincher at the end. The interviewer's words ("A West Virginian as governor of New York? How about it?") are delivered in a single dose, but they bridge two different images: a man who refuses to respond to them and, immediately afterwards—but in a completely different location—a woman who does respond. Once again, a single source of sound has been made to serve two unrelated images. Although one could view this as constituting deception (at least one of the two interviewees at the end cannot possibly be responding to the exact sound we are hearing), the purpose of this editing device in both places is obviously to quicken the pace rather than to fool the viewer in any way. Nonetheless, to the viewer who notices it, this device is bound to be an indicator that the ad is not entirely veridical.

Although this kind of evidence of artifice can be quite compelling, it does not in fact seem to be something most viewers notice easily. A case in point is the film *No Lies* (1973), a notorious example of a staged film designed to look like a documentary—in this instance, a cinéma-vérité short in which a male filmmaker interviewing a female rape victim responds to her story with doubt and with suggestions that she might have provoked the incident herself. As most people who have seen this film will probably agree, its attempt to conceal its staging is very successful. First-time viewers are typically quite surprised, if not shocked, when the credits at the film's end reveal that the two protagonists were both acting. In fact, I have heard one viewer who was deeply offended by the film's content argue that the admission of staging at the end is in fact a lie, cooked up after the fact by the filmmaker when he realized how odious his behavior had been.

As one would expect from our discussion of the Moore ad, it is commonly agreed that a major reason for the success of *No Lies* as a "documentary" is the impeccable acting of its two protagonists, especially the on-camera interviewee, actress Shelby Leverington. An article about the film by Mitchell Block (1975), its *real* director (not the actor who plays the fictional filmmaker in the film itself), makes it clear that the apparent spontaneity of Leverington's performance was actually the result of weeks of rehearsal and, more generally, that the film's attainment of a natural look required the most meticulous planning. As it happens, however, the film does contain one sure sign of its being staged. As with the Moore ad, this sign has to do with the continuation of action across an edit.

In order to enhance the cinéma-vérité quality, as well as for dramatic reasons, the film was designed to give the appearance of unfolding in real time—i.e., without any editing. Unfortunately, 16mm equipment, which was used in making the film, was limited to twelve-minute takes, whereas the script called for sixteen minutes of continuous dialogue. In order to circumvent this problem, Block introduced two edits. One of them is effectively masked by having the actress walk in front of the lens right before and right after the cut, producing the effect of continuous motion. In the other case, however, this procedure couldn't be used effectively. Consequently, although there is a marked switch in camera position, the action flows uninterruptedly—clearly an impossibility in the single-camera situation the film is trying to imitate. Nevertheless, hardly any viewer notices this cut without being told beforehand to look for it. In other words, this kind of editing, whose function is to integrate pieces of action into one continuous whole, seems not to attract the attention of the ordinary viewer. (Whether documentary filmmakers, who were presumably highly aware of the time limitations of the 16mm format, were more likely to look for this cut is an open question.)

Here, then, is an aspect of visual artifice whose detection appears to require specific priming of the viewer's eye, either through explicit instruction or through relevant prior experience. In the examples we have just considered, this kind of editing was applied to material that was itself artificial, completely staged. In such cases, the editing is only one element among the many that are typically employed to obtain the intended effect. However, such editing can become the primary locus of artifice when it is applied to material over which the filmmaker or TV producer does not have complete control—i.e., unstaged material or material in which the staging is not complete. An interesting example of this situation is provided by another political advertisement, this one from George Bush's campaign for the presidency in 1980.

In this ad, Bush is shown delivering a stirring speech at a political gathering. Such events are unlikely to be completely free of orchestration, of course, especially when they have been convened in support of a single candidate. Still, unless the participants have consciously conceived of the event as a piece of fiction, there is bound to be a considerable degree of spontaneity in their behavior; more to the point, the event can be said to have a real-life existence independent of the intentions of any filmmaker, TV producer, or advertiser. Consequently, an editor working with images derived from this kind of situation can be held accountable for his or her fidelity to reality, whereas accountability to the real event is an irrelevant notion when the only purpose of an event is to yield the images with which the editor is going to work. In this respect, the significant thing about the Bush ad is that its version of the political gathering and of Bush's speech contains certain sequences of images or juxtapositions of images and sounds that cannot conceivably have occurred in the "real" events.

The general strategy that has been followed in the editing of this ad is to cut back and forth between images of Bush and images of enthusiastic audience members. As Bush reaches the climax of his speech, the audience is shown responding with increasing fervor, the effect heightened by the traditional release of a cluster of balloons. Superficially, this appears to be a typical case of a forceful speaker firing up the crowd. However, if one looks at the ad more carefully, one notices that the words one is hearing on the soundtrack do not always seem to correspond to the movements of Bush's lips; that the long shots of the auditorium show a speaker up on stage, behind a podium, whereas the close-ups of Bush show him surrounded by reporters at what seems to be ground level; and that the figure behind the podium in the shot in which the balloons are released cannot be identified, because the camera's view of his face is blocked by the balloons.

What seems to have happened is that the editor (or whoever made the relevant decisions) preferred the close-ups of Bush, evidently taken during a question-and-answer session with reporters, to whatever material there was of him delivering the speech itself. These close-ups have thus been intercut with more general views of the auditorium, including an indistinct on-stage figure who might not even be Bush at all (the balloons could have been released while someone else, such as a master of ceremonies, was at the podium). All of this goes by very rapidly, and it is quite easy to miss both the long-shot/close-up discrepancy and the discrepancy between image and sound. As the case of *No Lies* has already suggested, the viewer's tendency to arrive at a mental synthesis of successive views may overwhelm any awareness of their distinctive qualities.

The kind of editing used in the Bush ad is not a rarity in political advertising. Another good example of its use is an ad produced for Howard Baker during his own campaign for the presidency in 1980. This ad, which has been called "the most dramatic" of the 1980 primaries (Diamond and Bates, 1984, p. 260), shows Baker giving a speech about the need for the United States to stop being pushed around. (This was the time of the Iran hostage crisis.) He gets a question from an angry Iranian in the audience: When the Shah's army was using U.S. money to kill Iranians, why wasn't Baker expressing concern for international law? "Because, my friend," Baker responds, "I'm interested in fifty Americans, that's why! And when those fifty Americans are released, then I'm perfectly willing to talk about that." The audience members applaud, and then, in a panning shot that sweeps the auditorium, they are shown rising to their feet for a standing ovation. But this final shot was put in after the fact: The standing ovation actually came at the conclusion of Baker's appearance.

This kind of editing is also likely to be encountered elsewhere on television, perhaps most commonly in taped interviews done on location with a single camera. As is well known, it is a frequent practice in such cases to take some extra shots of the interviewer asking the questions or pretending to respond to the answers after the interview itself has been concluded. These shots can then be inserted into the broadcast version of the interview, thus breaking up the monotony of a continuous shot of the interviewee—but also potentially giving the interviewee's words a coloration they did not have in their original context. The viewer's ability to tell that a certain shot "doesn't belong" may well depend to a large extent on reality-based judgments of implausibility: for example, that an interviewer's response doesn't seem to fit what the interviewee just said, or that the onset of the standing ovation seems unexpected. But the tendency to look for such discrepancies in the first place is undoubtedly contingent on specific knowledge about these aspects of editing, and this kind of knowledge can be said to be the key to the "literate" viewing of films or TV programs based on unstaged footage.

Unconcealed Artifice

The detection of artifice, whether in the form of staging or in the form of editing, is a crucial component of informed viewing in those cases in which artifice is likely to be concealed. But much of what people watch on television, and most of what they watch in the movies, is openly fictional. Unmasking the presence of staging or synthetic editing is not an issue with such material. Nevertheless, it can be argued that the considerations involved in the interpretation of this material are not unrelated to those we have just examined. Although very few fiction films pretend to be documentaries, it is a commonly accepted that most Hollywood movies, together with the fictional TV programs that are one of Hollywood's main products these days, adhere to a tradition of "illusionism" that encourages viewers to treat them as if they were a window on reality rather than fabrications created by teams of artists. According to this view, then, even when a film or TV program is openly fictional, in the sense that it is not trying to pass as a record of unstaged reality, the viewer's consciousness of the activity of the filmmaker or TV producer cannot be taken for granted. Detecting the presence of artifice may not be an issue in this case—but attending to the artifice is.

Illusionism

The assumption that Hollywood movies are particularly "illusionistic" and that this illusionism tends to suppress the audience's awareness of the movies' underlying artificiality is a central tenet of much of contemporary film scholarship. Typically, this phenomenon is seen as part of the process by which the ideological implications of mass-mediated entertainment are made to seem natural and inevitable (e.g., see Ray, 1985, and, for an equivalent argument regarding television, Fiske, 1987). Although this assumption is not unproblematic, it is a useful point of departure for the examination of viewers' interpretations of intentionality in fiction films and TV programs.

One sense in which Hollywood movies can be said to exhibit illusionism has to do with such things as costumes, props, sets, locations—the material environment in which a story unfolds. With a few exceptions, such as dream sequences, this environment is typically supposed to be that of recognizable or imaginable reality, and considerable effort is often expended in getting a good match. For example, even Alfred Hitchcock, whose films are hardly models of realism as far as their themes are concerned, apparently took some pride in achieving an authentic look in his sets and his locations, as well as in the physical appearance of actors playing supporting roles. In particular, his interviews with François Truffaut contain repeated references to cases in which special pains were taken to ensure this kind of authenticity, as when, in designing the set of an apartment for *Vertigo*'s protagonist, a retired San Francisco detective, Hitchcock sent a photographer to San Francisco to find some real retired detectives and take pictures of their apartments (Truffaut, 1967, p. 192). Similarly, one of his collaborators on *Psycho* remembered that Hitchcock had sent out his researchers to establish *"exactly"* what a car salesman in a certain part of California would be dressed like (Rebello, 1990, p. 56).

Despite such efforts, of course, no reasonably mature audience member is likely to mistake a Hitchcock film for a documentary. As was argued above, in connection with the Moore campaign ad, it is one thing to achieve a satisfyingly authentic look in a fictional context and quite another to convince an audience that the context is in fact not fictional. With regard to the issue of illusionism, however, the question raised by such attempts at authenticity is not whether they lead the viewer to misperceive the presence of staging but whether they lead one to overlook it.

That the typical audience member does in fact tend to overlook the ficticity of films and TV programs seems to be taken for granted without proof in much of the literature on illusionism. On the specific point which has just been outlined, however, there is some supportive empirical evidence. This evidence comes from a series of studies of viewers' interpretations of visual narratives (Custen, 1980; Messaris and Gross, 1977; Wawrzaszek, 1983; see also Gross, 1985; Worth and Gross, 1974). The consistent finding of these studies has been that even relatively knowledgeable viewers tend to talk about fictional characters and situations as if they were subject to the rules of everyday reality instead of the conventions of a medium and the intentions of its users.

An example of this tendency occurred in a study of viewers' responses to a short experimental film about a day in the life of an actress (Messaris, 1981). Viewers were asked to discuss a scene in which various "movie-industry types" are shown celebrating the opening of the actress's latest film. The costumes and the props used in this scene exhibit the usual exaggerations associated with stereotyped portrayals of movie people: A person playing a director, for instance, is identified by an ascot, dark glasses, a long cigarette holder, and so forth. Nevertheless, when viewers were asked to explain how they knew that this person and the others in the scene were movie types, almost three-quarters of the answers appealed exclusively to conceptions about real life, with no acknowledgment of the manufactured stereotypes present in these images. For example, one viewer said that "if I were to go to a Hollywood party, this is what I would expect to see," whereas another, in explaining her judgment that the people in this scene were wearing typically "show-business" clothes, argued that "at a premiere—though I've never been to one, I've always wanted to go to see one—I assume that people are dressed like that." Almost none of these viewers explicitly referred to the fictional stereotypes present in these images (e.g., in the words of one of the few exceptions, "the typical way they portray directors, you know, with the eyeglasses and everything").

The general conclusion such findings suggest, then, is that one of the barriers to viewers' awareness of artifice in Hollywood movies is the authentic look of the world portrayed in these movies—even when that authenticity is more a matter of convention than of actual fidelity to real-life prototypes. Indeed, this proposition may seem to be so self-evident as to make the presence of the supportive data irrelevant. All the same, it should be noted that the studies mentioned above do not address the question of how viewers respond to fictional worlds that do *not* make any pretense to authenticity. Is awareness of artifice heightened by nonnaturalistic genres (e.g., some kinds of fantasy) or the exceptional nonnaturalistic film? Furthermore—and perhaps this is the more important question—are audiences in cultures with a tradition of nonnaturalistic visual narrative any less likely than Hollywood audiences to respond to those narratives as if they were real? Might the surrender to artifice be less culture-bound a response to narrative than is often assumed in the literature on illusionism?

The "Invisible Style"

Another potential inhibitor of the awareness of artifice in Hollywood movies is the way in which the people and places and events of the narrative are translated into a sequence of visual images. This is a matter of cinematography and editing, and these areas have been the main focus of writings on illusionism. The notion that Hollywood techniques of cinematography and editing are characterized by the concealment of artifice is a standard premise in this literature and is encapsulated in the widely used term "invisible style." The precise sense in which this style is thought to be invisible varies somewhat from writer to writer, but the basic argument is usually that the style's unobtrusiveness stems from its subordination to the demands of the narrative. When camera work and editing are confined to following the action—as opposed to commenting on it or to acting independently of it— the viewer is encouraged to lose sight of the means of representation and become absorbed exclusively in the represented act itself.

A clear statement of this position is contained in André Bazin's well-known discussion of the evolution of cinema language. Bazin argues that it was this tendency to subordinate form to narrative that resulted in the almost complete disappearance in the 1930s of a device that had been quite popular during the previous decade: the use of editing for purposes of comparison or commentary. He claims that audiences were shocked when Fritz Lang used this device as late as 1935 in *Fury* in a series of shots juxtaposing cancan dancers with clucking chickens in a farmyard. He also argues that similar tendencies were responsible for the eclipse of such optical effects as superimpositions, and he suggests that even the close-up was being purged from U.S. movies (at the time when he was writing) because its "too violent impact . . . would make the audience conscious of the cutting" (Bazin, 1967, p. 32).

In addition to discussing the avoidance of devices such as these, which can be said to promote awareness of artifice, more recent writings on illusionism have examined the possibility that certain other devices whose popularity has, if anything, increased since Bazin's time might actually inhibit this awareness. One device that has been discussed in these terms is the shot/reverse-shot principle of shooting and editing. According to Jean-Pierre Oudart, the off-screen look, which is the linking element in shot/reverse-shot sequences, would be anti-illusionistic if it occurred by itself, without the complement of "matching" looks. Oudart's reasoning is that this single off-screen look would lead the viewer to become aware of the space outside the frame, a space that was occupied, during the making of the movie, by director, cameraperson, and crew. Awareness of this space is averted, however, when the off-screen look is provided with a fictional target—i.e., the fictional space from which the matching look is emanating. This putative effect Oudart refers to as "suture" (Oudart, 1990; see also Dayan, 1976; Rothman, 1976; and Silverman, 1983, ch. 5). A somewhat similar argument can be made about shots in which screen characters are shown looking directly into the camera. It is commonly assumed that such shots have the potential of reminding the audience members of their position as spectators. But, the argument goes, this potential is neutralized when such shots are ascribed to the subjective point of view of a fictional character "inside" the film itself.

Although some of these assumptions are not backed by any empirical evidence, the general tendency they ascribe to commercial movies—namely, the attempt to make sure that shot selection and editing appear to be "motivated" by the narrative—is observable not only in the movies themselves but also in filmmakers' accounts of the thinking that went into various formal choices. Two examples: Some time after the staircase murder in *Psycho* (the scene discussed earlier in this chapter), there is another scene in which Hitchcock wanted to use an overhead shot to conceal the killer's identity. But, as he told François Truffaut, he was concerned that if he simply cut to this shot from a more normal angle, the audience would notice the cut and become suspicious. His solution was to have the camera begin to rise earlier in the scene, while a character was walking up the stairs. This, Hitchcock argued, would give it a reason for being in the overhead position later (Truffaut, 1967, p. 208). In this instance "motivation" of a particular camera angle by the action also happened to disguise its true purpose.

More typically, however, the purpose of such motivation, from the point of view of the filmmaker, is to avoid obtrusiveness or the appearance of formalism. This view is expressed very clearly by Ralph Rosenblum, a prominent film editor, in the following statement: "Regardless of its extent or style, editing should not impress or call attention to itself. As an audience, we no more want to see the wheels and gears and levers responsible for the effect the film is having on us than we want to see the pencil marks on an author's first draft or the invisible wires in a magic show" (Rosenblum and Karen, 1979, p. 296). The application of this principle is illustrated in Rosenblum's description of why he wanted close-ups instead of a single long-shot in a certain scene from the film *Bad Company* (1972). Whereas the film's director is quoted by Rosenblum as arguing for the preservation of the "purity of the camera move," Rosenblum himself insists that what matters to the audience is clarity of the situation and contact with the action (p. 238).

If the subordination of editing to narrative serves the illusionistic tendencies of mainstream commercial movies, the refusal to edit in this way should promote awareness of artifice. Our brief review of "invisible editing" has suggested several possible ways in which a movie might draw attention to its own artificiality: injection of "similes" (e.g., Fritz Lang's chickens) into the narrative; shots in which characters look directly out at the camera/viewer; unmotivated camera angles; and so forth. Devices of this sort have often found a place in film or video work aimed at subverting the Hollywood code (e.g., in some of the films of Godard and of other members of the French New Wave). In such contexts, the use of these devices is often accompanied by the Brechtian assumption that awareness of artifice at the formal level also leads to awareness of ideology (see Elsaesser, 1990). However, this additional assumption is clearly not a necessary corollary of the notion that certain kinds of formal devices call attention to themselves.

Some indication of how audience members do in fact respond to these distancing devices is provided by the study mentioned earlier of viewers' interpretations of a short experimental film (Messaris, 1981). The film used in this study consisted of two sections, each of them characterized by a distinct style of shooting and editing. The first section was made according to the basic principles of the Hollywood style, in the sense that it did not contain any obtrusive formal devices. The second section, conversely, contained several such devices, including jump cuts, visual similes, and shots in which a character looks directly into the camera without any narrative motivation. The general procedure used in this study was to have viewers describe the film as a whole and then give their interpretations of a number of specific incidents. For present purposes, it is these more specific interpretations that constitute the relevant findings.

The major question in the analysis of the viewers' statements was whether their interpretations contained any reference to the intentions of the people who had made the film. We have already seen some examples of viewers' responses to the Hollywood-style section of this film. Now we will look at two sets of responses to the film's anti-illusionistic devices. One such device (discussed briefly in Chapter 4) involved the following juxtaposition: A woman is shown walking up to the entrance of a clothing store and going through the door; as she disappears inside, there is a direct cut to the interior of a church, and the woman is seen entering. This juxtaposition can be seen as a violation of Hollywood naturalism both by virtue of the direct transition between two nonadjacent locations and by virtue of what some viewers described as an overly obtrusive simile. As one viewer put it: "At that point I thought there was a . . . over-obvious . . . metaphor of fashionable store—church, you know, I thought kind of unsubtle" (pauses in original).

Nevertheless, despite this "over-obviousness," a substantial proportion of the viewers in this study (39 percent, to be exact) gave no indication of having taken this transition as anything other than a routine shift in narrative space and time. This type of response is illustrated in the following excerpt from one of the interviews:

> Oh, I'd forgotten entirely about the church. She walked in a side entrance, and . . . I think that may be the church down on Seventeenth Street, down in that neighborhood, but not the one on Rittenhouse Square.
> *Interviewer:* Why did you think it was there?
> *Respondent:* Because . . . it's the closest to Bonwit's, and I assume she was walking. She could have taken taxis in between, but if she was walking she could easily have walked.
> *Interviewer:* Well, why was the closest to Bonwit's . . . ?
> *Respondent:* Well, because I was down there myself one day and ended up in the church, too, went from the store to the church.

This exchange is an extreme instance of the use of personal experience as a point of reference in interpreting the scene in question. However, in its view of the film as a window onto an independent reality (in which there can be a question as to what means of transportation the protagonist took to get from one place to another), this response is not atypical of the answers of those viewers for whom the store/church transition was evidently not obtrusive enough to deflect them from an assumption of naturalistic narration.

A second set of interview excerpts will illustrate these issues with reference to another of the film's "obtrusive" devices, a lengthy close-up of the protagonist looking directly into the camera. Several viewers responded to this shot by questioning its place in the narrative and the intentions of the filmmaker. For instance, one viewer said that he "thought the camera was being used and . . . I didn't know what the intent was there if there was any." Another said that this shot "didn't really *say* anything about her face, there seemed to be no *reason* to keep the camera on her face that long. It just seemed kind of like a . . . some kind of *device*, some kind of *arty device*." Nevertheless, there were also several viewers who discussed this shot solely in terms of its relevance to the narrative, as in the following two instances: "I was trying to fantasize what she was thinking about . . . was she thinking about jumping off the bridge or was she just watching the water and wondering who she was." "Looking at her expression on her face, she didn't seem to be there just to enjoy the fresh air or anything, but, rather, she looked a little grim, and . . . looking at the river, and . . . she wasn't in a joyous mood, let's put it this way."

In general, the findings of this study indicate that there was a considerable difference between the two sections of the film in the extent to which viewers' interpretations contained any acknowledgment of intentionality. The overall frequency of interpretations falling into this category for the first section of the film (averaged over all the viewers and all the incidents covered by the interviews) was 22 percent. The corresponding figure for the second section of the film was 39 percent. These findings support the assumption that the invisible style of Hollywood cinema is indeed invisible—or, at any rate, more invisible than a style containing deliberate violations of the Hollywood canon.

With regard to visual literacy, there is also another interesting result in these findings. One of the purposes of this study was to compare the responses of "ordinary" viewers with those of "trained" viewers. In the terms of the study, ordinary viewers were simply people with no special experience in film, whereas trained viewers were people who did have such experience, either through film-study courses or through actual production experience. It was primarily the trained viewers with production experience who were responsible for the substantial jump in awareness of intentionality between the first section of the film and the second. Among these viewers, the share of interpretations indicating such awareness went from 27 percent in the first section of the film to 60 percent in the second, whereas the corresponding figures are 15 percent and 28 percent for the ordinary viewers and 24 percent and 29 percent for trained viewers with film-study experience. In short, there is evidence here that experience does indeed lead to greater awareness of the authorial presence behind the scenes—but mainly when this presence is intentionally obtrusive to begin with.

Visual Manipulation

Awareness of authorial presence is a basic component of the kind of visual literacy with which this chapter is concerned. The preceding discussion has dealt with detecting and attending to artifice in cases in which its presence is not obvious. Beyond detection and attention lie the analysis and evaluation of purpose. The viewer who has discerned misrepresentation in the editing of a news program or a documentary will also want to know what purpose might have been served if the intended impression had come across. The viewer who notices camera angles or points of view in a fiction film will also be concerned about their intended effect.

As suggested by the first example discussed in this chapter, the elevator-murder shot from *Dressed to Kill,* the competent analysis of purpose will require some familiarity with the ways in which visuals can be used to persuade, to (mis)inform, or to elicit an emotional response. Because new ways of using visuals for these purposes are constantly being devised, it would be inconceivable in principle to try to give a full list of techniques of visual manipulation (cf. Whittock, 1990). However, it is possible to give an outline of some of the major principles from which these techniques are derived. Three such principles, in particular, deserve special notice: the use of camera positioning to manipulate viewers' involvement with on-screen characters; the use of editing to manipulate contextual meaning; and the use of temporal or spatial juxtapositions to create mental associations. Aside from having wide ranges of applications, all three of these principles are particularly interesting in terms of their artistic and ideological implications.

Camera Positioning

An excellent illustration of the potential uses of camera positioning as a means of manipulating a viewer's involvement with on-screen characters occurs in a scene from Hitchcock's *North by Northwest* (1959). In this scene, the hero discovers that the villains intend to kill the heroine, and he tries to warn her without attracting their attention. The scene takes place in a house with a first-floor living room and a second-floor balcony that looks down on that living room. The heroine and the villains are in the living room. The hero is hiding on the balcony. He writes her a note in a monogrammed matchbook that he and she have joked about earlier in the film, and when no one is looking he tosses the matchbook down to her. It lands on the floor. She doesn't notice it. A moment later, one of the villains does. Without looking at it too closely, he picks it up, plays with it idly for a second or two, then puts it down on a coffee table in front of her. And now comes the part which illustrates the principle we are concerned with.

In discussing what happens next, it will be useful to look at the script for *North by Northwest* before we consider what actually takes place in the film itself. In the script, the woman finally notices the matchbook in the course of a shot described as "Low Angle—In Living Room." There is a transition to a close-up of her face. At first she is puzzled. Then she begins to realize what is happening, and she picks the matchbook up and opens it. At that point, the script's instructions about how her reaction should be filmed read as follows: "We are VERY CLOSE as she opens the [match] folder and reads Thornhill's message." (Lehman, 1959, p. 132). The script does not give a reason for this tight close-up, but it is easy to guess what that reason might have been: This is a moment of great tension in the narrative, the heroine's face will be registering—or attempting to conceal—powerful emotions, and a move to a tight close-up could therefore be seen as being in parallel with a rise in dramatic interest. Nine out of ten directors would undoubtedly have filmed the scene exactly as specified. But this is not how Hitchcock filmed it.

In the actual film, we not only do *not* get a close-up but we also are denied any clear view at all of the woman's face. Instead, she is filmed from behind, from a high angle, and from a considerable distance (see Figure 5.4)—in fact, from the point of view of the hero, who is surreptitiously witnessing the scene from the balcony behind her. Neither before she opens the matchbook nor after does the camera leave the balcony to go down to her level. In other words, there is a sharp contrast between the script's conception of this scene and the conception that went into the film itself. To anybody who is familiar with the methods of Hitchcock's films, the reasoning

Figure 5.4 Camera position as a means of manipulating viewer involvement.
Source: North by Northwest (directed by Alfred Hitchcock, MGM, 1959).

behind his unorthodox handling of this particular scene will not be a mystery: Rather than having his viewers participate in the sudden shock of the heroine's discovery, he preferred to subject them to the mounting suspense experienced by the hero.

In other words, this is a case in which a major change in the potential impact of a scene is associated with the revision of a set of purely visual devices (the action remains the same in both cases). All of these devices have to do with the positioning of the camera in relation to the characters in the scene. If we make the uncontroversial assumption that Hitchcock knew what he was doing, the use of these devices in this instance is a particularly clear illustration of the extent to which viewers' responses to fictional characters can be manipulated through visual means. Camera positioning can be analyzed in terms of three major variables—viz., distance, point of view, and angle—all of which are brought into play in the scene we have just examined.

As this example has indicated, both distance and point of view can be used to channel the viewer's involvement with the characters in a scene. In this particular case, the implications of the use of these variables were primarily artistic. (Of course, it could also be argued that this was one more example of Hollywood's tendency to adopt the male perspective.) In general, these two variables, particularly distance, are often used to reinforce the viewer's sympathy or identification with the protagonist(s) over the entire course of a fiction film. Certain directors, such as Hitchcock or De Palma, are quite rigorous about this principle. For example, in the scene we have been discussing, there are only two places in which Hitchcock uses either close-ups or point-of-view shots for anyone other than the hero or heroine. One of these exceptions has a purely informational purpose: A minor character spots the hero, who has been hiding, and a shot from her point of view makes this fact clear to the audience. The other exception occurs when one of the villains punches the other, and here a flurry of close-ups and subjective shots serves to inject the audience into the action.

Exceptions such as these, for informational purposes or for emphasis, are typically brief, and it seems unlikely that they would have any lasting influence on the audience's alignment with the characters in a feature-length movie. However, there are certain cases in which the departure from the perspective of the "good guys" is longer and more systematic, and in such cases the moral or ideological implications of the visuals can become particularly acute. One example of this kind of situation was illustrated at the beginning of this chapter in our discussion of the use of subjective shots to conceal the identity of the villain. This device, which is a staple of slasher movies, has often been criticized for encouraging identification with perpetrators of violence against women. Another common situation in which movies frequently adopt a morally troublesome perspective is the "suspenseful-burglary" scene. Here, of course, the burglar is often likely to be the protagonist of the whole movie, too, in which case the moral questions extend beyond the mere use of visuals.

In addition to serving the dramatic functions that motivate their use in fiction films, distance and point of view are also very commonly used as part of the persuasive apparatus in commercials. A study by Gable (1983) identified several interesting strategies, two of which are quite obvious and straightforward. In both cases, subjective point-of-view shots are the central element. In one case, they are used to put the audience in the position of the receiver of a persuasive message. In the other case, it is the perspective of the sender that is adopted.

The relative effectiveness of these techniques has been explored in an experiment by Galan (1986), in which the same action—a person eating a new brand of potato chips touts their virtues to a friend—was videotaped in three different ways: an "objective" version, showing both participants at all times; a "subjective-passive" version, in which the predominant point of view is that of the receiver of the message; and a "subjective-active" version, in which the persuader's point of view predominates. Galan hypothesized that the subjective versions would be more involving and therefore more persuasive, and she also hypothesized that the subjective-active version, which encourages vicarious participation with the act of praising the product, would be the most persuasive of the three. Her findings provided clear support for the first hypothesis and some weak support for the second. Furthermore—and this is the more important point for our purposes—Galan found that her subjects, who were all college students, were generally unaware that point of view was being used as a persuasive technique in the two subjective versions of the commercial.

The ordinary viewer's lack of attention to camera positioning is also attested to by research on camera angle. As a means of influencing viewers' responses to on-screen characters, the use of this variable has traditionally followed the well-known hypothesis that low camera angles, in which the camera is looking at a character from below, make a character appear stronger, whereas high camera angles make a character appear weaker. (Strength and weakness can be literal or metaphorical, depending on the context.) This hypothesis is among the most widely shared assumptions about the workings of the visual media, and its application has become routine not only in purely fictional contexts but also in such areas as advertising and the broadcasting of political events. For example, several print journalists covering the congressional Iran-Contra hearings (e.g., *The New Yorker,* 1987, p. 19; Rickey, 1987; see also Tomasulo, 1989, p. 88) argued that Oliver North might have benefited as a result of the low angle from which he was televised (although in this case any such effect was presumably inadvertent).

The general hypothesis about the effects of camera angles has been tested in several studies, of which the most relevant for our purposes is an experiment by Mandell and Shaw (1973) on the relationship between camera angle and viewers' ratings of a character in a news program. In this study, viewers were shown one of three versions of a fake news item inserted in a longer newscast comprising material actually used by a local station. The experimental news item, read by the station's actual newscaster, was about a (nonexistent) political appointee, who was shown from one of three angles: head-on, low (about twelve degrees below eye-level), and high (about twelve degrees above eye-level).

As expected, the lower the angle used, the higher the viewers' ratings of the "potency" of the "political appointee." Moreover—and, as with the Galan study, more crucial to this discussion—most viewers appeared to be unaware of the presence of this manipulation. The method Mandell and Shaw used to get at this issue was simply to ask viewers, at the conclusion of the study, "Do you have any comments about the camera angles used to photograph the people in the news stories?" Only thirteen viewers out of a total of seventy-eight who saw either the low- or high-angle version of the newscast indicated any awareness of the use of camera angle—this despite the fact that all the viewers were college students with at least one course in a department of radio, television, and motion pictures.

In general, then, notions about the influence of camera position on viewers' responses to on-screen characters have some empirical support, and there is also support for the idea that this influence operates out of viewers' awareness. The manipulation of viewers' responses through editing has not been studied as systematically as has camera position, at least in recent years, but here, too, there is some suggestive evidence. As indicated earlier, this aspect of editing will be examined with regard to two related topics: the manipulation of context within a single narrative location and time-frame, and the creation of mental associations through nonnarrative juxtapositions. Both topics were touched upon in Chapter 3, but here the emphasis will be on aesthetic or ideological consequences, rather than on intelligibility.

Narrative Editing

With regard to narrative editing, it was already noted, one of the tasks of the "literate" viewer is to beware of cases in which film or videotape of a real event (e.g., a political speech or an interview with a public figure) is reassembled in such a way as to give a false picture of the event (e.g., applause that didn't really occur or a question which wasn't really asked at a particular point in the event). However, even when falsification in this sense is not an issue (as, for example, in an openly fictional situation), the influence of context on interpretation is still a given, and the viewer who is interested in the relationship between meaning and intentions must still be concerned with the ways meaning has been shaped by editing.

In the case of reality-based films or TV programs, therefore, the viewer must be alert to the possibility of misleading editing even when it is clear that the real-life sequence and spatial ordering of the events are being observed. An example of this possibility is discussed in a study by Messaris, Eckman, and Gumpert (1979). This study involved an analysis of the pattern of shot selection in the broadcasts of the presidential debates of 1976. As anyone who has watched a televised political debate knows, it is a common practice in these programs to punctuate a candidate's remarks with brief shots of his or her opponents. The ostensible purpose of these shots is to indicate the opponent's response, and, indeed, they are typically referred to as "reaction shots."

However, when these shots in the 1976 debates were analyzed, it was not always clear that the candidate appearing in a reaction shot had actually "reacted" in any visible way. In several instances, for example, the camera would catch a candidate in the middle of making notes for his own subsequent remarks, his facial expression giving no indication that the notes were occasioned by anything the speaker had just said. A viewer who assumed that such shots were indeed indicative of a reaction, then, would be responding to context more than to content. There is some suggestion that this kind of response played a considerable role in the TV audience's overall perceptions of the three debates: The second debate, which contained twice as many reaction shots as the other two, was also judged the most confrontational—even though direct confrontation between Jimmy Carter and Gerald Ford occurred only in the third debate. In short, this is a case in which editing may have created a somewhat misleading impression without in any way departing from the sequence of events that actually occurred in the real-life sites in which the debates were held.

When this kind of editing is applied to fictional material, misrepresentation is of course no longer an issue, in the sense that there is now no real version of the events to which the editing is being applied. However, the possibility that a viewer may misattribute meaning to a performer rather than to the editing is clearly present in fictional situations, too. The classic illustrations of this aspect of editing, Lev Kuleshov's experiments from the early days of Soviet cinema, have been mentioned in Chapter 3. Aside from demonstrating how context affects interpretation, these experiments also suggest that with Kuleshov-style editing, too, viewers are not ordinarily aware of the visual devices responsible for their interpretations. This conclusion is implicit in the finding that the subjects in these experiments assumed they were viewing *actual,* rather than merely apparent, changes in actors' expressions as the context changed.

The artistic implications of the Kuleshov effect are illustrated very nicely in a story told by Edward Dmytryk, a major Hollywood director. Early in his career, Dmytryk worked as an editor on Leo McCarey's *Ruggles of Red Gap* (1935). In one of the scenes of this film, the star, Charles Laughton, had to recite the Gettysburg Address to a roomful of people. Unfortunately, a combination of nervousness and overacting kept marring his performance, and despite the fact that the scene was repeated about forty or fifty times, none of the takes was considered satisfactory. Convinced that the scene as originally planned would never work, Dmytryk put together a different version, in which most of the visual emphasis was on the faces of the people listening to Laughton rather than on Laughton himself. Both this version and one more closely conforming to the original conception—i.e., with more shots of Laughton himself in it—were then tested in previews, and the results were quite striking: Whereas the version emphasizing Laughton's actual performance drew deafening laughter from the audience, Dmytryk's "indirect" version won enthusiastic praise. The praise, however, was not for the editing; it was for Laughton, who, as a result of this film, would often be asked to deliver the Gettysburg Address during celebrations of Lincoln's birthday (Dmytryk, 1984, pp. 131–133).

Nonnarrative Juxtaposition of Images

The kind of editing illustrated in the example we have just looked at and in the presidential debates occurs as part of an overall narrative flow, which it does not disrupt. Consequently, it is not surprising to find that viewers do not ordinarily seem to be aware of the effects we have just examined. The kind of editing we will be considering next, however, is, on the face of it, more obtrusive, because it involves the juxtaposition of images with little or no narrative relationship to one another. Still, this kind of editing does have certain characteristics that may serve to dull awareness of its functioning. These possibilities will be discussed in connection with a specific example: a political advertisement used in the 1983 campaign for the office of mayor of Chicago. Speaking of this advertisement, political-campaign analyst Kathleen Hall Jamieson has said, "There is not a more powerful instance of 'reframing' [i.e., recontextualizing an opponent's attack] that I know of in the modern history of televised campaigning" (Jamieson, 1992a, p. 40).

The major-party candidates in this campaign were Bernard Epton, a Republican, and Harold Washington, a Democrat (the eventual winner). As described by one of Epton's campaign managers, the strategy of the Epton campaign was to make an issue of Washington's character on the grounds that he allegedly had had a number of legal and financial problems earlier in his career (Diamond and Bates, 1984, p. 361). However, Epton's ads used a tag line that could also be read as having other implications. The tag line was, "Epton for Mayor, before it's too late," and the reason it could be taken as more than just a personal attack was that a victory for Harold Washington would make him Chicago's first African-American mayor.

As a response to the presence of a racial issue in the contest, the Washington campaign ran the ad that concerns us here. This ad is a montage of fourteen different images, accompanied by a voiceover statement on the soundtrack. The first ten images, all of them still photographs, are as follows:

- a Ku Klux Klan gathering;
- John F. Kennedy, moments before his assassination;
- the Kennedy assassination;
- another view of the same;
- civil rights marchers attacked by police dogs;
- a U.S. soldier wounded in Vietnam;
- Dr. Martin Luther King, Jr., speaking from Memphis balcony;
- immediately following King assassination, companions pointing at gunman;
- victim of Kent State shootings;
- police clubbing a demonstrator at the 1968 Chicago Democratic convention.

This sequence is followed by a shot that begins as a freeze-frame and then "unfreezes." We see a white man pointing off-screen and shouting. Behind him is a crowd of other whites, some of them carrying Epton plackards (although these are barely visible). This image and the next two, which are also "live-action" shots, are accompanied by the sounds of the crowd (presumably recorded in sync with the images), but the audio quality is unclear; beyond the suggestion that people are chanting "Epton, Epton," it is impossible to make out what anybody is saying. The shot of the white crowd is followed by a shot of Harold Washington, who appears, by virtue of this juxtaposition, to be the object of whatever it is the white man in the previous shot is yelling; then there is a shot of another white man, shouting angrily (but indistinctly) and making a thumbs-down gesture, presumably, again, at Washington. This images freezes, and it is followed by the final image in the sequence, a photograph of Washington accompanied by the words, "Vote for Harold Washington."

The inference the viewer is expected to draw from these images is reinforced by a brief voiceover commentary that says that there have been some shameful moments in U.S. history and urges viewers to avoid repeating that history in the impending election. The effect is certainly overwhelming. I still remember the feeling of distress and revulsion that I experienced the first time I saw this ad's final group of images: a black man being vilified by an abusive white crowd. It was only after I had examined these images a few more times that I realized that perhaps I was seeing—and hearing—some things that were not actually there.

One of the things that cannot be determined upon repeated inspection of the ad is where exactly the white crowd was in relation to Harold Washington, as they do not appear together in the same shot (even though the real-life event from which these images were drawn was in fact a direct encounter between the protesters and Washington). But this is a kind of question we have already examined. The more interesting question for present purposes has to do with what the people in the crowd are shouting. When I first saw the ad, I had a powerful impression of having heard racist epithets and direct attacks on Washington, although I don't think I could have said, even then, exactly what those words were. Now, however, having gone over the ad's soundtrack any number of times, I think I can say conclusively that whatever it was I thought I had heard was a product of my own imagination. As I have already pointed out, the only words that can be made out at all in the sound accompanying the crowd shots are "Epton, Epton," and even that is not entirely clear. This does not mean, of course, that racial slurs were not shouted in the real-life event from which this ad was drawn. But whatever was said was not captured in the ad's soundtrack.

Perhaps I am making too much of my own reaction to this ad. I certainly do not want to suggest that my specific response—hearing racist abuse—should be expected of other viewers or was intended by the ad's producers. (However, see Grimes, 1990, for an interesting discussion of similar "misinterpretations" of TV programs.) But even if I did overreact and even if my reaction was idiosyncratic in this specific respect, I think it is fair to say that this reaction was in line with the more general goal of the ad's visual structure.

This ad is a good example of propositional editing, as discussed in Chapter 3. In particular, there are two major conceptual connections the viewer is expected to make among the images. First, the incidents depicted in the opening series of still photographs are to be linked together as instances of shameful moments in U.S. history. Second, the behavior of Harold Washington's opponents is to be taken as one further instance of such a moment. The research described at the conclusion of Chapter 3 suggests that viewers' awareness of the intended meaning of propositional editing cannot always be taken for granted. In this case, however, comprehension itself does not seem to me to be a primary issue (especially because the ad's message was also expressed more explicitly in the voice-over commentary). In fact, in a sense I think we could say that this is an instance in which the effectiveness of the ad may actually depend on a certain degree of *lack* of comprehension.

As I pointed out at the conclusion of Chapter 3, it may be possible for the conceptual connections put forth in advertising by means of propositional editing to do their work despite a viewer's lack of an articulable comprehension of the message. Repeated exposure to the combination of images in an ad may lead a viewer to form an unconscious mental association between the two without thinking explicitly about the nature of that association.

This kind of response to advertising is especially likely to be the aim when the implication of an ad's visuals might meet with resistance if viewers thought about it more consciously. For example, we can probably take it for granted that print ads for cigarettes are *not* courting an explicit awareness of the message when an image of the product is juxtaposed with scenes of unspoiled nature (implying that cigarettes do not contain harmful substances?), scenes of vigorous outdoor activity (implying that cigarettes do not cause ill health?), or scenes of friendly socializing (implying that cigarette smoke is not offensive to nonsmokers?). Of course, this is not to say that when an ad's message is intended to hold up to reasoned scrutiny, the unreflective response necessarily becomes irrelevant to its design. A print ad for a health product may contain extensive written documentation of its benefits and, at the same time, juxtapose an image of the product with a picture of a star athlete.

As far as the Washington ad is concerned, it seems to me that we are dealing with an unusual combination of circumstances. On the one hand, I would argue, this is a type of ad whose message should in principle be more effective the more explicitly it is stated. On the other hand, because of the uncertain spatial relationships and the indistinct soundtrack in the last set of images, I am not sure that a fully reflective viewing of the ad would lead to the intended effect. I wonder, for example, if my own reaction to these final images would have been as powerful if I had looked at them from the beginning as closely as I did later on.

We have here a situation, then, in which a relatively unreflective response might be more appropriate to the purposes of the ad but in which the standard means of securing such a response—viz., repeated exposure—might actually be counterproductive. Under the circumstances, the use of the initial series of ten images to set a pattern and "prime" the viewer seems a particularly apt strategy on the part of the ad's producers. Judging from my own response as well as the assessment by Jamieson cited earlier, it appears that this kind of strategy may indeed have the intended effect.

*   *   *

As with several of the other examples and situations discussed, then, the present case suggests that the kind of visual literacy with which this chapter has been concerned does not come naturally to most people. Whereas the ability to recognize the objects in an image, to make sense of a movie's space and time transitions, and to grasp the point of nonnarrative editing—as practiced on TV, at least—is something the typical viewer appears to acquire quite readily, the viewing skills required for the perception of intentionality appear to rest on exceptional experience or on explicit training.

As we have seen, an adequate response to intentionality may involve the detection of concealed staging; the detection of misrepresentation in cases in which images of real events have been rearranged through editing; attention to the purposes behind "invisible" editing; and awareness of the mechanisms of visual manipulation. Some of the skills these aspects of interpretation draw upon—for example, the ability to distinguish a fictional performance from real behavior—may not require any specific experience with visual media. For the most part, however, the ability to make these kinds of interpretations requires an explicit understanding, rather than merely a tacit grasp, of principles of visual composition and juxtaposition. Simply being able to infer the implied meaning is not enough here; the viewer must have a sense of how that meaning was produced. As the cases we have discussed have indicated, this sense is not a reliable by-product of viewing experience. In fact, much of what viewers see in the visual media actively discourages the development of this sense. We are therefore led to the conclusion that acquiring the kind of visual literacy this chapter has been concerned with may indeed be the challenge many advocates assume it to be.

6

Conclusion: Other Questions, Other "Literacies"

The argument I have developed in this book is summarized in Chapter 1. However, for those readers who may prefer a shorter overview, here is a capsule recapitulation of the main points:

1. What distinguishes images (including motion pictures) from language and from other modes of communication is the fact that images reproduce many of the informational cues that people make use of in their perception of physical and social reality. Our ability to infer what is represented in an image is based largely on this property, rather than on familiarity with arbitrary conventions (whereas the latter play a primary role in the interpretation of language, mathematics, and so on).

2. It follows from the above that visual literacy is unlikely to lead to any broader cognitive advantages analogous to those that result from learning a language. Because images *reproduce* aspects of our direct, unmediated experience rather than encoding it arbitrarily, familiarity with images does not entail the acquisition of a system of conceptual categories or of a set of analytical operators for ordering those categories. With regard to the one kind of cognitive advantage that might be expected to accrue most straightforwardly from visual literacy—viz., "spatial intelligence"—the empirical evidence is equivocal.

3. Although learning about visual conventions may not be a prerequisite for their interpretation or an avenue to enhanced cognitive functioning, such learning undoubtedly has significant consequences in two other areas: First, it gives the viewer a foundation for a heightened conscious appreciation of artistry; second, it is a prerequisite for the ability to see through the manipulative uses and ideological implications of visual images. Both of these consequences of visual literacy stem directly from the premise that the conventions of pictorial representation typically replicate real-world

165

informational cues and are therefore especially likely to operate outside of the average viewer's awareness.

Of the three points outlined above, this last one is the least likely to come as any news to readers familiar with scholarly arguments about the value of visual literacy. Indeed, the notion that visual literacy leads to critical viewing is typically the central feature of such arguments. With regard to this specific notion, therefore, the intent of this book has not been to advance a novel position but rather to spell out the details of *how* visual literacy might enhance critical viewing. Discussions of this subject often fail to give a systematic, concrete account of these connections. It is hoped that Chapter 5 will help to fill this gap in the literature.

Unlike the argument that visual literacy begets critical viewing, the other major positions taken in this book and outlined above are probably contrary to the views of a substantial number of people with a scholarly interest in matters relating to visual literacy. The notion that pictures may replicate the visual information that we get from the real world; that an inexperienced viewer might be able to make sense of her or his first encounter with pictorial information; that images do not play as significant a role as does language in the shaping of cognition—all these arguments go against a number of related views on visual literacy that tend to be held fairly firmly by their adherents. Because I believe that the perception of a contradiction is often mistaken and because, in any case, the views that are supposedly being contradicted deserve serious consideration, I would like to address this matter directly and in some detail.

Images and the Appearance of Reality

There may seem to be an irreconcilable difference between prevailing scholarly views and the arguments advanced in this book on the relationship between visual images and the appearance of the real world. Many writers have expended considerable energy in making the point that pictures are not replicas of reality and that photographic images in particular should not be thought of as objective records of the figures and events represented in them (see Snyder, 1980, for an unusually thorough exposition of such arguments; see also Roskill and Carrier, 1983). In a sense, therefore, this position's adherents may be said to have an "antirealist" conception of pictures, with an emphasis on the differences between pictures and the real-life appearance of objects and events. This position would seem to clash with a major premise of this book—namely, that we make sense of pictures largely on the basis of their reproduction of real-world informational cues. But the contradiction between these two views is—or should be—only a matter of relative emphasis, and the gap between them will appear unbridgeable only to someone whose thinking is confined to "either/or" terms.

The reason for the considerable emphasis on an antirealist view in scholarly writing on images has most likely been a perceived need to combat the "naive realism" that is often thought to be characteristic of the views of the general public. A typical expression of this assumption about ordinary people's attitudes toward photography, for example, is Lewis Hine's assertion that "the average person believes implicitly that the camera cannot falsify" (Hine, 1980, p. 111; see discussion in Stange, 1989, p. 86). This notion, coming from a photographer working in the early decades of this century, has been echoed through the years by such writers as Freund (1980) and Ritchin (1990), and similar concerns have been voiced about viewers' responses to other visual media (Caughey, 1984; Gumpert, 1977; Mitroff and Bennis, 1989; Stonehill, 1990). A prominent example of writing that seems motivated by a desire to combat such faith in images is Stuart Ewen's description of the various forms of visual artifice that go into the creation of the glamor industry's images of women and men (Ewen, 1988, pp. 87–89). If it is true that the broad public is unaware of the ways photographs can be manipulated, "exposés" of this sort may indeed serve a useful function.

Nevertheless, it is unclear to me that any of the revelations to which such writing typically gives rise truly contradict the principle that the interpretation of pictures is based on the same kinds of informational cues that viewers employ in making sense of real-world vision. The technique of airbrushing, which is one of Ewen's main concerns, illustrates this point quite clearly. One of the principal functions of airbrushing is to add shadow in order to enhance the apparent protuberance of various body parts. Most frequently, this takes the form of breast enlargement via darkened cleavage, but cheekbones, buttocks, and other areas can obviously be served in the same way. All this is clearly artificial, yet it just as clearly derives its effect from an analogy to the informational value of shadow in real-world vision.

More generally, even a cursory examination of the forms of visual artifice or manipulation that writings on this issue typically draw attention to should make it apparent, if it is not already self-evident, that an image can give a fake or misleading picture of reality yet remain faithful to the principles by which reality is apprehended. This point is manifestly true of all forms of image alteration designed to evade detection, from the retouching of a photograph to make someone look younger to the grafting of the head of one person onto the body of another to the politically motivated eradication of certain people from group portraits (see Jaubert, 1989, and Rockwell, 1989; see also Bossen, 1985, Lasica, 1989, and Reaves, 1989). It is also true of staged images intended to pass for real (such as the "recreated" Afghanistani war footage shown in a network news program) or images that have been cropped, edited, or selectively framed in such a way as to omit information contradicting the intended message. (This routine and, in cer-

tain respects, inevitable practice in news photography was analyzed most re-
vealingly in Lang and Lang's [1971] classic study of the selective emphasis
on footage of enthusiastic crowds during the televising of a parade in honor
of Gen. Douglas MacArthur.)

Indeed, it could be argued that in all such instances, successful visual
fakery or misrepresentation is crucially dependent on the capacity of an image to reproduce interpretational cues that viewers use in making sense of
unmediated reality. Whether this final point is true or not, I trust that it
should be evident by now that there is no necessary contradiction between
anything I have said in this book and the arguments of writers attempting to
dispel the "naive" view of images, especially photographic images, as faithful
copies of reality.

Images and Cultures

The second major area of apparent contradiction between the positions
taken in this book and certain widely held views on images is that of cross-
cultural differences in visual communication. The claim that many aspects of
images can be understood readily by first-time viewers is sometimes seen as
an attack on the principle that perception is shaped and therefore con-
strained by culture. The argument that images are capable of reproducing
real-world informational cues implies that cultures may vary in the degree of
realism of their images—a position sometimes taken as an assault on the
principle of cultural relativity in criteria of realism.

Emphasis on differences among cultures is currently very strong in academic thinking in the United States. In consequence, what might be called
the "anticulturalist" element in the ideas described in this book has occasionally been received with some hostility by colleagues and graduate students. Not wishing to appear iconoclastic unnecessarily, I will try to give a
precise account of the extent to which this book's premises do indeed clash
with the prevailing emphasis on cross-cultural difference, but I will also
point out certain aspects of the matter with regard to which any appearance
of a contradiction is illusory.

To begin with, it seems to me an obviously unassailable principle that
cultural differences do erect some barriers to the cross-cultural understanding of images. The crucial question is: What *kinds* of barriers? The
depiction of culture-specific objects or practices is one obvious source of
potential difficulty in cross-cultural communication through images, but,
conceptually, it does not seem—to me, at least—particularly interesting. For
example, there can be little doubt that people who have spent all of their
lives in a small rural community will encounter many unfamiliar actions and
situations in a movie about life in a big city, and vice versa. But does such an
observation tell us anything significant (nonobvious) about the nature of

cross-cultural visual communication or, indeed, of cultural differences in general?

Somewhat more interesting, perhaps, are cases in which objects or situations that may appear on the surface to be common to two different cultures are found in fact to have divergent connotations for the members of each. With regard to visual communication, instances of this sort are likely to be particularly significant when the source of "misunderstanding" is a specifically visual convention (as opposed to general cultural values). An example of this is described by Anne Dumas in a study of cultural differences in the interpretation of U.S. magazine advertising. Dumas interviewed a group of Chinese graduate students attending a university in the United States on their responses to a set of advertising images whose captions and product labels had been removed. The Chinese students' responses were compared with those of a group of U.S. natives studying in the same field at the same university.

One of the images, taken from an ad for a financial-services company, shows a man having a cup of tea on a balcony overlooking a big city. It is early morning, and the man's clothes and grooming suggest that he is a businessman. To a viewer who is familiar with the imagery of U.S. advertising, the situation should be familiar: a financially successful person with an upper-floor view of the city in which he has "made it." Variations of this image can be found in contemporary ads for such things as liquor, cosmetics, and VCRs, and the historical antecedents of this visual convention may well go back as far as the advertising of the 1920s (Marchand, 1985, pp. 238–247). However, to Dumas's Chinese respondents, who had only recently come to the United States, the connotations of wealth and power in the image of the man on the balcony were not at all apparent. Instead, many of them constructed hypothetical scenarios to account for the absence of family members in a scene of a man having breakfast (Dumas, 1988).

This example is a clear case of the shaping of pictorial interpretation by specifically visual past experience. Nonetheless, there is still an important distinction to be made between the kind of visual literacy exhibited by, or lacking in, Dumas's respondents and the visual skills that have thus far been the primary focus of this book. The kind of visual experience entailed in Dumas's example has to do with (1) exposure to specific visual *subject matter* (a person at a window overlooking a city) and (2) the *implicit connotations* of the image. By contrast, for the most part this book has been concerned with (1) exposure to the *structural principles* of still and moving images (e.g., contrasts in illumination; changes in camera positioning; eye-line matching) and (2) the *explicit* content of the image. As Dumas's example makes clear, there can be no question regarding the existence of significant cultural differences in the area of visual literacy she was concerned with, and because I have not dealt with this area in any detail thus far, I will take a closer look at it in a later section of this chapter. But what of my primary subject—visual literacy in the sense of structural or syntactic competence? Do my arguments about the cultural transparency of much of visual syntax mean that culture does not play a constraining role in this area of visual interpretation?

The answer to this question is complicated and depends, to a certain extent, on one's conception of culture. The theory developed in this book assumes as a starting point that many of the structural or "syntactic" rules that people use in making sense of their real-world visual environments (e.g., rules for isolating objects from their backgrounds, rules for perceiving depth) do not differ substantially from one culture to another. From this assumption it follows that, to the extent that images from one culture are capable of reproducing real-world visual syntax, their interpretation should not pose substantial problems to first-time viewers from another culture. I have offered theoretical arguments and cited empirical evidence in support of these latter possibilities, but I have not accounted explicitly for the validity of the initial assumption of cross-cultural uniformity in real-world perceptual principles. Despite the existence of considerable empirical support for the propositions I have based on this assumption, readers inclined to see differences rather than similarities between cultures may find this assumption itself questionable. Fortunately, this assumption, too, has been tested empirically; however, the research results in this area can be read rather differently depending on one's own prior inclinations.

The classic study of cross-cultural differences in visual perception was performed by Segall, Campbell, and Herskovits (1966), who investigated how people from a wide variety of cultural backgrounds responded to optical illusions. The study was based on the assumption that certain optical illusions will work only if the viewer unconsciously applies to the two-dimensional, illusion-producing design certain interpretational habits normally used in one's real, three-dimensional environment (for example, the tendency to interpret an inclined quadrilateral as being "in reality" a rectangle viewed obliquely). It was hypothesized that if visual perception is shaped by culture, then people from physical environments lacking the necessary visual stimuli (for example, a non-industrial society without rectangular structures, or a jungle-dwelling society cut off from long-distance views) should not be susceptible to the relevant optical illusions.

The results of this study did indeed uncover some cross-cultural differences in susceptibility to the illusions consistent with the overall hypothesis. However, those differences that did occur were primarily matters of degree rather than kind (i.e., susceptibility to the illusions at some level was virtually universal among the various cultures tested); furthermore, the differences were not large, despite the use of a highly refined measurement instrument.

Committed cultural relativists might perceive clear support for their views in these results. However, in my view, a more balanced summary of the study's findings would yield the conclusion that, although the particular physical environment of one's culture may make one more or less sensitive to certain visual cues, a base-level set of common perceptual processes is the shared property of all people.

This conclusion is supported by a number of studies suggesting that a variety of perceptual abilities, such as the ability to infer depth from occlusion or the ability to discriminate between a human face and other objects of comparable shape and size, may actually develop out of inborn (species-wide) starting points (see Aslin et al., 1981; Granrud, 1992; Hochberg, 1978; Hofsten and Lindhagen, 1980). However, the existence of such genetic origination is not a prerequisite of the assumption that all cultures share a basic set of perceptual principles; one can just as well argue that common visual habits are acquired through learning because of the fundamental commonalities affecting all people on this earth regardless of their specific cultural backgrounds.

The physiology of human eyes and the principles of the atmospheric propagation of light are the same across the globe, and all normally functioning human beings must be able to distinguish objects from their backgrounds, to identify those objects, to calculate distances and directions of motion, and so forth. These shared requirements of daily life might be expected to lead to cross-cultural commonalities in processes of visual interpretation even in the absence of any genetic "hard-wiring" of such processes in people's brains. If the term "culture" can be legitimately applied to the physical aspects of the environment in which a person is brought up and if, moreover, the term is not restricted only to those features in which environments differ, then the assumption of cross-cultural commonality in basic principles of visual perception is perfectly consistent with the view that visual processes are always shaped by culture. Of course, to anyone who finds such a broad conception of "culture" unacceptable, the assumption of cross-cultural commonality will undoubtedly appear to be a denial of the role of culture in this area of human behavior.

Whichever of these perspectives one chooses to take, it should be remembered that the assumption that people from different cultures share a basic visual syntax is only a preliminary element in the theory developed in this book. If this assumption were to be taken away entirely, the theory would lose some of its more interesting implications, but its central propositions regarding the capacity of images to replicate real-world visual syntax would not be affected in any fundamental way. These propositions and their corollaries would now have to be seen as applying only *within* any one culture rather than across cultures, but the theory's predictions regarding the ability of first-time viewers (from that particular culture) to interpret images would remain in force, as would its implications in the areas of general cognitive consequences, aesthetic appreciation, and awareness of manipulation.

My own view, as I have already indicated, is that there are good reasons to believe in a substantial degree of cross-cultural similarity in basic visual syntax. However, I am willing to concede that there may be exceptions to this principle, both in the form of cultures with unique features (e.g., people living in dense jungles, with no opportunities for truly long-distance perception) and more significantly in the form of those aspects of visual syntax having to do with social rather than physical perception. To distinguish between social and physical perception is not always a simple matter, but a couple of concrete examples may make the point clearer.

In discussing the meaning and interpretation of transitions from medium-shot to close-up, I argued that one possible (contextually determined) real-world analogue of this device might be the heightened interpersonal involvement resulting from closer physical proximity. In view of the common, species-wide basis for this aspect of the meaning of proximity—its grounding in the activities of sexual contact, physical aggression, and nurturing of the young—a good argument can be made in favor of the idea that all cultures should recognize a positive relationship between proximity and intimacy, even if, as some research has shown, cultures do vary with respect to the precise distance that signals a transition from one degree of intimacy to another (Watson, 1970). Nevertheless, it is conceivable in principle that some (or many, or most) cultures will be found on close inspection to have developed proxemic conventions totally unrelated to the one I am assuming here (for example, an inverse relationship between proximity and intimacy, or no relationship at all). In that case, I would simply have to say that my interpretation of the Hollywood convention for moving to a close-up would be irrelevant to any such cultures, and the members of those cultures would undoubtedly see that convention as something arbitrary and unrelated to their real-world experience.

Another example that we might look at along these lines is that of Kuleshov-style editing—i.e., the juxtaposition of a character's face with some contextual object that shapes the viewer's perception of the face's expression. In my earlier discussion of this device, I pointed out that the interaction of contextual and facial cues is generally assumed to be a universal feature of the act of interpreting expressions, and in that regard Kuleshov-style editing would appear to be an analogue of a pan-cultural process of real-world visual interpretation. It is also worth noting that research projects that have looked systematically at the cross-cultural distribution of facial expressions have tended to find evidence of pan-cultural similarities in the way in which people interpret certain basic facial expressions, such as smiles or scowls (Ekman, 1980; see also Buck, 1984.)

All the same, nothing precludes the possibility, unlikely though it may seem, that there may be some cultures whose members do not make use of contextual cues in interpreting facial expressions and for whom, therefore, the Kuleshov effect would be a purely cinema-specific convention requiring specifically cinematic literacy of its viewers. Kuleshov-style editing would also appear "unnatural" to a viewer whose culture did not encompass the specific facial expression or associated contextual cues referred to in any particular instance of this type of editing.

With regard to both close-ups and the Kuleshov effect, then, when it comes to the more social aspects of perception—e.g., the perception of interpersonal intimacy or the meaning of a facial expression—the likelihood that there will be some cross-cultural differences in visual syntax increases. With regard to the more physical aspects of perception, though, the assumption of cross-cultural commonalities in perceptual processes is probably more secure because the constraints on cultural variation are stronger. To put it another way: The members of a culture could choose to teach their young that apparently converging parallel lines (in the real world) signify *smaller* distance, or that an occluding object is *farther* away than that which it occludes, or that the visual impressions resulting from successive views of a scene should *not* be summed up into a unified conception of that scene— but each of these cultural precepts would suffer prompt contradiction in the course of a child's own exploration of its physical environment.

At this physical level, then, we would expect substantial perceptual uniformity across cultures, which in turn should facilitate cross-cultural understanding of aspects of images modeled on this common visual syntax. Because there is also considerable empirical support for this conclusion, it seems to me that, when all is said and done, we are indeed justified in concluding that cultural differences do not have the absolute force in this area of experience that is taken for granted, I think, by many scholars today.

This observation brings us to a related question with particularly significant implications for the issue of cultural relativity: If pictures are capable of reproducing features of real-world visual syntax and if there are cross-cultural commonalities in that syntax, is it legitimate to rank cultures with respect to the degree to which their pictorial styles succeed in replicating the features of this common real-world visual syntax? Aren't perceptions of the "realism" of a picture purely relative to the internal standards of any particular culture?

From what I have said so far, it should be evident that I do indeed believe that we can make certain meaningful distinctions between cultural styles of pictorial representation on a scale of greater or lesser fidelity to the principles of real-world visual perception. For example, let us imagine a culture that employs reverse linear perspective in its pictures—i.e., constructs its pictures on the basis of a conceptual framework of parallel lines that *diverge* as they recede into the distance. (As J. J. Gibson [1971, p. 30] has pointed out, such a convention could not possibly be applied consistently across the entire space of a picture, although certain writers have imagined its existence in the pictures of China and other "non-Western" cultures.) I would have no hesitation in saying that, *with regard to that specific feature,* the pictorial style in question is less realistic than a style employing the more familiar Western convention of linear perspective.

Another example of a representational style that I would readily label as less realistic, *in one specific respect,* than many types of Western pictures is that of the Native American cultures of the Pacific Northwest (e.g., Tlingit, Haida, Kwakiutl). In the two-dimensional images produced in these cultures, the forms of various animals are often conflated or folded into each other in such a way as to violate the structural relationships of body parts in the real world (Holm, 1965, pp. 11–13; Stewart, 1979, pp. 32–39). For example, a head will appear inside a torso, or an eye will appear inside an arm. According to the specific criterion of fidelity to the visible bodily structures of real animals, this pictorial style seems self-evidently less realistic than, say, the kinds of illustrations of animals typically found in U.S. textbooks.

I don't mean to suggest, however, that judgments of realism—in the specific sense of fidelity to real-world visual syntax—are always, or even often, as simple as in the examples I have just given (cf. Hagen, 1986). Compare traditional Egyptian painting to the styles of Hellenistic or Roman art. Egyptian painting traditionally avoided foreshortening in its representation of human figures (hence the characteristic combination of a frontal view of the upper torso with a side view of the head, arms, and legs), whereas the development of Greek and Roman art can be seen in certain respects as a movement toward increasingly more pronounced uses of foreshortening. Because Egyptian painting and these latter styles form part of a continuous tradition, in that there are evident historical influences linking developments in the later styles with precedents in the earlier one, it may be tempting to see the move toward foreshortening as part of the greater drive toward realism commonly assumed to have been a major motive of Greek and Roman artists up to the Christian era.

However, if we ask how well these styles approximate the informational cues available to a viewer in the real world, it is not at all clear to me that there is an obvious choice to be made between them. It is true that a foreshortened figure can encode information about its relative orientation to the viewer, whereas an unforeshortened figure by itself lacks that capacity. But an unforeshortened figure typically gives a more accurate representation of its structure, which radical foreshortening can sometimes render completely unrecognizable. In view of these circumstances, unless one has some a priori reason for weighing one of these criteria more heavily than the other, a simple assessment of the relative degree of realism of these two figural styles does not seem appropriate.

Much the same could undoubtedly be said of any number of stylistic comparisons of this sort that one might choose to perform. Therefore, although I do believe that relative judgments of pictorial fidelity to real-world visual syntax are feasible, I also think that, as in all of the examples cited above, such judgments must be very specific as to the criterion of comparison. I should probably add—although I would hope this goes without saying—that the kind of assessment of realism I have been discussing here is meant to be independent of any judgment of artistic merit. For example, to my eyes the "unrealistic" style of the Pacific Northwest is also the most elegant of any of the artistic traditions to have emerged in North America in recent times—and I would certainly include the European-American tradition in this evaluation.

The absence of any necessary relationship between realism and artistic merit is surely one reason for the existence, in certain cultures, of marked preferences for relatively unrealistic representational conventions. However, a committed cultural relativist might ask: Even if we accept the proposition that there is a meaningful external standard for comparing the realism of various pictorial styles, isn't it true that what appears unrealistic to an outsider could, by the internal standards of a particular culture, seem perfectly true-to-life? Might it not be the case that people prefer "unrealistic" styles simply because, to them, the styles do *not* seem unrealistic? An adequate answer to this question must, it seems to me, encompass several points.

To begin with, it is surely true that a wide variety of representational styles can appear realistic to the people who practice them, for precisely the reasons discussed earlier. But does that mean that *every* culture considers its own representational style realistic? This I very much doubt. Although there is a certain sentimental strain of art theory that insists Picasso really did see the world as a cubist jumble of fractured planes or that El Greco was astigmatic, the history of Western art has presumably taught us that fidelity to appearances is often a minor motive in the making of images. Shouldn't people from non-Western cultures be credited with having had the same insight? (See also Burch, 1979, p. 75; Sullivan, 1979, ch. 3.) Assuming this point is granted, the more pertinent question in this general area is whether there is any reason to believe that people whose cultures *do* in fact value representational realism are ever likely to judge the images of another culture as being more realistic than their own. I suspect that a strict cultural relativist would probably find such a possibility inconceivable; and yet it is not hard to find evidence that supports it. This evidence revolves around the convention of linear perspective.

Although linear perspective is typically assumed to have originated as an invention of Filippo Brunelleschi and/or other artists of the Florentine Renaissance, Edgerton (1975) has shown persuasively that its principles had been worked out at least as early as the Alexandrian period and that a written description of these principles in a work by Ptolemy is the likely source for the "rediscovery" of linear perspective in fifteenth-century Florence. This would appear to be a clear case, then, of the borrowing of an external representational device that appeared to the borrowers to offer a better match to real-world visual principles than did their own earlier conventions. It might be objected, of course, that the kind of borrowing this story illustrates was not really cross-cultural but rather simply the revival of an ancestral practice within one continuous culture. The same cannot be said, however, of two subsequent events in the history of the spread of linear perspective: its incorporation into Persian miniatures and its adoption as a genre of Japanese wood-block printmaking. Furthermore, although the importation of examples of linear perspective into China did not lead to borrowing of this device on the same scale as in these other two cases, there is clear evidence, in early Chinese responses to Western painting, of a sense of regret at the lack of an equivalent technique in traditional Chinese art (Danto, 1989, p. 472).

These examples speak directly to the more general point of this discussion of images and culture: that at the level of visual syntax, there is sufficient cross-cultural commonality in real-world perceptual processes to serve as a basis for communication between different cultures. With regard to visual syntax, then, the notion that pictorial interpretation is always dependent on culture-specific visual literacy does not seem tenable. The argument that culture-specific visual literacy erects barriers to cross-cultural communication becomes much more viable when one is dealing with visual *subject matter*. In particular, within this area, the term "visual literacy" would seem to be an appropriate label to describe a viewer's familiarity with specific images or sets of images that have played a role in her or his culture's visual heritage (as in the example of Dumas's study of Chinese and U.S. students discussed above). Although this sense of visual literacy has not been the prime concern of this book, it does overlap with many of the issues we have discussed thus far, and the time has now come to take a brief look at it directly.

Familiarity with Visual Subject Matter

A useful way to approach this kind of visual literacy is to ask a practical question: Is this a type of knowledge that is worth building into the educational curriculum of our schools? There are at least three possible reasons one might want to answer "yes." The first of these has already been dealt with in the context of our more general examination of aesthetics and ideology in Chapter 5: Knowledge of precedents can sharpen a viewer's appreciation of skill and awareness of manipulative intent. A second, equally straightforward reason would be the argument that certain images, primarily photographs, have been so intimately and significantly intertwined with the social developments from which they emerged that the teaching of history, among other things, seems almost inconceivable without some reference to these images (see Goldberg, 1991). The civil rights marcher being attacked by police dogs; the exhausted woman seeking refuge in a camp for Depression-era migrants; the Vietnamese children fleeing a napalm attack on their village—these are only a few of the many images that have played significant roles in the evolution of the events they recorded. That such images should be a part of basic courses in U.S. history seems an unassailable proposition. Such images also might be worthy candidates for inclusion on the kinds of cultural-literacy lists that various writers have developed in recent years (Hirsch et al., 1988; Simonson and Walker, 1988, pp. 191–200).

A third argument for the kind of visual literacy we are considering now is related to the one above but may be somewhat less obvious. There are certain images about which one might want to instruct younger generations because of the role they have played as a reference point in the public life of older generations. The art of Norman Rockwell may be the best example of what I have in mind here. My only encounter with Rockwell in an academic setting took place many years ago, in an art history course in college, in which the instructor once got his daily quota of laughs by treating us to ten minutes of heavy sarcasm at the expense of one of Rockwell's *Saturday Evening Post* covers. But I don't think one has to argue about the relative merits of Rockwell and, say, Jackson Pollock in order to make the point that Rockwell is worth knowing about if one wants to know about his society and his times.

What is at issue is not how accurately Rockwell reflected the national character (which is, in any case, a fictitious entity) nor what effect Rockwell's work may have had on the values of his contemporaries (although, to the extent that there was such an effect, we might want to consider his work for inclusion in the type of imagery discussed in reason number two above). Rather, it seems to me that Rockwell's distinction lies in the fact that his work became—for believers and unbelievers alike—a common standard against which to measure character and values (see Olson, 1983). Even today, an advertising photographer can speak of capturing a "Rockwellian" mood in one of his images (a Nikon ad of little leaguers in front of a small rural church, photographed by Dewitt Jones [1989]), whereas debunkers of the mythical past can go after their quarry by going after Rockwell.

Rockwell aside, now, an especially interesting manifestation of this cultural process occurs in the case of certain well-known images that frequently serve as the bases of mass-mediated parodies (see Figure 6.1). In such instances, the original image's power as a frame of reference is expressed directly in visual form by virtue of the parody. Pride of place among

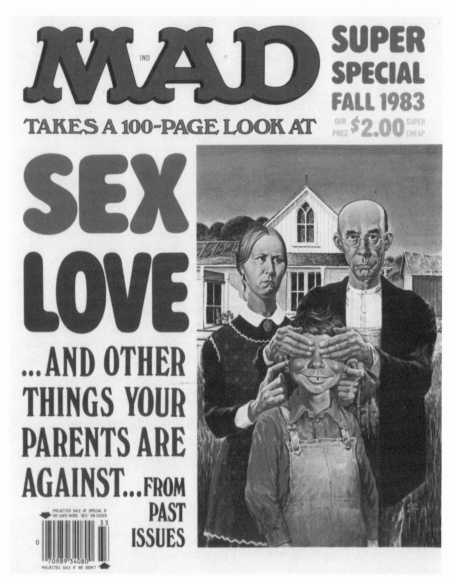

Figure 6.1 Visual culture: Alfred E. Neuman meets *American Gothic. Source:* The *MAD Super Special Fall 1983* cover is reprinted with permission of E. C. Publications, Inc. Copyright © 1983.

the relatively small number of American images in this category surely belongs to Grant Wood's *American Gothic,* which has provided the theme for several generations of variations on the nature of this country's identity. In contrast to the works of Norman Rockwell, whose meaning most commentators seem to feel is only too clear, there is an ineffable quality about Wood's attitude toward the subjects of this image, and this quality is also present to some degree in two other frequently parodied images, James Montgomery Flagg's World War I "I Want You" poster and the painting that is usually referred to as *Whistler's Mother.* The ambivalent note in these images is characteristic of a certain American attitude toward the past (also present very strongly in some of the films of John Ford) and may partly explain why these specific images have attained their unusual status in the national consciousness. Some degree of ambivalence also seems present in Steinberg's famous *New Yorker* cover, whose view of the United States as seen from Manhattan was for some time (and may still be) a ready metaphor for American class relationships and regional differences.

In an informal attempt to get some sense of how widespread people's knowledge of such images actually is, I have recently been testing my students' familiarity with a number of historical photographs, as well as with some frequently parodied images of the kind discussed above. Because the courses in which I have been doing this all deal specifically with visual communication, the results can probably be taken as an indication of the likely upper limit of this form of visual literacy among the broader college-age population.

All of the various historical photographs I tested were associated with events that happened before most of my students were born, but two had particularly high recognition rates: Walker Evans's 1936 photograph of an Alabama sharecropper's wife and Alfred Eisenstaedt's picture of a sailor kissing a woman on the day World War II ended. In a class of twenty-nine undergraduates (all U.S.-born), 83 percent knew that Evans's picture had been taken during the Depression (despite the fact that this photograph is a facial close-up with no obvious signs of poverty or distress), and 73 percent accurately identified the circumstances of the Eisenstaedt picture. The corresponding figures were even higher for U.S.-born graduate students, and, interestingly, even graduate students from other countries had recognition rates of 50 percent or more for these two images.

However, none of the other photographs I have tested so far has had a recognition rate higher than 50 percent among my undergraduates. For example, only 47 percent were able to give even an approximate description (e.g., a World War II battle) of the correct circumstances in Joe Rosenthal's photograph of the Marines raising the flag on Iwo Jima (others thought the scene had occurred in Vietnam, Korea, or, in one case, the Civil War). Similar recognition rates were typical of such images as the civil rights marcher attacked by dogs (several students thought it was something that had happened in South Africa) or the assassination of Martin Luther King, Jr. (several thought the people on the balcony in this scene were pointing at something in the sky).

In testing students' familiarity with the original sources of mass-mediated parodies, my method has been to show them a parody and ask them to identify the original image on which it was based. This yardstick has tended to yield relatively high recognition rates for parodies whose original form was itself a mass-mediated image, such as Uncle Sam, correctly identified as a recruiting poster figure by 83 percent of undergraduates, or Steinberg's *New Yorker* cover, which 63 percent of undergraduates were able to name as the prototype of a parody in which a different city took the place of New York. It is worth noting that in neither of these two cases could the students have had any substantial familiarity with the actual prototypes of these images—i.e., the poster itself or the magazine cover in its original appearance.

In contrast to parodies based on mass-mediated images, parodies of "high art" tended to have lower recognition rates. For example, only 37 percent recognized the image of Whistler's mother (in an advertising parody that actually contained the words, "A sale to make a mother whistle"). Because the students' exposure to either type of work would typically have come from reproductions rather than from the original, differences in accessibility, in and of themselves, are probably not the main reason for these differences in recognition rates. In any event, these numbers, together with those cited earlier in connection with the historical photographs, give us some sense, perhaps, of the potential scope of any educational efforts directed at raising students' levels of this type of visual literacy.

"Production Literacy"

One other aspect of visual literacy deserves some comment before we bring this chapter to a close. As I pointed out from the very beginning, this book's primary focus has been on the interpretation of images, rather than their creation. However, because one of the aims of this chapter is to examine relevant issues that did not fit into the book's main compass, this may be the place to say a few words about visual literacy in the sense of experience in the *production* of images, as opposed to their interpretation.

The capacity to produce an image in accord with the conventions of a certain culture or interpretive community obviously requires a multitude of manual and/or technical skills that people typically have to work hard to acquire (although "point-and-shoot" photography and parallel developments in video technology have recently made this aspect of production considerably easier). However, from the theoretical perspective this book has attempted to develop, the more interesting question about production has to do with its conceptual, not its technical, aspects. It has been argued here that ordinary competence in real-world perceptual skills may provide a "shortcut" to the interpretation of certain visual conventions, enabling viewers to understand these conventions without having encountered them before in a manufactured image. Might anything like this occur in the *production* of an image? Are there any visual conventions that creators could be expected to come up with spontaneously, purely on the basis of their real-world visual competence?

On the face of it, this may appear to be a hopelessly hypothetical question, as it conjures up a situation in which a person is motivated and technically equipped to produce an image yet has somehow never seen an image before. However, this situation has in fact been approximated, with very interesting results, in Sol Worth and John Adair's experiment with Navajo filmmakers (in which Navajos with little or no prior exposure to movies were taught the technical rudiments of filmmaking and then produced their own films). Worth and Adair's analysis of these films was chiefly aimed at uncovering parallels between the films' structure and various culture-specific elements of Navajo life. The authors' point in this analysis was that different cultural backgrounds should lead to different production conventions, and it is probably fair to say that they would not have been very receptive to the suggestion that cross-cultural similarities in visual processes might actually serve as the basis for cross-cultural similarities in first-time producers' cinematic conventions. Nevertheless, an episode they themselves highlight in their account of the experiment provides quite clear support for the latter proposition.

This episode involved an interaction between Sol Worth and Johnny Nelson, one of the Navajo filmmakers. Nelson had learned how to operate a camera and how to splice shots together, and he was now exploring on his own the conceptual aspects of filmmaking. In the course of planning a scene about a horse, he suddenly turned to Worth, who was present as an observer, and asked the following question: If he took many different shots of parts of the horse and then edited them together, would viewers see the edited sequence as adding up to a single horse? Greatly excited, Worth managed to respond with social-scientific neutrality: What did he, Nelson, think? Yes, Nelson answered, "I think this is so with movies." As Worth indicates, here we have the independent invention of the standard Hollywood convention of breaking up scenes into partial shots (Worth and Adair, 1972, pp. 95–96). In Chapter 3, it was argued that even an inexperienced *viewer* of film or television should be able to make sense of this convention because of its basis in the universal perceptual principle of constructing a coherent mental image from successive fragmentary views. Now we see evidence for the extension of this principle into the realm of *production*.

In a certain sense, of course, this implied equation between the phenomenon documented by Worth and the ability of inexperienced viewers to interpret images is misleading. My argument with regard to interpretation was that viewers can go automatically, without having to think about it, from real world to image, whereas in Worth's story it is clear that Nelson arrived at the principle of scene breakdown after considerable experimentation and reflection. This is in fact a highly significant aspect of the event described by Worth. It is an excellent illustration of the potential—perhaps inevitable—link between practical experience in a visual medium and heightened awareness of the workings of the visual process. It suggests, in other words, that *conscious, analytical* literacy in visual interpretation may flow from literacy in production.

This is a possibility I have touched upon before in this book, most notably in Chapter 5, in connection with my research on the relationship between viewers' prior experience and their conscious awareness of various aspects of visual manipulation. Here I will briefly review the aspects of this research which were most relevant to the issue of a connection between production experience and interpretational awareness.

In the first of two related studies (Messaris, 1981), a film containing both Hollywood-style editing and certain experimental elements was shown to three sets of students: (1) filmmakers with substantial production experience, including some cases of professional employment; (2) students who had taken courses in film theory and analysis; (3) students with no formal background or experience in film. In their interpretations of the Hollywood-style section of the film used in this study, the three kinds of students reacted fairly similarly: Regardless of their background, they tended not to make any explicit references to visual conventions or to the fact that this film, like any other, was an artificial, intentional creation. Instead, in what may be seen as a reflection of Hollywood's "invisible style," they tended to discuss the events in the film in more "naturalistic" terms, as if these events had actually occurred in reality. (Examples of this interpretational tendency were given in Chapter 5.)

In their dealing with the more experimental parts of the film, however, the three groups of students did differ according to their backgrounds. Many of the viewers without special experience still seemed to be struggling to disentangle a naturalistic narrative from the disjunctive editing and other non-Hollywood devices in these parts of the film, but the other two groups were now much more likely to deal explicitly with intentionality and with the making and breaking of conventions. Furthermore, this tendency was particularly pronounced for the students with direct production experience.

The significance of production experience was confirmed in a second, follow-up study with older viewers (Messaris and Nielsen, 1989). This time the experienced group was composed of full-time production professionals from two big-city TV stations, who were compared with a more educated (college and above) and a less educated (high school or less) group of viewers from the same area. The study investigated these viewers' interpretations of two examples of propositional editing, taken from a political campaign film and from a TV commercial. As in the latter part of the first study, there were pronounced differences among the three groups: Once again, the viewers with production experience were much more likely to express awareness of the visual conventions tested in this study, although education in and of itself also appeared to increase awareness to a certain extent.

Taken together, then, the findings of these two studies suggest that, at least when it comes to the more obtrusive or openly manipulative devices characteristic of much of advertising and of some forms of non-Hollywood cinema, awareness of manipulative conventions and intent is heightened by direct production experience. However, the Hollywood style of naturalistic storytelling may indeed be more stubbornly invisible, in the sense that even people who have made films themselves may be lulled into overlooking its artifice and manipulative intent. In a world as permeated by attempts at visual manipulation as ours is, these findings point to one possible avenue for increasing viewers' awareness of intent: training in production. However, even a method as labor-intensive as that may not always be enough.

References

Abelman, Robert. 1990. "You Can't Get There from Here: Children's Understanding of Time-Leaps on Television." *Journal of Broadcasting and Electronic Media,* 34(4): 469–476.

Acker, Steve R., and Tiemens, Robert K. 1981. "Children's Perceptions of Changes in Size of Televised Images." *Human Communication Research,* 7(4): 340–346.

Arlen, Michael. 1980. *Thirty Seconds.* New York: Penguin.

Arnheim, Rudolf. 1969. *Visual Thinking.* Berkeley and Los Angeles: University of California Press.

———. 1988. *The Power of the Center: A Study of Composition in the Visual Arts.* The New Version. Berkeley and Los Angeles: University of California Press.

Aslin, Richard N.; Alberts, Jeffrey R.; and Petersen, Michael R. (Eds.). 1981. *Development of Perception: Psychobiological Perspectives.* New York: Academic Press.

Bachmann, Gideon. 1965. Interview with John Huston. *Film Quarterly,* 19(1). Reprinted in Andrew Sarris (Ed.), *Interviews with Film Directors.* New York: Avon Books, 1967, pp. 253–273.

Baines, J. 1985. "Color Terminology and Color Classification: Ancient Egyptian Color Terminology and Polychromy." *American Anthropologist,* 87: 282–297.

Balázs, Béla. 1952. *Theory of the Film: Character and Growth of a New Art.* Trans. Edith Bone. New York: Dover, 1970.

Bang, Molly. 1991. *Picture This: Perception and Composition.* Boston: Bulfinch Press.

Bateson, Gregory. 1972. *Steps to an Ecology of Mind.* New York: Ballantine Books.

Baugh, Albert C., and Cable, Thomas. 1978. *A History of the English Language.* 3rd ed. Englewood Cliffs, N.J.: Prentice-Hall.

Bazin, André. 1967. *What Is Cinema?* Volume I. Trans. Hugh Gray. Berkeley and Los Angeles: University of California Press.

Bell, Tracey. 1992. "Decentration as a Predictor of Comprehension of Cross-Cutting." M.A. Thesis, Annenberg School for Communication, University of Pennsylvania.

Berger, John. 1972. *Ways of Seeing.* New York: Penguin Books.

Berger, Klaus. 1992. *Japonisme in Western Painting from Whistler to Matisse.* Trans. David Britt. New York: Cambridge University Press.

Berlin, Brent, and Kay, Paul. 1969. *Basic Color Terms: Their Universality and Evolution.* Berkeley and Los Angeles: University of California Press.

185

Birdwhistell, Ray L. 1970. *Kinesics and Context: Essays on Body Motion Communication*. Philadelphia: University of Pennsylvania Press.

Block, Mitchell. 1975. "The Filming of NO LIES." *Filmmakers Newsletter*, February, pp. 18–20.

Bloom, A. H. 1981. *The Linguistic Shaping of Thought: A Study in the Impact of Language on Thinking in China and the West*. Hillsdale, N.J.: Lawrence Erlbaum Associates.

Bordwell, David. 1985. *Narration in the Fiction Film*. Madison: The University of Wisconsin Press.

Bordwell, David; Staiger, Janet; and Thompson, Kristin. 1985. *The Classical Hollywood Cinema: Film Style and Mode of Production to 1960*. New York: Columbia University Press.

Bordwell, David, and Thompson, Kristin. 1986. *Film Art: An Introduction*. 2nd ed. New York: Knopf.

Bossen, Howard. 1985. "Zone V: Photojournalism, Ethics, and the Electronic Age." *Studies in Visual Communication*, 11(3): 22–32.

Bowser, Eileen. 1983. "Toward Narrative, 1907: The Mill Girl." In John L. Fell (Ed.), *Film Before Griffith*. Berkeley and Los Angeles: University of California Press, pp. 330–338.

Branigan, Edward. 1985. "The Point-of-View Shot." In Bill Nichols (Ed.), *Movies and Methods: An Anthology*, Volume II. Berkeley and Los Angeles: University of California Press.

———. 1986. "'Here Is a Picture of No Revolver!' The Negation of Images, and Methods for Analyzing the Structure of Pictorial Statements." *Wide Angle*, 8(3–4): 8–17.

Brown, James. 1991. *Television Critical Viewing Skills Education: Major Literacy Projects in the United States and Selected Countries*. Hillsdale, N.J.: Lawrence Erlbaum Associates.

Bruce, Vicki, and Green, Patrick. 1990. *Visual Perception: Physiology, Psychology, and Ecology*. Hillsdale, N.J.: Lawrence Erlbaum Associates.

Bruno, Vincent J. 1977. *Form and Color in Greek Painting*. New York: W. W. Norton.

Buck, Ross. 1984. *The Communication of Emotion*. New York: Guilford Press.

Burch, Noël. 1979. *To the Distant Observer: Form and Meaning in the Japanese Cinema*. Rev. and Ed. Annette Michelson. Berkeley and Los Angeles: University of California Press.

Calvert, Sandra L. 1988. "Television Production Feature Effects on Children's Comprehension of Time." *Journal of Applied Developmental Psychology*, 9: 263–273.

Carey, John. 1982. "Conventions and Meaning in Film." In Sari Thomas (Ed.), *Film Culture: Explorations of Cinema in Its Social Context*. Metuchen, N.J.: Scarecrow Press, pp. 110–125.

Carroll, John B., and Casagrande, Joseph B. 1958. "The Function of Language Classification in Behavior." In E. E. Maccoby, T. M. Newcomb, and E. L. Hartley (Eds.), *Readings in Social Psychology*, 3rd ed. New York: Holt, Rinehart and Winston, pp. 18–31.

Carroll, John M. 1980. *Toward a Structural Psychology of Cinema*. The Hague: Mouton Publishers.

Carroll, Noël. 1985. "The Power of Movies." *Daedalus,* 114(4): 79–103.

———. 1988. *Mystifying Movies: Fads and Fallacies in Contemporary Film Theory.* New York: Columbia University Press.

Cassidy, M. F., and Knowlton, J. Q. 1983. "Visual Literacy: A Failed Metaphor?" *Educational Communication and Technology Journal,* 31: 67–90.

Caughey, John L. 1984. *Imaginary Social Worlds: A Cultural Approach.* Lincoln and London: University of Nebraska Press.

Chideya, F. 1991. "Surely for the Spirit, but also for the Mind." *Newsweek,* December 2, p. 61.

Clifton, N. Roy. 1983. *The Figure in Film.* Newark: University of Delaware Press.

Cohen, Jodi R. 1987. "The Television Generation, Television Literacy, and Television Trends." Paper presented to the Eastern Communication Association, Syracuse, N.Y., May 18–21.

Comuntzis, Georgette M. 1987. "Children's Comprehension of Changing Viewpoints in Visual Presentations." Paper presented at the Visual Communication Conference, Alta, Utah, July 26–29.

Comuntzis-Page, Georgette. 1991. "Perspective-Taking Theory: Shifting Views from Sesame Street." Paper presented at the Fifth Annual Visual Communication Conference, Breckenridge, Colo., July 29.

Cook, Bruce L. 1981. *Understanding Pictures in Papua New Guinea.* Elgin, Ill.: David C. Cook Foundation.

Cooper, Robert L., and Spolsky, Bernard (Eds.). 1991. *The Influence of Language on Culture and Thought: Essays in Honor of Joshua A. Fishman's Sixty-Fifth Birthday.* Berlin and New York: Mouton de Gruyter.

Craig, Robert L. 1992. "Advertising as Visual Communication." *Communication,* 13(3): 165–179.

Custen, George F. 1980. "Film Talk: Viewers' Responses to a Film as a Socially Situated Event." Ph.D. Dissertation, University of Pennsylvania.

Danto, Arthur C. 1989. "Ming and Qing Paintings." *The Nation,* 249(13): 469–472.

Davies, John. 1991. "Linking Media Literacy to Critical Thinking: An Opportunity for Education." *Telemedium,* Second Quarter, pp. 3–4.

Dayan, Daniel. 1976. "The Tutor-Code of Classical Cinema." In Bill Nichols (Ed.), *Movies and Methods: An Anthology.* Berkeley and Los Angeles: University of California Press, pp. 438–451.

Deregowski, Jan B. 1968. "Difficulties in Pictorial Depth Perception in Africa." *British Journal of Psychology,* 59: 195–204.

———. 1980. *Illusions, Patterns and Pictures: A Cross-Cultural Perspective.* New York: Academic Press.

Deregowski, Jan B.; Muldrow, E. S.; and Muldrow, W. F. 1972. "Pictorial Recognition in a Remote Ethiopian Population." *Perception,* 1: 417–425.

Diamond, Edwin, and Bates, Stephen. 1984. *The Spot: The Rise of Political Advertising on Television.* Cambridge, Mass.: The MIT Press.

Diawara, Manthia. 1988. "Popular Culture and Oral Traditions in African Film." *Film Quarterly,* 41(3): 6–14.

Dika, Vera. 1990. *Games of Terror: Halloween, Friday the 13th, and the Films of the Stalker Cycle.* Cranbury, N.J.: Fairleigh Dickinson University Press.

Dmytryk, Edward. 1984. *On Film Editing: An Introduction to the Art of Film Construction.* Boston: Focal Press.

Dondis, Donis A. 1973. *A Primer of Visual Literacy.* Cambridge, Mass.: The MIT Press.

Dressler, William W., and Robbins, Michael C. 1975. "Art Styles, Social Stratification, and Cognition: An Analysis of Greek Vase Painting." *American Ethnologist,* 2(3): 427–434.

Dumas, Anne Andrée. 1988. "Cross-Cultural Analysis of People's Interpretation of Advertising Visual Cliches." M.A. Thesis, Annenberg School for Communication, University of Pennsylvania.

Dunning, William V. 1991. *Changing Images of Pictorial Space: A History of Spatial Illusions in Painting.* Syracuse, N.Y.: Syracuse University Press.

Dusenbury, Katharine A. 1990. "Inexperienced Viewers' Understanding of Pictorial Materials: The Results of a Survey in Lesotho, Africa." M.A. Thesis, Annenberg School for Communication, University of Pennsylvania.

Dyer, Gillian. 1989. *Advertising as Communication.* New York: Routledge.

Ebong, Enoh T. 1989. "Visual Images in Political Advertisements: An Analysis of Their Informational Content and Their Demographic Appeal." M.A. Thesis, Annenberg School for Communication, University of Pennsylvania.

Edgerton, Samuel Y., Jr. 1975. *The Renaissance Rediscovery of Linear Perspective.* New York: Icon Editions.

———. 1991. *The Heritage of Giotto's Geometry: Art and Science on the Eve of the Scientific Revolution.* Ithaca, N.Y.: Cornell University Press.

Eisenstein, Sergei. 1957. *Film Form and The Film Sense.* Trans. and Ed. Jay Leyda. Cleveland: Meridian Books.

———. 1944. "Dickens, Griffith, and the Film Today." In Sergei Eisenstein, *Film Form and The Film Sense,* Trans. and Ed. Jay Leyda. Cleveland: Meridian Books, 1957, pp. 195–255.

Ekman, Paul. 1980. *The Face of Man: Expressions of Universal Emotions in a New Guinea Village.* New York: Garland Press.

Elgin, Catherine Z. 1984. "Representation, Comprehension, and Competence." *Social Research,* 51(4): 905–925.

Elsaesser, Thomas. 1990. "From Anti-Illusionism to Hyper-Realism: Bertolt Brecht and Contemporary Film." In Pia Kleber and Colin Visser (Eds.), *Re-Interpreting Brecht: His Influence on Contemporary Drama and Film.* New York: Cambridge University Press.

Ewen, Stuart. 1988. *All Consuming Images: The Politics of Style in Contemporary Culture.* New York: Basic Books.

Fagioli, Marco, and Materassi, Mario. 1985. "Some Notes on Kuniyoshi, the Projected Shadow, and Yoshitsune." *Impressions,* 11: 1–2.

Fell, John L. 1974. *Film and the Narrative Tradition.* Berkeley and Los Angeles: University of California Press.

Fischer, John L. 1961. "Art Styles as Cultural Cognitive Maps." *American Anthropologist,* 63(1): 79–93.

Fiske, John. 1987. *Television Culture.* London and New York: Methuen.

Forbes, Norma E., and Lonner, Walter J. 1980. *The Sociocultural and Cognitive Effects of Commercial Television on Previously Television-Naive Rural Alaskan*

Children. Final Report to the National Science Foundation (Grant No. BNS–78-25687).

Forbes, Norma E.; Ashworth, Clark; Lonner, Walter J.; and Kasprzyk, D. 1984. *Social and Cognitive Effects of the Introduction of Television on Rural Alaskan Native Children.* Final Report Submitted to the Alaska Council on Science and Technology (Contract No. 33–82). Fairbanks: Center for Cross-Cultural Studies, University of Alaska.

Foss, Sonja K., and Kanengieter, Marla R. 1991. "Expansion of Communication Fundamentals Courses to Include Visual Literacy." Paper presented to the Speech Communication Association, Atlanta, November 2.

Freud, Sigmund. 1952. *On Dreams.* Trans. James Strachey. New York: Norton.

Freund, Gisèle. 1980. *Photography and Society.* Boston: David R. Godine.

Frith, Uta, and Robson, Jocelyn E. 1975. "Perceiving the Language of Films." *Perception,* 4: 97–103.

Gabbadon, Donna. 1992. "Children's Comprehension of Flashbacks: A Study of Inexperienced and Experienced Jamaican Child Viewers." M.A. Thesis, Annenberg School for Communication, University of Pennsylvania.

Gable, Gregory C. 1983. "Point of View in Television Advertising." M.A. Thesis, Annenberg School for Communication, University of Pennsylvania.

Galan, Leslie S. 1986. "The Use of Subjective Point of View in Persuasive Communication." M.A. Thesis, Annenberg School for Communication, University of Pennsylvania.

Galassi, Peter. 1981. *Before Photography: Painting and the Invention of Photography.* Boston: New York Graphic Society.

Gardner, Howard. 1983. *Frames of Mind: The Theory of Multiple Intelligences.* New York: Basic Books.

——— (with Jaglom, Leona). 1985. "Cracking the Codes of Television: The Child as Anthropologist." In Peter D'Agostino (Ed.), *Transmission.* New York: Tanam Press, pp. 93–102.

Gaudreault, André. 1979. "Detours in Film Narrative: The Development of Cross-Cutting." *Cinema Journal,* 19: 39–59.

Gibson, James J. 1971. "The Information Available in Pictures." *Leonardo,* 4: 27–35.

———. 1982. *Reasons for Realism: Selected Essays of James J. Gibson.* Ed. Edward Reed and Rebecca Jones. Hillsdale, N.J.: Lawrence Erlbaum Associates.

———. 1986. *The Ecological Approach to Visual Perception.* Hillsdale, N.J.: Lawrence Erlbaum Associates.

Goldberg, Vicki. 1991. *The Power of Photography: How Photographs Changed Our Lives.* New York: Abbeville Press.

Gombrich, E. H. 1960. *Art and Illusion: A Study in the Psychology of Pictorial Representation.* A. W. Mellon Lectures in the Fine Arts, 1956. Princeton: Princeton University Press.

———. 1972. "The Visual Image." *Scientific American,* 227(3): 82–96.

———. 1982. *The Image and the Eye.* Ithaca, N.Y.: Cornell University Press.

———. 1984. "Representation and Misrepresentation." *Critical Inquiry,* 11.

Goodman, Nelson. 1976. *Languages of Art: An Approach to a Theory of Symbols.* 2nd ed. Indianapolis: Hackett.

Granrud, Carl (Ed.). 1992. *Visual Perception and Cognition in Infancy.* Hillsdale, N.J.: Lawrence Erlbaum Associates.

Greenfield, Patricia Marks. 1984. *Mind and Media: The Effects of Television, Video Games, and Computers.* Cambridge, Mass.: Harvard University Press.

Greenfield, Patricia Marks, and Beagles-Roos, Jessica. 1988. "Radio vs. Television: Their Cognitive Impact on Children of Different Socioeconomic and Ethnic Groups." *Journal of Communication,* 38(2): 71–92.

Gregory, Richard L. 1970. *The Intelligent Eye.* New York: McGraw-Hill.

———. 1990. *Eye and Brain: The Psychology of Seeing.* 4th ed. Princeton: Princeton University Press.

Griffith, D. W. 1926. "Pace in the Movies." *Liberty Magazine,* Museum of Modern Art Archive, New York. Quoted in Jesionowski (1987).

Griffith, Mrs. D. W. 1975. *When the Movies Were Young.* New York: Benjamin Blom.

Grimes, Tom. 1989. "The Consequences of 'Grabbing B-Roll' in Television News: Why Semantic Audio and Video Redundancy is Crucial to Recognition." Paper presented to the Association for Education in Journalism and Mass Communication, Washington, D.C.

———. 1990. "Encoding TV News Messages into Memory." *Journalism Quarterly,* 67(4): 757–766.

Gross, Larry. 1973a. "Art as the Communication of Competence." *Social Science Information,* 12(5): 115–121.

———. 1973b. "Modes of Communication and the Acquisition of Symbolic Competence." In George Gerbner, Larry Gross, and William Melody (Eds.), *Communications Technology and Social Policy.* New York: Wiley, pp. 189–208.

———. 1985. "Life vs. Art: The Interpretation of Visual Narratives." *Studies in Visual Communication,* 11(4): 2–11.

Gumpert, Gary. 1977. "The Ambiguity of Perception." *Et Cetera,* 34(2): 192–203.

Gumpert, Gary, and Cathcart, Robert. 1985. "Media Grammars, Generations, and Media Gaps." *Critical Studies in Mass Communication,* 2(1): 23–35.

Hagen, Margaret A. 1980. "Generative Theory: A Perceptual Theory of Pictorial Representation." In Margaret A. Hagen (Ed.), *The Perception of Pictures,* Vol. II, *Durer's Devices: Beyond the Projective Model of Pictures.* New York: Academic Press, pp. 3–46.

———. 1986. *Varieties of Realism: Geometries of Representational Art.* New York: Cambridge University Press.

Hagen, Margaret A., and Johnson, Margaret M. 1977. "Hudson Pictorial Depth Perception Test: Cultural Content and Question with a Western Sample." *Journal of Social Psychology,* 101: 3–11.

Hamdi, Narjes; Knirk, Fred; and Michael, William B. 1982. "Differences between American and Arabic Children in Performance on Measures of Pictorial Depth Perception: Implications for Valid Interpretation of Test Scores Based on Items Reflecting Dissimilar Cultural Content." *Educational and Psychological Measurement,* 42: 285–296.

Hatcher, Evelyn P. 1988. *Visual Metaphors: A Methodological Study in Visual Communication.* Albuquerque: University of New Mexico Press.

Herrnstein, R. J. 1984. "Objects, Categories, and Discriminative Stimuli." In H. L.

Roitblat, T. G. Bever, and H. S. Terrace (Eds.), *Animal Cognition.* Hillsdale, N.J.: Lawrence Erlbaum Associates, pp. 233–261.

Hine, Lewis. 1980. "Social Photography." In Alan Trachtenberg (Ed.), *Classic Essays on Photography.* New Haven: Leete's Island Books.

Hirsch, E. D., Jr.; Kett, Joseph F.; and Trefil, James. 1988. *The Dictionary of Cultural Literacy.* Boston: Houghton Mifflin.

Hobbs, Renée; Frost, Richard; Davis, Arthur; and Stauffer, John. 1988. "How First-Time Viewers Comprehend Editing Conventions." *Journal of Communication,* 38(4): 50–60.

Hobbs, Renée, and Frost, Richard. 1989. "Comprehending Transitional Editing Conventions: No Experience Necessary?" Paper presented at the Seventh International Conference on Culture and Communication, Philadelphia, October 7.

Hochberg, Julian E. 1978. *Perception.* 2nd ed. Englewood Cliffs, N.J.: Prentice-Hall.

———. 1983. "Pictorial Functions in Perception." *Art Education,* March, pp. 15–18.

———. 1984. "The Perception of Pictorial Representations." *Social Research,* 51(4): 841–862.

Hochberg, Julian E., and Brooks, Virginia. 1962. "Pictorial Recognition as an Unlearned Ability: A Study of One Child's Performance." *American Journal of Psychology,* 75: 624–628.

———. 1978. "The Perception of Motion Pictures." In Edward C. Carterette and Morton P. Friedman (Eds.), *Handbook of Perception,* Volume X. New York: Academic Press.

von Hofsten, Claes, and Lindhagen, Karin. 1980. "Perception of Visual Occlusion in 4½-Month-Old Infants." *Uppsala Psychological Reports,* 290.

Holland, Norman N. 1989. "Film Response from Eye to I: The Kuleshov Experiment." *The South Atlantic Quarterly,* 88(2): 415–442.

Hollander, Anne. 1989. *Moving Pictures.* New York: Knopf.

Holm, Bill. 1965. *Northwest Coast Indian Art: An Analysis of Form.* Seattle: University of Washington Press.

Homer, William Innis. 1964. *Seurat and the Science of Painting.* Cambridge, Mass.: The MIT Press.

Hudson, William. 1960. "Pictorial Depth Perception in Subcultural Groups in Africa." *Journal of Social Psychology,* 52: 183–208.

———. 1967. "The Study of the Problem of Pictorial Perception among Unacculturated Groups." *International Journal of Psychology,* 2: 89–107.

von Humboldt, Wilhelm. 1836. *On Language: The Diversity of Human Language-Structure and Its Influence on the Mental Development of Mankind.* Trans. Peter Heath. New York: Cambridge University Press.

Ives, Colta F. 1974. *The Great Wave: The Influence of Japanese Woodcuts on French Prints.* Boston: New York Graphic Society.

Jacobs, Lewis. 1968. *The Rise of the American Film: A Critical History.* New York: Teachers College Press.

Jaglom, Leona, and Gardner, Howard. 1981. "Decoding the Worlds of Television." *Studies in Visual Communication,* 7(1): 33–47.

Jamieson, Kathleen Hall. 1984. *Packaging the Presidency: A History and Criticism of Presidential Campaign Advertising.* New York: Oxford University Press.

————. 1992a. "Dirty Politics." *The Pennsylvania Gazette,* 91(1): 38–43.

————. 1992b. *Dirty Politics: Deception, Distraction, and Democracy.* New York: Oxford University Press.

Jaubert, Alain. 1989. *Making People Disappear: An Amazing Chronicle of Photographic Deception.* Washington: Pergamon-Brassey's.

Jesionowski, Joyce E. 1987. *Thinking in Pictures: Dramatic Structure in D. W. Griffith's Biograph Films.* Berkeley and Los Angeles: University of California Press.

Johansson, Gunnar. 1982. "Visual Space Perception through Motion." In Alexander Wertheim, Willem Wagenaar, and Herschel Leibowitz (Eds.), *Tutorials on Motion Perception.* New York: Plenum.

Jones, Dewitt. 1989. "Fall Classic." *Outdoor Photographer,* 5(8): 10, 23.

Kaplan, Stuart Jay. 1990. "Visual Metaphors in the Representation of Communication Technology." *Critical Studies in Mass Communication,* 7(1): 37–47.

————. 1992. "A Conceptual Analysis of Form and Content in Visual Metaphors." *Communication,* 13(3): 197–209.

Kauffmann, Stanley, with Bruce Henstell, Eds. 1972. *American Film Criticism: From the Beginnings to Citizen Kane.* New York: Liveright.

Kay, Paul, and Kempton, Willett. 1984. "What Is the Sapir-Whorf Hypothesis?" *American Anthropologist,* 86(1): 65–79.

Kennedy, John M. 1983. "What Can We Learn about Pictures from the Blind?" *American Scientist,* 71: 19–26.

————. 1984. "How Minds Use Pictures." *Social Research,* 51(4): 885–904.

Kennedy, John M., and Ross, Abraham S. 1975. "Outline Picture Perception by the Songe of Papua." *Perception,* 4: 391–406.

Kepplinger, Hans Mathias. 1991. "The Impact of Presentation Techniques: Theoretical Aspects and Empirical Findings." In Frank Biocca (Ed.), *Television and Political Advertising.* Hillsdale, N.J.: Lawrence Erlbaum Associates, pp. 173–194.

Kessler, Hope. 1970. "The Effect of Varying the Length of Edemes Related to Meaning Inferences from Films." M.A. Thesis, Annenberg School for Communication, University of Pennsylvania.

Kilbride, Philip L., and Robbins, Michael C. 1969. "Pictorial Depth Perception and Acculturation among the Baganda." *American Anthropologist,* 71(2): 293–301.

Kipper, Philip. 1990. "A New Interpretive Strategy for Television's Changing Visual World." Paper presented at the Fourth Annual Visual Communication Conference, Northstar, Calif.

Korac, Nada. 1988. "Functional, Cognitive and Semiotic Factors in the Development of Audiovisual Comprehension." *Educational Communication and Technology Journal,* 36(2): 67–91.

Kozloff, Sarah. 1988. *Invisible Storytellers: Voice-Over Narration in American Fiction Film.* Berkeley and Los Angeles: University of California Press.

Krieger, Murray. 1984. "The Ambiguities of Representation and Illusion: An E. H. Gombrich Retrospective." *Critical Inquiry,* 11: 181–194.

Kubovy, Michael. 1986. *The Psycholology of Perspective and Renaissance Art.* New York: Cambridge University Press.

Kuleshov, Lev. 1974. *Kuleshov on Film: Writings by Lev Kuleshov*. Trans. and Ed. Ronald Levaco. Berkeley and Los Angeles: University of California Press.

Lakoff, George. 1987. *Women, Fire, and Dangerous Things: What Categories Reveal about the Mind*. Chicago: University of Chicago Press.

Lang, Kurt, and Lang, Gladys Engel. 1971. "The Unique Perspective of Television and Its Effect: A Pilot Study." In W. Schramm and D. F. Roberts (Eds.), *The Process and Effects of Mass Communication*, rev. ed. Urbana: University of Illinois Press, pp. 169–188.

Lasica, J. D. 1989. "Photographs that Lie." *Washington Journalism Review*, 11(5): 22–25.

Layton, Robert. 1991. *The Anthropology of Art*. 2nd ed. New York: Cambridge University Press.

Leach, Eleanor W. 1988. *The Rhetoric of Space: Literary and Artistic Representations of Landscape in Republican and Augustan Rome*. Princeton: Princeton University Press.

Lee, Ellen Wardwell. 1990. *Seurat at Gravelines: The Last Landscapes*. Bloomington and Indianapolis: Indiana University Press.

Lehman, Ernest. 1959. *North by Northwest*. The MGM Library of Film Scripts. New York: Viking Press.

Lesser, Wendy. 1991. *His Other Half: Men Looking at Women through Art*. Cambridge, Mass.: Harvard University Press.

Lloyd-Kolkin, Donna, and Turner, Kathleen. 1989. "Media Literacy Education Needs for Elementary Schools: A Survey." Paper presented to the International Visual Literacy Association, Scottsdale, AZ, October 30.

Lonner, Walter J.; Thorndike, Robert M.; Forbes, Norma E.; and Ashworth, Clark. 1985. "The Influence of Television on Measured Cognitive Abilities: A Study with Native Alaskan Children." *Journal of Cross-Cultural Psychology*, 16(3): 355–380.

Lucy, John A. 1992a. *Grammatical Categories and Cognition: A Case Study of the Linguistic Relativity Hypothesis*. New York: Cambridge University Press.

————. 1992b. *Language Diversity and Thought: A Reformulation of the Linguistic Relativity Hypothesis*. New York: Cambridge University Press.

MacKinnon, Kenneth. 1990. *Misogyny in the Movies: The De Palma Question*. Newark: University of Delaware Press.

Mamet, David. 1985. *House of Games*. New York: Grove Press.

————. 1991. *On Directing Film*. New York: Penguin.

Mandell, Lee M., and Shaw, Donald L. 1973. "Judging People in the News—Unconsciously: Effect of Camera Angle and Bodily Activity." *Journal of Broadcasting*, 17(3): 353–362.

Marchand, Roland. 1985. *Advertising the American Dream*. Berkeley and Los Angeles: University of California Press.

Marr, David. 1982. *Vision: A Computational Investigation into the Human Representation and Processing of Visual Information*. New York: W. H. Freeman.

McBride, Joseph. 1982. *Hawks on Hawks*. Berkeley and Los Angeles: University of California Press.

McGinnis, Joe. 1969. *The Selling of the President*. New York: Penguin.

Meadowcroft, Jane D., and Reeves, Byron. 1989. "Influence of Story Schema Development on Children's Attention to Television." *Communication Research*, 16: 352–374.

Meringoff, Laurene K.; Vibbert, Martha M.; Char, Cynthia A.; Fernie, David E.; Banker, Gail S.; and Gardner, Howard. 1983. "How Is Children's Learning from Television Distinctive? Exploiting the Medium Methodologically." In Jennings Bryant and Daniel R. Anderson (Eds.), *Children's Understanding of Television: Research on Attention and Comprehension*. New York: Academic Press, pp. 151–179.

Messaris, Paul. 1981. "The Film Audience's Awareness of the Production Process." *Journal of the University Film Association*, 33(4): 53–56.

———. 1982. "To What Extent Does One Have to Learn to Interpret Movies?" In Sari Thomas (Ed.), *Film/Culture: Explorations of Cinema in Its Social Context*. Metuchen, N.J.: Scarecrow Press, pp. 168–183.

———. 1983. "Family Conversations about Television." *Journal of Family Issues*, 4(2): 293–308.

———. 1987. "Mothers' Comments to Their Children about the Relationship between Television and Reality." In Thomas R. Lindlof (Ed.), *Natural Audiences: Qualitative Research of Media Uses and Effects*. Norwood, N.J.: Ablex Publishing Corporation, pp. 95–108.

———. 1989. "Associational Imagery in Magazine Advertisements." Paper presented at the Third Annual Visual Communication Conference, Park City, Utah, June 24.

———. 1990. "Ethics in Visual Communication." Broadcast Education Association *Feedback*, 31(4): 2–5, 22–24.

———. 1992. "Visual 'Manipulation': Visual Means of Affecting Responses to Images." *Communication*, 13: 181–195.

Messaris, Paul; Eckman, Bruce; and Gumpert, Gary. 1979. "Editing Structure in the Televised Versions of the 1976 Presidential Debates." *Journal of Broadcasting*, 23: 359–369.

Messaris, Paul, and Gross, Larry. 1977. "Interpretations of a Photographic Narrative by Viewers in Four Age Groups." *Studies in the Anthropology of Visual Communication*, 4(2): 99–111.

Messaris, Paul, and Nielsen, Karen. 1989. "Viewers' Interpretations of Associational Montage: The Influence of Visual 'Literacy' and Educational Background." Paper Presented to the Association for Education in Journalism and Mass Communication, Washington, D.C., August 12.

Messaris, Paul, and Sarett, Carla. 1981. "On the Consequences of Television-Related Parent-Child Interaction." *Human Communication Research*, 7(3): 226–244.

Metallinos, Nikos. 1992. "Visual Literacy: Suggested Theories for the Study of Television Picture Perception." *Journal of Visual Literacy*, 12(1): 57–72.

Metz, Christian. 1974. *Film Language: A Semiotics of the Cinema*. Trans. Michael Taylor. New York: Oxford University Press.

———. 1982. *The Imaginary Signifier: Psychoanalysis and Cinema*. Trans. Celia Britton, Annwyl Williams, Ben Brewster, and Alfred Guzzetti. Bloomington: Indiana University Press.

Meyrowitz, Joshua. 1986. "Television and Interpersonal Behavior: Codes of Perception and Response." In Gary Gumpert and Robert Cathcart (Eds.), *Inter/Media: Interpersonal Communication in a Media World,* 3rd ed. New York: Oxford University Press, pp. 253–272.

Michaels, Eric. 1986. *The Aboriginal Invention of Television in Central Australia 1982–1986.* Canberra: Australian Institute of Aboriginal Studies.

Miller, Mark Crispin. 1990. "Hollywood: The Ad." *The Atlantic Monthly,* April, pp. 41–54.

Mitchell, Greg. 1988. "How Hollywood Fixed an Election." *American Film,* 14(2): 26–31.

Mitroff, Ian I., and Bennis, Warren. 1989. *The Unreality Industry: The Deliberate Manufacturing of Falsehood and What It Is Doing to Our Lives.* New York: Birch Lane Press.

Monaco, James. 1981. *How to Read a Film: The Art, Technology, Language, History, and Theory of Film and Media.* Rev. ed. New York: Oxford University Press.

Morello, John T. 1988a. "Argument and Visual Structuring in the 1984 Mondale-Reagan Debates: The Medium's Influence on the Perception of Clash." *Western Journal of Speech Communication,* 52: 277–290.

———. 1988b. "Visual Structuring of the 1976 and 1984 Nationally Televised Presidential Debates." *Central States Speech Journal,* 39(3–4): 233–243.

Morgan, John, and Welton, Peter. 1992. *See What I Mean: An Introduction to Visual Communication.* 2nd ed. London: Edward Arnold.

Morreale, Joanne. 1991. *A New Beginning: A Textual Frame Analysis of the Political Campaign Film.* Albany, N.Y.: State University of New York Press.

Morris, L. Robert, and Raskin, Lawrence. 1992. *Lawrence of Arabia: The 30th Anniversary Pictorial History.* Foreword by Martin Scorsese. New York: Anchor Books.

Mshelia, Ayuba Yabilar, and Lapidus, Leah Blumberg. 1990. "Depth Picture Perception in Relation to Cognitive Style and Training in Non-Western Children." *Journal of Cross-Cultural Psychology,* 21(4): 414–433.

Mulvey, Laura. 1975. "Visual Pleasure and Narrative Cinema." *Screen,* 16(3): 6–18.

———. 1989. *Visual and Other Pleasures.* Bloomington and Indianapolis: Indiana University Press.

Musser, Charles. 1991. *Before the Nickelodeon: Edwin S. Porter and the Edison Manufacturing Company.* Berkeley and Los Angeles: University of California Press.

The New Yorker, July 20, 1987. "Notes and Comment," pp. 19–20.

Ohri, Kusum Uppal. 1981. "A Study of the Assessment of the Pictorial Depth Perception of Indian Children on Specific Pictorial Depth Discrimination Tasks." Ph.D. Dissertation, University of Maryland.

Olson, David R. (Ed.). 1974. *Media and Symbols: The Forms of Expression, Communication, and Education.* Yearbook of the National Society for the Study of Education. Chicago: University of Chicago Press.

Olson, Lester C. 1983. "Portraits in Praise of a People: A Rhetorical Analysis of Norman Rockwell's Icons in Franklin D. Roosevelt's 'Four Freedoms' Campaign." *Quarterly Journal of Speech,* 69: 15–24.

Omari, I. M., and McGintie, W. H. 1974. "Some Pictorial Artifacts in Studies of African Children's Pictorial Depth Perception." *Child Development,* 45: 535–539.

Oudart, Jean-Pierre. 1990. "Suture." In Nick Browne (Ed.), *Cahiers du Cinema*

1969–1972: The Politics of Representation. Cambridge, Mass.: Harvard University Press.

Panofsky, Erwin. 1991. *Perspective as Symbolic Form.* Trans. Christopher S. Wood. New York: Zone Books.

Pasolini, Pier Paolo. 1962. Statement. *Film Culture,* 24. Reprinted in Andrew Sarris (Ed.), *Interviews with Film Directors.* New York: Avon Books, 1967, pp. 366–370.

Penn, Roger. 1971. "Effects of Motion and Cutting Rate in Motion Pictures." *AV Communication Review,* 19(1): 29–50.

Picard, Gilbert. 1968. *Roman Painting.* Greenwich, Conn.: New York Graphic Society.

Pittman, Robert W. 1990. "We're Talking the Wrong Language to 'TV Babies.'" *The New York Times,* September 30, p. 19.

Pocius, Gerald L. 1979. "Hooked Rugs in Newfoundland: The Representation of Social Structure in Design." *Journal of American Folklore,* 92: 273–284.

Polan, Dana. 1986. "The 'Kuleshov Effect' Effect." *Iris,* 4(1).

Prazdny, K. 1980. "Egomotion and Relative Depth from Optical Flow." *Biological Cybernetics,* 36: 87–102.

Prince, Stephen. 1988. "The Pornographic Image and the Practice of Film Theory." *Cinema Journal,* 27(2): 27–39.

———. 1990. "Are There Bolsheviks in Your Breakfast Cereal?" In Sari Thomas and William A. Evans (Eds.), *Communication and Culture: Language, Performance, Technology, and Media* (Norwood, N.J.: Ablex Publishing Corporation), pp. 180–184.

Prince, Stephen, and Hensley, Wayne. 1992. "The Kuleshov Effect: Recreating the Classic Experiment." *Cinema Journal,* 31(2): 59–75.

Pudovkin, V. I. 1958. *Film Technique and Film Acting.* Trans. and Ed. Ivor Montagu. New York: Grove Press.

Rachman, S. 1966. "Sexual Fetishism: An Experimental Analogue." *Psychological Record,* 16: 293–296.

Rachman, S., and Hodgson, R. J. 1968. "Experimentally-Induced 'Sexual Fetishism': Replication and Development." *Psychological Record,* 18: 25–27.

Ramage, Nancy H., and Ramage, Andrew. 1991. *Roman Art: Romulus to Constantine.* New York: Harry N. Abrams.

Ramsaye, Terry. 1926. *A Million and One Nights: A History of the Motion Picture.* New York: Simon & Schuster.

Ray, Robert B. 1985. *A Certain Tendency of the Hollywood Cinema, 1930–1980.* Princeton: Princeton University Press.

Reaves, Shiela. 1989. "Digital Alteration of Photographs in Magazines: An Examination of the Ethics." Paper presented to the Association for Education in Journalism and Mass Communication, Washington, D.C.

Rebello, Stephen. 1990. *Alfred Hitchcock and the Making of* Psycho. New York: Dembner Books.

Reisz, Karel, and Millar, Gavin. 1968. *The Technique of Film Editing.* 2nd ed. New York: Hastings House.

Rice, M.; Huston, A.; and Wright, J. 1986. "Replays as Repetitions: Young Children's Interpretation of Television Forms." *Journal of Applied Developmental Psychology,* 7: 61–76.

Richter, Gisela Marie Augusta. 1970. *Perspective in Greek and Roman Art.* New York: Phaidon.

Rickey, Carrie. 1987. "Right out of 'Mr. Smith': North takes his cues from Jimmy Stewart." *The Philadelphia Inquirer,* July 13, p. E1.

Ritchin, Fred. 1990. *In Our Own Image: The Coming Revolution in Photography.* New York: Aperture.

Rockwell, Paul. 1989. "Fighting the Fires of Racism: Blacks Challenge the I.A.F.F." *The Nation,* 249(10): 714–718.

Rosenblum, Ralph, and Karen, Robert. 1979. *When the Shooting Stops . . . the Cutting Begins: A Film Editor's Story.* New York: Penguin Books.

Roskill, Mark, and Carrier, David. 1983. *Truth and Falsehood in Visual Images.* Amherst: University of Massachusetts Press.

Rothman, William. 1976. "Against 'The System of the Suture.'" In Bill Nichols (Ed.), *Movies and Methods: An Anthology* (Berkeley and Los Angeles: University of California Press), pp. 451–459.

Saint-Martin, Fernande. 1990. *Semiotics of Visual Language.* Bloomington and Indianapolis: Indiana University Press.

Salomon, Gavriel. 1979. *Interaction of Media, Cognition, and Learning: An Exploration of How Symbolic Forms Cultivate Mental Skills and Affect Knowledge Acquisition.* San Francisco: Jossey-Bass Publishers.

Salt, Barry. 1983. "The Early Development of Film Form." In John L. Fell (Ed.), *Film Before Griffith.* Berkeley and Los Angeles: University of California Press, pp. 284–298.

Sapir, Edward. 1921. *Language.* New York: Harcourt, Brace, & World.

Sarris, Andrew (Ed.). 1967. *Interviews with Film Directors.* New York: Avon Books.

de Saussure, Ferdinand. 1966. *Course in General Linguistics.* Trans. Wade Baskin. New York: McGraw-Hill.

Schwartz, Barry. 1981. *Vertical Classification: A Study in Structuralism and the Sociology of Knowledge.* Chicago: University of Chicago Press.

Scribner, Sylvia, and Cole, Michael. 1981. *The Psychology of Literacy.* Cambridge, Mass.: Harvard University Press.

Segall, Marshall H. 1979. *Cross-Cultural Psychology: Human Behavior in Global Perspective.* Monterey, Calif.: Brooks Cole Publishing Company.

Segall, Marshall H.; Campbell, Donald T.; and Herskovits, Melville J. 1966. *The Influence of Culture on Visual Perception.* Indianapolis: Bobbs-Merrill.

Silverman, Kaja. 1983. *The Subject of Semiotics.* New York: Oxford University Press.

Simonson, Rick, and Walker, Scott. 1988. *The Graywolf Annual Five: Multi-Cultural Literacy.* Saint Paul, Minn.: Graywolf Press.

Smith, Robin; Anderson, Daniel R.; and Fischer, Catherine. 1985. "Young Children's Comprehension of Montage." *Child Development,* 56(4): 962–971.

Snyder, Joel. 1980. "Picturing Vision." *Critical Inquiry,* 6(3): 499–526.

Spain, Sikandra. 1983. "Factors Affecting Pictorial Comprehension in Non-Literates: Results of a Survey in the Gambia, West Africa." M.A. Thesis, Annenberg School for Communication, University of Pennsylvania.

Stange, Maren. 1989. *Symbols of Ideal Life: Social Documentary Photography in America 1890–1950.* New York: Cambridge University Press.

Stephenson, Ralph, and Phelps, Guy. 1989. *The Cinema as Art.* Rev. ed. New York: Penguin Books.

Stewart, Hilary. 1979. *Looking at Indian Art of the Northwest Coast*. Seattle: University of Washington Press.

Stonehill, Brian. 1990. "The Show-Me Decade." *The Christian Science Monitor*, January 2.

Stout, Roy G. 1984. "Pavlov Founded Advertising Because He Showed that Imagery Could Be Transferred." *Television/Radio Age*, 31: 160.

Sullivan, Michael. 1979. *Symbols of Eternity: The Art of Landscape Painting in China*. Stanford, Calif.: Stanford University Press.

————. 1989. *The Meeting of Eastern and Western Art*. Rev. and exp. ed. Berkeley and Los Angeles: University of California Press.

Tiemens, Robert K.; Hellweg, Susan A.; Kipper, Philip; and Phillips, Stephen L. 1985. "An Integrative Verbal and Visual Analysis of the Carter-Reagan Debate." *Communication Quarterly*, 33: 34–42.

Tomasulo, Frank P. 1989. "Colonel North Goes to Washington: Observations on the Intertextual Re-presentation of History." *Journal of Popular Film and Television*, 17: 82–88.

Tomlinson, Madeline C. 1991. "History and Analysis of Conventions Encoding Subjective Mental Processes." M.A. Thesis, Annenberg School for Communication, University of Pennsylvania.

Truffaut, François. 1967. *Hitchcock*. With Helen G. Scott. New York: Simon & Schuster.

Tufte, Edward R. 1990. *Envisioning Information*. Cheshire, Conn.: Graphics Press.

Turim, Maureen. 1989. *Flashbacks in Film: Memory and History*. New York: Routledge.

Wachtel, Edward. 1984. "The Impact of Television on Space Conception." In Sari Thomas (Ed.), *Studies in Mass Communication and Technology: Selected Proceedings from the Fourth International Conference on Culture and Communication*. Norwood, N.J.: Ablex Publishing Corporation, pp. 168–174.

Wade, Nicholas J., and Swanston, Michael. 1991. *Visual Perception: An Introduction*. New York: Routledge.

Wartofsky, Marx. 1979. "Picturing and Representing." In Calvin Nodine and David Fischer (Eds.), *Views of Pictorial Representation: Making, Perceiving and Interpreting*. New York: Praeger.

————. 1984. "The Paradox of Painting: Pictorial Representation and the Dimensionality of Visual Space." *Social Research*, 51(4): 863–883.

Watson, O. Michael. 1970. *Proxemic Behavior: A Cross-Cultural Study*. The Hague: Mouton Publishers.

Wawrzaszek, Laura. 1983. "Children's Interpretations of a Videotaped Story: A Partial Replication." M.A. Thesis, Annenberg School for Communication, University of Pennsylvania.

Weale, R. A. 1982. *Focus on Vision*. Cambridge, Mass.: Harvard University Press.

Welch, Renate L.; Huston-Stein, Aletha; Wright, John C.; and Plehal, Robert. 1979. "Subtle Sex-Role Cues in Children's Commercials." *Journal of Communication*, 29(3): 202–209.

Welch, Stuart Cary. 1972. *A King's Book of Kings: The Shah-nameh of Shah Tahmasp*. New York: The Metropolitan Museum of Art.

White, John. 1987. *The Birth and Rebirth of Pictorial Space*. 3rd ed. Cambridge, Mass.: The Belknap Press of Harvard University Press.

Whittock, Trevor. 1990. *Metaphor and Film*. New York: Cambridge University Press.

Whorf, Benjamin Lee. 1956. *Language, Thought, and Reality: Selected Writings of Benjamin Lee Whorf*. Ed. John B. Carroll. Cambridge, Mass.: The MIT Press.

Willemen, Paul. 1983. "Cinematic Discourse: The Problem of Inner Speech." In Stephen Heath and Patricia Mellencamp (Eds.), *Cinema and Language*. Frederick, Md.: University Publications of America, pp. 141–167.

Williams, Joseph M. 1975. *Origins of the English Language*. New York: Free Press.

Williams, Martin T. 1980. *Griffith: First Artist of the Movies*. New York: Oxford University Press.

Williams, Tannis MacBeth, and Harrison, L. F. 1986. "Television and Cognitive Development." In Tannis MacBeth Williams (Ed.), *The Impact of Television: A Natural Experiment in Three Communities*. Orlando: Academic Press.

Wilson, John. 1983. "Comments on Work with Film Preliterates in Africa." *Studies in Visual Communication*, 9(1): 30–35.

Worth, Sol. 1982. "Pictures Can't Say Ain't." In Sari Thomas (Ed.), *Film Culture: Explorations of Cinema in Its Social Context*. Metuchen, N.J.: Scarecrow Press, pp. 97–109.

Worth, Sol, and Adair, John. 1972. *Through Navajo Eyes: An Exploration in Film Communication and Anthropology*. Bloomington: Indiana University Press.

Worth, Sol, and Gross, Larry. 1974. "Symbolic Strategies." *Journal of Communication*, 24(4): 27–39.

Zettl, Herbert. 1990. *Sight Sound Motion: Applied Media Aesthetics*. 2nd ed. Belmont, Calif.: Wadsworth Publishing Company.

Zimmerman, Robert R., and Hochberg, Julian. 1970. "Responses of Infant Monkeys to Pictorial Representations of a Learned Visual Discrimination." *Psychonomic Science*, 18(5): 307–308.

Zuckerman, Cindy I. 1990. "Rugged Cigarettes and Sexy Soap: Brand Images and the Acquisition of Meaning through Associational Juxtaposition of Visual Imagery." M.A. Thesis, The Annenberg School for Communication, University of Pennsylvania.

About the Book and Author

Post-industrial humankind is inundated daily with visual images. Televisions transmit their blue haze into dark living rooms; advertisements and billboards bombard us at every turn; movies evoke tears, outrage, or hilarity; and the visual arts elicit strong emotional and intellectual responses. At almost every moment, several visual images are warring for our attention in order to make a claim, sell a product, or call us to action. Faced with visual overload, how do we interpret these images? What is happening when a picture moves us? What process takes place in our minds as we respond to such visual devices as close-ups, camera angles, and flashbacks?

This book provides a foundation for answering these questions. Encouraging his readers to become "visually literate," Paul Messaris takes them on a journey through four major conceptual levels of understanding: imparting visual literacy as a prerequisite for comprehending visual media; creating awareness of the general cognitive consequences of visual literacy; making us alert to visual manipulation; and promoting aesthetic appreciation of the images we see. Taken together, these approaches provide a comprehensive view of how visual images are produced and interpreted, and of what their potential social consequences may be.

Paul Messaris is associate professor of communication at The Annenberg School for Communication at the University of Pennsylvania. He has conducted research on viewers' awareness of visual manipulation in movies and advertising, and on parent-child discussions about television. He has also taught 16mm film production.

Index